D0856076

Contemporary

New England

Stories

Contemporary

New England
Stories

Edited by

C. Michael Curtis
Senior Editor, *The Atlantic*

The Globe Pequot Press

Old Saybrook, Connecticut

"A Father's Story" by Andre Dubus. Copyright 1983 by Andre Dubus. Reprinted with permission of the author.
"The Afterlife" by John Updike. Reprinted by permission; © 1986 by John Updike. Originally in *The New Yorker*.
"The President of the Argentine" by John Cheever. Copyright 1976 by John Cheever. Reprinted with permission of Wylie, Aitken & Stone, Inc.
"Tyler and Brina" from *Inventing the Abbots* by Sue Miller. Copyright © 1987 by Sue Miller. Reprinted by permission of HarperCollins Publishers Inc.
"Stand" from *Skating in the Dark* by David Michael Kaplan. Copyright © 1991 by David Michael Kaplan. Reprinted by permission of Pantheon Books, a division of Random House, Inc.
"The Black Hand Girl" by Blanche McCrary Boyd. Copyright 1988 by Blanche M. Boyd. Reprinted with permission of the author.
"Lies" from *Emperor of the Air* by Ethan Canin. Copyright 1988 by Ethan Canin. Reprinted with permission of Houghton Mifflin Co.
"Way to the Dump" by E.S. Goldman. Copyright 1987 by E.S. Goldman. Reprinted with permission of the author.
"Apache" by David Huddle. Copyright 1987 by David Huddle and Bread Loaf Writers' Conference. Reprinted with permission of the author and University Press of New England.
"In a Father's Place" from *In a Father's Place* by Christopher Tilghman. Copyright © 1990 by Christopher Tilghman. Reprinted by permission of Farrar, Straus & Giroux, Inc.
"Helping" by Robert Stone. Copyright 1987 by Robert Stone. Reprinted with permission of Donadio

& Ashworth, on behalf of the author.
"Clothing" by John L'Heureux. Copyright 1984 by John L'Heureux. Reprinted with permission of the author.
"The Skater" by Joy Williams. Copyright 1984 by Joy Williams. First appeared in *Esquire*. Reprinted with permission of International Creative Management, on behalf of the author.
"Graduation" from *A Glimpse of Scarlet and Other Stories* by Roxana Robinson. Copyright © 1991 by Roxana Robinson. Reprinted by permission of HarperCollins Publishers Inc.
"Jungle Video" from *Men Under Water* by Ralph Lombreglia. Copyright © 1990 by Ralph Lombreglia. Used by permission of Doubleday, a division of Bantam Doubleday Dell Publishing Group, Inc.
"Rue" by Susan Dodd. Reprinted from *Old Wives' Tales* by Susan Dodd by permission of the University of Iowa Press. Copyright 1984 by Susan Dodd.
"Thanksgiving Day" from *Monkeys* by Susan Minot. Copyright © 1986 by Susan Minot. Used by permission of the publisher, Dutton, an imprint of New American Library, a division of Penguin Books USA Inc.
"Offerings" by Joyce Kornblatt. Copyright 1985 by Joyce Kornblatt. Reprinted with permission of the author.
"Palais de Justice" from *Ellis Island & Other Stories* by Mark Helprin. Copyright © 1976, 1977, 1979, 1980, 1981 by Mark Helprin. Used by permission of Delacorte Press/Seymour Lawrence, a division of Bantam Doubleday Dell Publishing Group, Inc.
"Company" from *Blood Relations* by Roberta Silman. Copyright © 1977 by Roberta Silman. By permission of Little, Brown and Company.

Library of Congress Cataloguing-in-Publication Data

Contemporary New England Stories / edited by C. Michael Curtis. — 1st ed.

    p. cm.

    ISBN 1-56440-067-0

    1. Short stories, American—New England. 2. American fiction—20th century. 3. New England—Fiction. I. Curtis, C. Michael.

    PS648. N38C66 1992

    813' .01083274—dc20

                          92-26894
                            CIP

BOOK DESIGN BY NANCY FREEBORN

Manufactured in the United States of America
First Edition/First Printing

This one is for Elizabeth Cox,
a long story with no end in sight.

CONTENTS

INTRODUCTION

C. Michael Curtis

What *is* a New England story? What, for that matter, is a New England attitude or stance towards the world? These questions perplex anthologists, but possibly no one else other than clothing manufacturers, highway architects, television programmers, and people who make ice cream. Some New Englanders, plainly, endure the burden of a traceable family heritage that spins itself back to a Liverpool agnostic or perhaps a sneak thief. Never mind: The Mayflower erased any such invidious distinction and brought to these unbending shores folks who, simply by virtue of being first, and then hardy, created lineage—a connection to the past that has filled a lot of men's clubs in and around Boston and put in place a sense of entitlement that has traumatized more than one fragile psyche in recent (and no doubt past) years. This affliction is sometimes known as "blue blood," and it is widely thought to go hand in hand with a predisposition to gout, various ailments of the nervous system, and an obsessive interest in propriety.

Many New Englanders, however, didn't arrive on the Mayflower; nor did they descend from those who did. Many were looking for Yankee Stadium and went too far on Interstate 95; others may have been vacationing and ran out of money. Whatever brought them to New England, they stayed, and after a generation or two they began to take pleasure in muggy summer days, hail storms, and roads built to accommodate roughly half the number of vehicles that crowd them daily. An old New England axiom declares: "If you don't like the weather, wait a minute." This posture—half defiance, half pridefulness—suggests still another index of the New England mood. Where the weather is concerned, nothing can be taken for granted. Snow may fall in April; a December day may well heat up to eighty degrees. A New Englander knows this and is never caught off guard. But a lifetime spent coping with the improbable has consequences. In acute cases, some New Englanders fully expect the sun to rise one day in the West, and they carry bags of rock salt in the trunk of their cars even during the hottest summer days.

New England is also hilly. Not mountainous, but hilly. This means that getting places is not easy, but neither is it dramatically difficult. From an Aristotelian perspective, this "golden mean" may be attractive. But the psyche needs grand conquests, or the chance to recover from apparently crushing defeats. Surmounting the Berkshires is a little like having to put more gasoline in your lawnmower, and the most one can say about traversing the White Mountains is that if you get above the timberline, you're either in a hot air balloon or in the wrong state.

Churches. New England has a great many houses of worship, at least in part because it was settled by people who were unhappy with the Church of England, or with Rome, or with Martin Luther; or who simply had a scheme of their own they wanted to try out—usually having to do with wearing black clothes and making sure everyone behaved. Whatever the reason, all New England towns need steeples, and steeples usually come with churches. Competitiveness being what it is, along with theological fractiousness, most New England towns have several churches and quite a lot of people and institutions who want everyone to behave, including clergy, businesses, schoolchildren, town leaders, and candidates for political office, national as well as local.

Central heating. The cold and extended New England winters have persuaded the home-building industry to equip houses with heating systems that don't depend entirely on one's willingness to haul, split, and stack firewood. Central heating brings families closer together—at least during the first four or five months of the year—and has led to a lot of deeply reflective thinking about early childhood trauma, fraternal insults, parental possessiveness, parental indifference, or garden variety anomie.

As one can easily see, these factors of geography, climate, cultural history, and population density explain why New England stories often tend to be introspective, overheated (or under-heated), occasionally high-minded, often philosophical, sometimes quite violent, aggressively sexual, and usually built around the lives of characters who went to Harvard, wanted to go to Harvard, went instead to Yale, hang around

Harvard Square, or want you very badly to know how little the Harvard question means to them.

As New Englanders go, I barely qualify. I moved to Boston almost thirty years ago to become an editor at *The Atlantic*. I had never lived in New England before, nor had anyone in my family, though I have an older brother who has a summer home on "the Cape" (that's what everyone in New England calls Cape Cod) and whose children have subsequently settled in and around Boston (two of them, of course, went to Harvard, as did this brother). I, by contrast, had lived chiefly in upstate New York (I went to Cornell, a university that competes with Harvard in athletics but not in very much else) and in rural Arkansas, an area in which population density and central heating are not obvious problems. Concerning New England, I think of myself as in a transition stage. Although I've lived in a number of Victorian homes in and around Boston, I have never heard any of them referred to as "the Curtis house." They are usually described, in my hearing, as the house owned by whoever lived there before me. Perhaps that means my time will come, though long after I'm out of hearing range. Even after thirty years, I still think New Englanders sound funny, that they expect much too much of the Red Sox, that their religiosity is more procedural than deeply felt, and that their highways were built with the conviction that automobiles could not possibly replace the horse-drawn buggy, and therefore need not be wide, permanent, or especially well-designed.

The stories in this collection no doubt reflect my various confusions about what New England is and isn't. One story starts in New England and shifts resolutely to England—as if on spring break. Another locates itself physically (though not emotionally) along the Maryland shore. Still others, like so many transplants from Iowa or Arizona, make fertile use of Boston and New England landmarks, on the way to investigations of human frailties or appetites that are hardly unique to this region. The qualities that might tempt one to think "New England story" are probably not the qualities that make the story most memorable or artistically sound. Setting can do a lot: It can drive characters indoors; it can bring them face to face with people they could meet only in, for example, a Combat Zone bar; and it can bring them into a world where social placement depends on where one went to school, or even lived, as an undergraduate.

Some of the writers were born and educated in New England. Several went to Harvard (John Updike and Mark Helprin were Harvard undergraduates; Ethan Canin, Sue Miller, and John L'Heureux were graduate students or Bunting Fellows at Harvard; and Susan Dodd taught there). Several others—not native New Englanders—now live there (Andre Dubus, Ralph Lombreglia, David Huddle, and Christopher Tilghman, for example). And others (like Joyce Kornblatt, Susan Minot, and the late John Cheever) were born in or near Boston, then travelled south to establish careers in writing or related fields. Non-New Englanders, like Roberta Silman, Roxana Robinson, David Kaplan, and Robert Stone, have family in the region or summer homes, or several periods of apprenticeships in New England. And I have taught intermittently in Harvard's undergraduate college, Extension School, and Kennedy Institute for nearly twenty years.

One might well point out that only a handful of writers, those stranded helplessly on the other side of the Rockies, can't be said to belong to one or another of these catagories. But that is simply another truth about New England. The region has more universities per square mile than any other area of like size in the country. It almost surely has, as well, more actively publishing writers, more PEN meetings, more failed novelists, more novels-in-progress, and more bad poetry than any such locale on earth. Every sophomore English major in New England, as well as every cab driver and every brooding victim of domestic conflict, has a story to tell and access to writing classes, hospitable editors, extension courses, and either private or community mental health practitioners who will urge them to exorcise their demons in writing.

The stories in this collection tap into one or more of the many themes that may be said to characterize New England fiction. And most, if not all, of the writers are infected, in one way or another, by the traditions and expectations of the region. The collection may be seen as a sampler, with all the variety and surprise that connotes. At the very least, it brings together some of America's most distinguished writers, represented here by stories that will encourage their readers to stay off the highways, turn up the heat, forgive the Red Sox, and, perhaps, listen to their pastor.

Contemporary
New England
Stories

A FATHER'S STORY

Andre Dubus

My name is Luke Ripley, and here is what I call my life: I own a stable of thirty horses, and I have young people who teach riding, and we board some horses too. This is in northeastern Massachusetts. I have a barn with an indoor ring, and outside I've got two fenced-in rings and a pasture that ends at a woods with trails. I call it my life because it looks like it is, and people I know call it that, but it's a life I can get away from when I hunt and fish, and some nights after dinner when I sit in the dark in the front room and listen to opera. The room faces the lawn and the road, a two-lane country road. When cars come around the curve northwest of the house, they light up the lawn for an instant, the leaves of the maple out by the road and the hemlock closer to the window. Then I'm alone again, or I'd appear to be if someone crept up to the house and looked through a window: a big-gutted gray-haired guy, drinking tea and smoking cigarettes, staring out at the dark woods across the road, listening to a grieving soprano.

My real life is the one nobody talks about anymore, except Father Paul LeBoeuf, another old buck. He has a decade on me: he's sixty-four, a big man, bald on top with gray at the sides; when he had hair, it was black. His face is ruddy, and he jokes about being a whiskey priest, though he's not. He gets outdoors as much as he can, goes for a long walk every morning, and hunts and fishes with me. But I can't get him on a horse anymore. Ten years ago I could badger him into a trail ride; I had to give him a Western saddle, and he'd hold the pommel and bounce through the woods with me, and be sore for days. He's looking at seventy with eyes that are younger than many I've seen in people in their twenties. I do not remember ever feeling the way they seem to; but I was lucky, because even as a child I knew that life would try me, and I must be strong to endure, though in those days I expected to be tortured and killed for my faith, like the saints I learned about in school.

Father Paul's family came down from Canada, and he grew up speaking more French than English, so he is different from the Irish priests who abound up here. I do not like to make general statements, or even to hold general beliefs, about people's blood, but the Irish do seem happiest when they're dealing with misfortune or guilt, either their own or somebody else's, and if you think you're not a victim of either one, you can count on certain Irish priests to try to change your mind. On Wednesday nights Father Paul comes to dinner. Often he comes on other nights too and once, in the old days when we couldn't eat meat on Fridays, we bagged our first ducks of the season on a Friday, and as we drove home from the marsh, he said: For the purposes of Holy Mother Church, I believe a duck is more a creature of water than land, and is not rightly meat. Sometimes he teases me about never putting anything in his Sunday collection, which he would not know about if I hadn't told him years ago. I would like to believe I told him so we could have philosophical talk at dinner, but probably the truth is I suspected he knew, and I did not want him to think I so loved money that I would not even give his church a coin on Sunday. Certainly the ushers who pass the baskets know me as a miser.

I don't feel right about giving money for buildings, places. This starts with the pope, and I cannot respect one of them till he sells his house and everything in it, and that church too, and uses the money to feed the poor. I have rarely, and maybe never, come across saintliness, but I feel certain it cannot exist in such a place. But I admit, also, that I know very little, and maybe the popes live on a different plane and are tried in ways I don't know about. Father Paul says his own church, St. John's, is hardly the Vatican. I like his church: it is made of wood, and has a simple altar and crucifix, and no padding on the kneelers. He does not have to lock its doors at night. Still it is a place. He could say Mass in my barn. I know this is stubborn, but I can find no mention by Christ of maintaining buildings, much less erecting them of stone or brick, and decorating them with pieces of metal and mineral and elements that people still fight over like barbarians. We had a Maltese woman taking riding lessons, she came over on the boat when she was ten, and once she told me how the nuns in Malta used to tell the little girls that if they wore jewelry, rings and bracelets and necklaces, in purgatory snakes would coil around their fingers and wrists and throats. I do not believe in frightening children or telling them lies, but if those nuns saved a few girls from devotion to things, maybe they were right. That Maltese woman laughed about it, but I noticed she wore only a watch, and that with a leather strap.

The money I give to the church goes in people's stomachs, and on their backs, down in New York City. I have no delusions about the worth of what I do, but I feel it's better to feed somebody than not. There's a priest in Times Square giving shelter to runaway kids, and some Franciscans who run a bread line; actually it's a morning line for coffee and a roll, and Father Paul calls it the continental breakfast for winos and bag ladies. He is curious about how much I am sending and I know why: he guesses I send a lot, he has said probably more than tithing, and he is right; he wants to know how much because he believes I'm generous and good, and he is wrong about that; he has never had much money and does not know how easy it is to write a check when you have everything you will ever need, and the figures are mere numbers, and represent no sacrifice at all. Being a real Catholic is too hard; if I were one, I would do with my house and barn what I want the pope to do with his. So I do not want to impress Father Paul, and when he asks me how much, I say I can't let my left hand know what my right is doing.

He came on Wednesday nights when Gloria and I were married, and the kids were young; Gloria was a very good cook (I assume she still is, but it is difficult to think of her in the present), and I liked sitting at the table with a friend who was also a priest. I was proud of my handsome and healthy children. This was long ago, and they were all very young and cheerful and often funny, and the three boys took care of their baby sister, and did not bully or tease her. Of course they did sometimes, with that excited cruelty children are prone to, but not enough so that it was part of her days. On the Wednesday after Gloria left with the kids and a U-Haul trailer, I was sitting on the front steps, it was summer, and I was watching cars go by on the road, when

Father Paul drove around the curve and into the driveway. I was ashamed to see him because he is a priest and my family was gone, but I was relieved too. I went to the car to greet him. He got out smiling, with a bottle of wine, and shook my hand, then pulled me to him, gave me a quick hug, and said: "It's Wednesday, isn't it? Let's open some cans."

With arms about each other we walked to the house, and it was good to know he was doing his work but coming as a friend too, and I thought what good work he had. I have no calling. It is for me to keep horses.

In that other life, anyway. In my real one I go to bed early and sleep well and wake at four forty-five, for an hour of silence. I never want to get out of bed then, and every morning I know I can sleep for another four hours, and still not fail at any of my duties. But I get up, so have come to believe my life can be seen in miniature in that struggle in the dark of morning. While making the bed and boiling water for coffee, I talk to God: I offer Him my day, every act of my body and spirit, my thoughts and moods, as a prayer of thanksgiving, and for Gloria and my children and my friends and two women I made love with after Gloria left. This morning offertory is a habit from my boyhood in a Catholic school; or then it was a habit, but as I kept it and grew older it became a ritual. Then I say the Lord's Prayer, trying not to recite it, and one morning it occurred to me that a prayer, whether recited or said with concentration, is always an act of faith.

I sit in the kitchen at the rear of the house and drink coffee and smoke and watch the sky growing light before sunrise, the trees of the woods near the barn taking shape, becoming single pines and elms and oaks and maples. Sometimes a rabbit comes out of the treeline, or is already sitting there, visible till the light finds him. The birds are awake in the trees and feeding on the ground and the little ones, the purple finches and titmice and chickadees, are at the feeder I rigged outside the kitchen window; it is too small for pigeons to get a purchase. I sit and give myself to coffee and tobacco, that get me brisk again, and I watch and listen. In the first year or so after I lost my family, I played the radio in the mornings. But I overcame that, and now I rarely play it at all. Once in the mail I received a questionnaire asking me to write down everything I watched on television during the week they had chosen. At the end of those seven days I wrote in *The Wizard of Oz* and returned it. That was in winter and was actually a busy week for my television, which normally sits out the cold months without once warming up. Had they sent the questionnaire during baseball season, they would have found me at my set. People at the stables talk about shows and performers I have never heard of, but I cannot get interested; when I am in the mood to watch television, I go to a movie or read a detective novel. There are always good detective novels to be found, and I like remembering them next morning with my coffee.

I also think of baseball and hunting and fishing, and of my children. It is not painful to think about them anymore, because even if we had lived together, they would be gone now, grown into their own lives, except Jennifer. I think of death too, not sadly, or with fear, though something like excitement does run through me, something more quickening than the coffee and tobacco. I suppose it is an intense interest, and an outright distrust: I never feel certain that I'll be here watching birds eating at tomorrow's daylight. Sometimes I try to think of other things, like the rabbit that is warm and breathing but not there till twilight. I feel on the brink of something about the life of the senses, but either am not equipped to go further, or am not interested enough to concentrate. I have called all of this thinking, but it is not, because it is unintentional; what I'm really doing is feeling the day, in silence, and that is what Father Paul is doing too on his five- to ten-mile walks.

When the hour ends I take an apple or carrot, and I go to the stable and tack up a horse. We take good care of these horses, and no one rides them but students, instructors, and me, and nobody rides the horses we board unless an owner asks me to. The barn is dark and I turn on lights and take some deep breaths, smelling the hay and horses and their manure, both fresh and dried, a combined odor that you either like or you don't. I walk down the wide space of dirt between stalls, greeting horses, joking with them about their quirks, and choose one for no reason at all other than the way it looks at me that morning. I get my old English saddle that has smoothed and darkened through the years, and go into the stall, talking to this beautiful creature who'll swerve out of a canter if a piece of paper blows in front of him, and if the barn catches fire and you manage to get him out he will, if he can get away from you, run back into the fire, to his stall. Like the smells that surround them, you either like them or you don't.

I love them, so am spared having to try to explain why. I feed one the carrot or apple and tack up and lead him outside where I mount, and we go down the driveway to the road and cross it and turn northwest and walk then trot then canter to St. John's.

A few cars are on the road, their drivers looking serious about going to work. It is always strange for me to see a woman dressed for work so early in the morning. You know how long it takes them, with the makeup and hair and clothes, and I think of them waking in the dark of winter or early light of other seasons, and dressing as they might for an evening's entertainment. Probably this strikes me because I grew up seeing my father put on those suits he never wore on weekends or his two weeks off, and so am accustomed to the men, but when I see these women I think something went wrong, to send all those dressed-up people out on the road when the dew hasn't dried yet. Maybe it's because I so dislike getting up early, but am also doing what I choose to do, while they have no choice. At heart I am lazy, yet I find such peace and delight in it that I believe it is a natural state, and in what looks like my laziest periods I am closest to my center. The ride to St. John's is fifteen minutes. The horses and I do it in all weather; the road is well plowed in winter, and there are only a few days a year when ice makes me drive the pickup. People always look at someone on horseback, and for a moment their faces change and many drivers and I wave to each other. Then at St. John's, Father Paul and five or six regulars and I celebrate the Mass.

Do not think of me as a spiritual man whose every thought during those twenty-five minutes is at one with the words of the Mass. Each morning I try, each morning I fail, and know that always I will be a creature who, looking at Father Paul and the altar, and uttering prayers, will be distracted by scrambled eggs, the weather, and memories and daydreams that have nothing to do with the sacrament I am about to receive. I can receive, though: the Eucharist, and also, at Mass and at other times, moments and even minutes of contemplation. But I cannot achieve contemplation, as some can; and so, having to face and forgive my own failures, I have learned from them both the necessity and the wonder of ritual. For ritual allows those who cannot will themselves out of the secular to perform the spiritual as dancing allows the tongue-tied man a ceremony of love. And, while my mind dwells on breakfast, or Major or Duchess tethered under the church eave, there is, as I take the Host from Father Paul and place it on my tongue and return to the pew, a feeling that I am thankful I have not lost in the forty-eight years since my first Communion. At its center is excitement; spreading out from it is the peace of certainty. Or the certainty of peace. One night Father Paul and I talked about faith. It was long ago, and all I remember him saying: Belief is believing in God; faith is believing that God believes in you. That is the excitement, and the peace; then the Mass is over, and I go into the sacristy and we have a cigarette and chat, the mystery ends, we are two men talking like any two men on a morning in America, about baseball, plane crashes, presidents, governors, murders, the sun, the clouds. Then I go to the horse and ride back to the life people see, the one in which I move and talk, and most days I enjoy it.

It is late summer now, the time between fishing and hunting, but a good time for baseball. It has been two weeks since Jennifer left, to drive home to Gloria's after her summer visit. She is the only one who still visits; the boys are married and have children, and sometimes fly up for a holiday, or I fly down or west to visit one of them. Jennifer is twenty, and I worry about her the way fathers worry about daughters but not sons. I want to know what she's up to, and at the same time I don't. She looks athletic, and she is: she swims and runs and of course rides. All my children do. When she comes for six weeks in summer, the house is loud with girls, friends of hers since childhood, and new ones. I am glad she kept the girl friends. They have been young company for me and, being with them, I have been able to gauge her growth between summers. On their riding days, I'd take them back to the house when their lessons were over and they had walked the horses and put them back in the stalls, and we'd have lemonade or Coke, and cookies if I had some, and talk until their parents came to drive them home. One year their breasts grew, so I wasn't startled when I saw Jennifer in July. Then they were driving cars to the stable, and beginning to look like young women, and I was passing out beer and ashtrays and they were talking about college.

When Jennifer was here in summer, they were at the house most days. I would say generally that as they got older they became quieter, and though I enjoyed both, I sometimes missed the giggles and shouts. The quiet voices, just low enough for me not to hear from wherever I was, rising and falling in proportion to my distance from them, frightened me. Not that I believed they were planning or recounting anything really wicked, but there was a female seriousness about them, and it was secretive, and of course I thought: love, sex. But it was more than that: it was womanhood they were entering, the deep forest of it, and no matter how many women and men too are saying these days that there is little difference between us, the truth is that men find their way into that forest only on clearly marked trails while women move about in it like birds. So hearing Jennifer and her friends talking so quietly, yet intensely, I wanted very much to have a wife.

But not as much as in the old days, when Gloria had left but her presence was still in the house as strongly as if she had only gone to visit her folks for a week. There were no clothes or cosmetics, but potted plants endured my neglectful care as long as they could, and slowly died; I did not kill them on purpose, to exorcise the house of her, but I could not remember to water them. For weeks, because I did not use it much, the house was as neat as she had kept it, though dust layered the order she had made. The kitchen went first: I got the dishes in and out of the dishwasher and wiped the top of the stove, but did not return cooking spoons and potholders to their hooks on the wall, and soon the burners and oven were caked with spillings, the refrigerator had more space and was spotted with juices. The living room and my bedroom went next; I did not go into the children's rooms except on bad nights when I went from room to room and looked and touched and smelled, so they did not lose their order until a year later when the kids came for six weeks. It was three months before I ate the last of the food Gloria had cooked and frozen: I remember it was a beef stew, and very good. By then I had four cookbooks, and was boasting a bit, and talking about recipes with women at the stables, and looking forward to cooking for Father Paul. But I never looked forward to cooking at night only for myself, though I made myself do it; on some nights I gave in to my daily temptation, and took a newspaper or detective novel to a restaurant. By the end of the second year, though, I had stopped turning on the radio as soon as I woke in the morning, and was able to be silent and alone in the evening too, and then I enjoyed my dinners.

It was not hard to live through a day, if you can live through a moment. What creates despair is the imagination, that pretends there is a future, and insists on predicting millions of moments, thousands of days, and so drains you that you cannot live the moment at hand. That is what Father Paul told me in those first two years, on some of the bad nights when I believed I could not bear what I had to: the most painful loss was my children, then the loss of Gloria whom I still loved despite or maybe because of our long periods of sadness that rendered us helpless, so neither of us could break out of it to give a hand to the other. Twelve years later I believe ritual would have healed us more quickly than the repetitious talks we had, perhaps even kept us healed. Marriages have lost that, and I wish I had known then what I know now, and we had performed certain acts together every day, no matter how we felt, and perhaps then we could have subordinated feeling to action, for surely that is the essence of love. I know this from my distractions during Mass, and during everything else I do, so that my actions and feelings are seldom one. It does happen every day, but in proportion to everything else in a day, it is rare, like joy. The third most painful loss, which became second and sometimes first as months passed, was the knowledge that I could never marry again, and so dared not even keep company with a woman.

On some of the bad nights I was bitter about this with Father Paul, and I so pitied myself that I cried, or nearly did, speaking with damp eyes and breaking voice. I believe that celibacy is for him the same trial it is for me, not of the flesh, but the spirit: the heart longing to love. But the difference is he chose it, and did not wake one day to a life with thirty horses. In my anger I said I had done my service to love and chastity, and I told him of the actual physical and spiritual pain of practicing rhythm: nights of striking the mattress with a fist, two young animals lying side by side in heat, leaving the bed to pace, to smoke, to curse, and too passionate to question, for we were so angered and oppressed by our passion that we could see no further than our loins. So now I understand how people can be enslaved for generations before they throw down their tools or use them as weapons, the form of their slavery—the cotton fields, the shacks and puny cupboards and untended illnesses—absorbing their emotions and thoughts until finally they have little or none at all to direct their clarity and energy at the owners and legislators. And I told him of the trick of passion and its slaking: how during what we had to believe were safe periods, though all four children were conceived at those times, we were able with some coherence to question the tradition and reason and justice of the law against birth control, but not with enough conviction to soberly act against it, as though regular satisfaction in bed tempered our revolutionary as well as our erotic desires. Only when abstinence drove us hotly away from each other did we receive an urge so strong it lasted all the way to the drugstore and back; but always, after release, we threw away the remaining condoms; and after going through this a few times, we knew what would happen, and from then on we submitted to the calendar she so precisely marked on the bedroom wall. I told him that living two lives each month, one as celibates, one as lovers, made us tense and short-tempered, so we snapped at each other like dogs.

To have endured that, to have reached a time when we burned slowly and could gain from bed the comfort of lying down at night with one who loves you and whom you love, could for weeks on end go to bed tired, and peacefully sleep after a kiss, a touch of the hands, and then to be thrown out of the marriage like a bundle from a moving freight car, was unjust, was intolerable, and I could not or would not muster the strength to endure it. But I did, a moment at a time, a day, a night, except twice, each time with a different woman and more than a year apart, and this was so long ago that I clearly see their faces in my memory, can hear the pitch of their voices, and the way they pronounced words, one with a Massachusetts accent, one midwestern, but I feel as though I only heard about them from someone else. Each rode at the stables and was with me for part of an evening; one was badly married, one divorced, so none of us was free. They did not understand this Catholic view, but they were understanding about my having it, and I remained friends with both of them until the married one left her husband and went to Boston, and the divorced one moved to Maine. After both those evenings, those good women, I went to Mass early while Father Paul was still in the confessional, and received his absolution. I did not tell him who I was, but of course he knew, though I never saw it in his eyes. Now my longing for a wife comes only once in a while, like a cold: on some late afternoons when I am alone in the barn then I lock up and walk to the house, daydreaming, then suddenly look at it and see it empty, as though for the first time, and all at once I'm weary and feel I do not have the energy to broil meat, and I think of driving to a restaurant, then shake my head and go on to the house, the refrigerator, the oven; and some mornings when I wake in the dark and listen to the silence and run my hand over the cold sheet beside me; and some days in summer when Jennifer is here.

Gloria left first me then the church, and that was the end of religion for the children, though on visits they went to Sunday Mass with me, and still do, out of a respect for my life that they manage to keep free of patronage. Jennifer is an agnostic, though I doubt she would call herself that, any more than she would call herself any other name that implied she had made a decision, a choice, about existence, death, and God. In truth she tends to pantheism, a good sign I think; but not wanting to be a father who tells his children what they ought to believe, I do not say to her that Catholicism includes pantheism, like onions in stew. Besides, I have no missionary instincts and do not believe everyone should or even could live with the Catholic faith. It is Jennifer's womanhood that renders me awkward. And womanhood now is frank, not like when Gloria was twenty and there were symbols: high heels and cosmetics and dresses, a cigarette, a cocktail. I am glad that women are free now of false modesty and all its attention paid the flesh; but still it is difficult to see so much of your daughter, to face the deep and unabashed sensuality of women, with no tricks of the eyes and mouth to hide the pleasure she feels at having a strong young body. I am certain, with the way things are now, that she has very happily not been a virgin for years. That does not bother me. What bothers me is my certainty about it, just from watching her walk across a room or light a cigarette or pour milk on cereal.

She told me all of it, waking me that night when I had gone to sleep listening to the wind in the trees against the house, a wind so strong that I had to shut all but the lee windows, and still the house cooled; told it to me in such detail and so clearly that now, when she has driven the car to Florida, I remember it all as though I had been a passenger in the front seat, or even at the wheel. It started with a movie, then beer and driving to the sea to look at the waves in the night and the wind, Jennifer and Betsy and Liz. They drank a beer on the beach and wanted to go in naked but were afraid they would drown in the high surf. They bought another six-pack at a grocery store in New Hampshire, and drove home. I can see it now, feel it: the three girls and the beer and the ride on country roads where pines curved in the wind and the big deciduous trees swayed and shook as if they might leap from the earth. They would have some windows partly open so they could feel the wind; Jennifer would be playing a cassette, the music stirring them, as it does the young, to memories of another time, other people and places in what is for them the past.

She took Betsy home, then Liz, and sang with her cassette as she left the town west of us and started home, a twenty-minute drive on the road that passes my house. They each had four beers, but now there were twelve empty bottles in the bag on the floor at the passenger seat, and I keep focusing on their sound against each other when the car shifted speeds or changed directions. For I want to understand that one moment out of all her heart's time on earth, and whether her history had any bearing on it, or whether her heart was then isolated from all it had known, and the sound of those bottles urged it. She was just leaving town, accelerating past a nightclub on the right, gaining speed to climb a long gradual hill, then she went up it, singing, patting the beat on the steering wheel, the wind loud through her few inches of open window, blowing her hair as it did the high branches alongside the road, and she looked up at them and watched the top of the hill for someone drunk or heedless coming over it in part of her lane. She crested to an open black road, and there he was: a bulk, a blur, a thing running across her headlights, and she swerved left and her foot went for the brake and was stomping air above its pedal when she hit him, saw his legs and body in the air, flying out of her light, into the dark. Her brakes were screaming into the wind, bottles clinking in the fallen bag, and with the music and wind inside the car was his sound already a memory but as real as an echo, that car-shuddering thump as though she had struck a tree. Her foot was back on the accelerator. Then she shifted gears and pushed it. She ejected the cassette and closed the window. She did not start to cry until she knocked on my bedroom door, then called: "Dad?"

Her voice, her tears, broke through my dream and the wind I heard in my sleep, and I stepped into jeans and hurried to the door, thinking harm, rape, death. All were in her face, and I hugged her and pressed her cheek to my chest and smoothed her blown hair, then led her weeping to the kitchen and sat her at the table where still she could not speak, nor look at me; when she raised her face it fell forward again, as of its own weight, into her palms. I offered tea and she shook her head, so I offered beer twice then she shook her head, so I offered whiskey and she nodded. I had some rye that Father Paul and I had not finished last hunting season, and I poured some over ice and set it in front of her and was putting away the ice but stopped and got another glass and poured one for myself too, and brought the ice and bottle to the table where she was trying to get one of her long menthols out of the pack, but her fingers jerked like severed snakes, and I took the pack and lit one for her and took one for myself. I watched her shudder with her first swallow of rye, and push hair back from her face, it is auburn and gleamed in the overhead light, and I remembered how beautiful she looked riding a sorrel; she was smoking fast, then the sobs in her throat stopped, and she looked at me and said it, the words coming out with smoke: "I hit somebody. With the *car*."

Then she was crying and I was on my feet, moving back and forth, looking down at her asking Who? Where? Where? She was pointing at the wall over the stove, jabbing her fingers and cigarette at it, her other hand at her eyes, and twice in horror I actually looked at the wall. She finished the whiskey in a swallow and I stopped pacing and asking and poured another, and either the drink or the exhaustion of tears quieted her, even the dry sobs, and she told me; not as I tell it now, for that was later as again and again we relived it in the kitchen or living room, and if in daylight fled it on horseback out on the trails through the woods, and if at night walked quietly around in the moonlit pasture, walked around and around it, sweating through our clothes. She told it in bursts, like she was a child again, running to me, injured from play. I put on boots and a shirt and left her with the bottle and her streaked face and a cigarette twitching between her fingers, pushed the door open against the wind, and eased it shut. The wind squinted and watered my eyes as I leaned into it and went to the pickup.

When I passed St. John's I looked at it, and Father Paul's little white rectory in the rear, and wanted to stop, wished I could as I could if he were simply a friend who sold hardware or something. I had forgotten my watch but I always know the time within minutes, even when a sound or dream or my bladder wakes me in the night. It was nearly two; we had been in the kitchen about twenty minutes; she had hit him around one-fifteen. Or her. The road was empty and I drove between blowing trees; caught for an instant in my lights, they seemed to be in panic. I smoked and let hope play her tricks on me; it was neither man nor woman but an animal, a goat or calf or deer on the road; it was a man who had jumped away in time, the collision of metal and body glancing not direct, and he had limped home to nurse bruises and cuts. Then I threw the cigarette and hope both out the window and prayed that he was alive, while beneath that prayer, a reserve deeper in my heart, another one stirred: that if he were dead, they would not get Jennifer.

From our direction, east and a bit south, the road to that hill and the nightclub beyond it and finally the town is, for its last four or five miles, straight through farming country. When I reached that stretch I slowed the truck and opened my window for the fierce air; on both sides were scattered farmhouses and barns and sometimes a silo, looking not like shelters but like unsheltered things the wind would flatten. Corn bent toward the road from a field on my right, and always something blew in front of me: paper, leaves, dried weeds, branches. I slowed approaching the hill, and went up it in second, staring through my open window at the ditch on the left side of the road, its weeds alive, whipping, a mad dance with the trees above them. I went over the hill and down and, opposite the club, turned right onto a side street of houses, and parked there, in the leaping shadows of trees. I walked back across the road to the club's parking lot, the wind behind me, lifting me as I strode, and I could not hear my boots on pavement. I walked up the hill, on the shoulder, watching the branches above me, hearing their leaves and the creaking trunks and the wind. Then I was at the top, looking down the road and at the farms and fields; the night was clear, and I could see a long way; clouds scudded past the half-moon and stars, blown out to sea.

I started down, watching the tall grass under the trees to my right, glancing into the dark of the ditch, listening for cars behind me; but as soon as I cleared one tree, its sound was gone, its flapping leaves and rattling branches far behind me, as though the greatest distance I had at my back was a matter of feet, while ahead of me I could see a barn two miles off. Then I saw her skid marks: short, and going left and downhill, into the other lane. I stood at the ditch, its weeds blowing; across it were trees and their moving shadows, like the clouds. I stepped onto its slope, and it took me sliding on my feet then rump to the bottom where I sat still, my body gathered to itself, lest a part of me should touch him. But there was only tall grass, and I stood, my shoulders reaching the sides of the ditch, and I walked uphill, wishing for the flashlight in the pickup, walking slowly, and down in the ditch I could hear my feet in the grass and on the earth, and kicking cans and bottles. At the top of the hill I turned and went down, watching the ground above the ditch on my right, praying my prayer from the truck again, the first one, the one I would admit, that he was not dead, was in fact home, and began to hope again, memory telling me of lost pheasants and grouse I had shot, but they were small and the colors of their home, while a man was either there or not; and from that memory I left where I was and while walking the ditch under the wind was in the deceit of imagination with Jennifer in the kitchen, telling her she had hit no one, or at least had not badly hurt anyone, when I realized he could be in the hospital now and I would have to think of a way to check there, something to say on the phone. I see now that, once hope returned, I should have been certain what she prepared me for; ahead of me, in high grass and the shadows of trees, I saw his shirt. Or that is all my mind would allow itself: a shirt, and I stood looking at it for the moments it took my mind to admit the arm and head and the dark length covered by pants. He lay face down, the arm I could see near his side, his head turned from me, on its cheek.

"Fella?" I said. I had meant to call, but it came out quiet and high, lost inches from my face in the wind. Then I said, "Oh God," and felt Him in the wind and the sky moving past the stars and moon and the fields around me, but only watching me as He might have watched Cain or Job, I did not know which, and I said it again, and wanted to sink to the earth and weep until I slept there in the weeds. I climbed, scrambling up the side of the ditch, pulling at clutched grass, gained the top on hands and knees, and went to him like that, panting, moving through the grass as high and higher than my face, crawling under that sky, making sounds too like some animal, there being no words to let him know I was here with him now. He was long; that is the word that came to me, not tall. I kneeled beside him, my hands on my legs. His right arm was by his side, his left arm straight out from the shoulder, but turned, so his palm was open to the tree above us. His left cheek was clean shaven, his eye closed, and there was no blood. I leaned forward to look at his open mouth and saw the blood on it, going down into the grass. I straightened and looked ahead at the wind blowing past me through grass and trees to a distant light, and I stared at the light, imagining someone awake out there, wanting someone to be, a gathering of old friends, or someone alone listening to music or painting a picture, then I figured it was a night light at a farmyard whose house I couldn't see. *Going.* I thought. *Still going.* I leaned over again and looked at dripping blood.

So I had to touch his wrist, a thick one with a watch and expansion band that I pushed up his arm, thinking *he's left-handed,* my three fingers pressing his wrist and all I felt was my tough fingertips on that smooth underside flesh and small bones, then relief, then certainty. But against my will, or only because of it, I still don't know, I touched his neck, ran my fingers down it as if petting, then pressed and my hand sprang back as from fire. I lowered it again, held it there until it felt that faint beating that I could not believe. There was too much wind. Nothing could make a sound in it. A pulse could not be felt in it, nor could mere fingers in that wind feel the absolute silence of a dead man's artery. I was making sounds again; I grabbed his left arm and his waist, and pulled him toward me, and that side of him rose, turned, and I lowered him to his back, his face tilted up toward the tree that was groaning, the tree and I the only sounds in the wind. Turning my face from his, looking down the length of him at his sneakers, I placed my ear on his heart, and heard not that but something else, and I clamped a hand over my exposed ear, heard something liquid and alive, like when you pump a well and after a few strokes you hear air and water moving in the pipe, and I knew I must raise his legs and cover him and run to a phone, while still I listened to his chest, thinking *raise with what? cover with what?* and amid the liquid sound I heard the heart then lost it, and pressed my ear against bone, but his chest was quiet, and I did not know when the liquid had stopped, and do not know when I heard air, a faint rush of it, and whether under my ear or at his mouth or whether I heard it at all. I straightened and looked at the light, dim and yellow. Then I touched his throat, looking him full in the face. He was blond and young. He could have been sleeping in the shade of a tree, but for the smear of blood from his mouth to this hair, and the night sky, and the weeds blowing against his head, and the leaves shaking in the dark above us.

I stood. Then I kneeled again and prayed for his soul to join in peace and joy all the dead and living; and doing so, confronted my first sin against him, not stopping for Father Paul, who could have given him the last rites, and immediately then my second one, or, I saw then, my first, not calling an ambulance to meet me there, and I stood and turned into the wind, slid down the ditch and crawled out of it, and went up the hill and down it, across the road to the street of houses whose people I had left behind forever, so that I moved with stealth in the shadows to my truck.

When I came around the bend near my house, I saw the kitchen light at the rear. She sat as I had left her, the ashtray filled, and I looked at the bottle, felt her eyes on me, felt what she was seeing too: the dirt from my crawling. She had not drunk much of the rye. I poured some in my glass, with the water from melted ice, and sat down and swallowed some and looked at her and swallowed some more, and said: "He's dead."

She rubbed her eyes with the heels of her hands, rubbed the cheeks under them, but she was dry now.

"He was probably dead when he hit the ground. I mean, that's probably what killed—"

"Where was he?"

"Across the ditch, under a tree."

"Was he—did you see his face?"

"No. Not really. I just felt. For life, pulse. I'm going out to the car."

"What for? Oh."

I finished the rye, and pushed back the chair, then she was standing too.

"I'll go with you."

"There's no need."

"I'll go."

I took a flashlight from a drawer and pushed open the door and held it while she went out. We turned our faces from the wind. It was like on the hill, when I was walking, and the wind closed the distance behind me: after three or four steps I felt there was no house back there. She took my hand, as I was reaching for hers. In the garage we let go, and squeezed between the pickup and her little car, to the front of it, where we had more room, and we stepped back from the grill and I shone the light on the fender, the smashed headlight turned into it, the concave chrome staring to the right, at the garage wall.

"We ought to get the bottles," I said.

She moved between the garage and the car, on the passenger side, and had room to open the door and lift the bag. I reached out, and she gave me the bag and backed up and shut the door and came around the car. We sidled to the doorway, and she put her arm around my waist and I hugged her shoulders.

"I thought you'd call the police," she said.

We crossed the yard, faces bowed from the wind, her hair blowing away from her neck, and in the kitchen I put the bag of bottles in the garbage basket. She was working at the table: capping the rye and putting it away, filling the ice tray, washing the glasses, emptying the ashtray, sponging the table.

"Try to sleep now," I said.

She nodded at the sponge circling under her hand, gathering ashes. Then she dropped it in the sink and, looking me full in the face, as I had never seen her look, as perhaps she never had, being for so long a daughter on visits (or so it seemed to me and still does: that until then our eyes had never seriously met), she crossed to me from the sink, and kissed my lips, then held me so tightly I lost balance, and would have stumbled forward had she not held me so hard.

I sat in the living room, the house darkened, and watched the maple and the hemlock. When I believed she was asleep I put on *La Bohème*, and kept it at the same volume as the wind so it would not wake her. Then I listened to *Madame Butterfly*, and in the third act had to rise quickly to lower the sound: the wind was gone. I looked at the still maple near the window, and thought of the wind leaving farms and towns and the coast, going out over the sea to die on the waves. I smoked and gazed out the window. The sky was darker, and at daybreak the rain came. I listened to *Tosca*, and at six-fifteen went to the kitchen where Jennifer's purse lay on the table, a leather shoulder purse crammed with the things of an adult woman, things she had began accumulating only a few years back, and I nearly wept, thinking of what sandy foundations they were: driver's license, credit card, disposable lighter, cigarettes, checkbook, ballpoint pen, cash, cosmetics, comb, brush, Kleenex, these the rite of passage from childhood, and I took one of them—her keys—and went out, remembering a jacket and hat when the rain struck me, but I kept going to the car, and squeezed and lowered myself into it, pulled the seat belt over my shoulder and fastened it and backed out, turning in the drive, going forward into the road, toward St. John's and Father Paul.

Cars were on the road, the workers, and I did not worry about any of them noticing the fender and light. Only a horse distracted them from what they drove to. In front of St. John's is a parking lot; at its far side, past the church and at the edge of the lawn, is an old pine, taller than the steeple now. I shifted to third, left the road, and aiming the right headlight at the tree, accelerated past the white blur of church, into the black trunk growing bigger till it was all I could see, then I rocked in that resonant thump she had heard, had felt, and when I turned off the ignition it was still in my ears, my blood, and I saw the boy flying in the wind. I lowered my forehead to the wheel. Father Paul opened the door, his face white in the rain.

"I'm all right."

"What happened?"

"I don't know. I fainted."

I got out and went around to the front of the car, looked at the smashed light, the crumpled and torn fender.

"Come to the house and lie down."

"I'm all right."

"When was your last physical?"

"I'm due for one. Let's get out of this rain."

"You'd better lie down."

"No. I want to receive."

That was the time to say I wanted to confess, but I have not and will not. Though I could now, for Jennifer is in Florida, and weeks have passed, and perhaps now Father Paul would not feel that he must tell me to go to the police. And, for that very reason, to confess now would be unfair. It is a world of secrets, and now I have one from my best, in truth my only, friend. I have one from Jennifer too, but that is the nature of fatherhood.

Most of that day it rained, so it was only in early evening, when the sky cleared, with a setting sun, that two little boys, leaving their confinement for some play before dinner, found him. Jennifer and I got that on the local news, which we listened to every hour, meeting at the radio, standing with cigarettes, until the one at eight o'clock; when she stopped crying, we went out and walked on the wet grass, around the pasture, the last of sunlight still in the air and trees. His name was

Patrick Mitchell, he was nineteen years old, was employed by CETA, lived at home with his parents and brother and sister. The paper next day said he had been at a friend's house and was walking home, and I thought of that light I had seen, then knew it was not for him; he lived on one of the streets behind the club. The paper did not say then, or in the next few days, anything to make Jennifer think he was alive while she was with me in the kitchen. Nor do I know if we—if I— could have saved him.

In keeping her secret from her friends, Jennifer had to perform so often, as I did with Father Paul and at the stables, that I believe the acting, which took more of her than our daylight trail rides and our night walks in the pasture, was her healing. Her friends teased me about wrecking her car. When I carried her luggage out to the car on that last morning, we spoke only of the weather for her trip—the day was clear, with a dry cool breeze—and hugged and kissed, and I stood watching as she started the car and turned it around. But then she shifted to neutral and put on the parking brake and unclasped the belt, looking at me all the while, then she was coming to me, as she had that night in the kitchen, and I opened my arms.

I have said I talk with God in the mornings, as I start my day, and sometimes as I sit with coffee, looking at the birds, and the woods. Of course He has never spoken to me, but that is not something I require. Nor does He need to. I know Him, as I know the part of myself that knows Him, that felt Him watching from the wind and the night as I knelt over the dying boy. Lately I have taken to arguing with Him, as I can't with Father Paul who, when he hears my monthly confession, has not and will not hear anything of failure to do all that one can to save an anonymous life, of injustice to a family in their grief, of deepening their pain at the chance and mystery of death by giving them nothing—no one—to hate. With Father Paul, I feel lonely about this, but not with God. When I received the Eucharist while Jennifer's car sat twice-damaged, so redeemed, in the rain, I felt neither loneliness nor shame, but as though He were watching me, even from my tongue, intestines, blood, as I have watched my sons at times in their young lives when I was able to judge but without anger, and so keep silent while they, in the agony of their youth, decided how they must act; or found reasons, after their actions, for what they had done. Their reasons were never as good or as bad as their actions, but they needed to find them, to believe they were living by them, instead of the awful solitude of the heart.

I do not feel the peace I once did: not with God, nor the earth, or anyone on it. I have begun to prefer this state, to remember with fondness the other one as a period of peace I neither earned nor deserved. Now in the mornings while I watch purple finches driving larger titmice from the feeder, I say to Him: I would do it again. For when she knocked on my door then called me, she woke what had flowed dormant in my blood since her birth, so that what rose from the bed was not a stable owner or a Catholic or any other Luke Ripley I had lived with for a long time, but the father of a girl.

And He says: I am a Father too.

Yes, I say, as You are a Son Whom this morning I will receive; unless You kill me on the way to church, then I trust You will receive me. And as a Son You made Your plea.

Yes, He says, but I would not lift the cup.

True, and I don't want You to lift it from me either. And if one of my sons had come to me that night, I would have phoned the police and told them to meet us with an ambulance at the top of the hill.

Why? Do you love them less?

I tell Him no, it is not that I love them less, but that I could bear the pain of watching and knowing my sons' pain, could bear it with pride as they took the whip and nails. But You never had a daughter, and if You had, You could not have borne her passion.

So, He says, you love her more than you love Me.

I love her more than I love truth.

Then you love in weakness, He says.

As You love me, I say, and I go with an apple or carrot out to the barn.

THE AFTERLIFE

John Updike

The Billingses, so settled in their ways, found in their fifties that their friends were doing sudden, surprising things. Mitch Lothrop, whom Carter and Jane had always rather poked fun at as stuffy, ran off with a young Jamaican physical therapist, and Augustina, who had seemed such a mouse all those years—obsessed with her garden and her children's educations—took it rather raucously in stride, buying herself a new wardrobe of broad-shouldered dresses, putting a prodigiously expensive new slate roof on the Weston house, and having in as a new companion another woman, a frilly little blue-eyed person who worked in Boston as a psychologist for the Department of Social Services. Ken McEvoy, on the other hand, was one day revealed in the newspapers as an embezzler who over the course of twenty years had stolen between two and five million from his brokerage firm; nobody, including the IRS, knew exactly how much. The investigation had evidently been going on for ages, during which time Ken and Molly had been showing up at cocktail parties and dinner parties and zoning hearings and church suppers with not a hair out of place, smiling and looking as handsome a couple as ever. Even now, with the indictment in the paper and the pleabargaining stage under way, they continued to appear at gatherings, Ken quite hilarious and open about it all and basking at the center of attention; he had always seemed rather stiff and shy before. What had he done with all the money? It was true they had two foreign cars, and a place on the Cape, and trips to Europe in the years they didn't go to Florida, but then so did everybody, more or less.

And then the Billingses' very dearest friends, Frank and Lucy Eggleston, upped and moved to England. It was something, Frank confided, they had thought about for years; they detested America, the way it was going—the vulgarity, the crowdedness, the violence. They both, Frank and Lucy, were exceptionally soft-spoken and virtual teetotalers, with health diets and peaceable hobbies; Frank did watercolors, Lucy bird-watched. A juncture came in his career when the corporation asked him to move to Texas; he opted to take early retirement instead, and with his savings and a little inheritance of hers, plus the ridiculous price their house brought—ten times what they had paid for it in the early sixties—they moved to England, at a time when the pound was low against the dollar. Why defer a dream, they asked the Billingses, until you're too old to enjoy it? They found a suitable house not in one of the pretty counties south of London but up in Norfolk, where, as one of Lucy's early letters put it, "the sky is as big as they say the sky of Texas is."

The letters were less frequent than the Billingses had expected, and on their side they proved slower than they had promised to arrange a visit to their transplanted friends. Three years had gone by before they at last, after some days in London to adjust to the time change and the currency and the left-right confusion, took a train north, got off at a station beyond Cambridge, and were greeted in the damp and windy spring twilight by a bouncy, bog-hatted shadow they recognized as Frank Eggleston. He had put on weight, and had acquired that rosy English complexion and an un-American way of clearing his throat several times in rapid succession. As they drove along the A-11, and then navigated twisting country roads, Carter seemed to hear Frank's accent melt, becoming less clipped and twitchy as his passengers and he talked and warmed the car's interior with their growly, drawling Americanness.

After many a turning in the dark, they arrived at Flinty Dell—a name no natives, surely, would have given the slightly gaunt mustard brick house, with its many gables and odd-sized, scattered windows, behind its high wall and bristlings of privet. Lucy seemed much as ever; a broad-faced strawberry blonde, she had always worn sweaters and plaid pleated skirts and low-heeled shoes for her birding walks, and here this same outfit seemed a shade more chic and less aggressively "sensible" than it had at home. Her pleasant plain looks, rather lost in the old crowd of heavily groomed suburban wives, had bloomed in this climate; her manner, as she showed them the house and their room upstairs, seemed to Carter somehow blushing, bridal. She escorted them through a maze of brightly papered rooms and awkward little hallways, up one set of stairs then down another, and on through the kitchen to a mud room, where she and Frank outfitted themselves with scarves and Wellingtons and fat leather gloves and canes and riding crops and rakes and shovels for their dealings with the constantly invigorating out-of-doors. A barn went with the place, where they boarded horses. The village church was just across the pasture and through the wood on a path. Some obscure duke's vast estate stretched all about, with miles and miles of wonderful riding. And then there were fens, and a priory ruin, and towns where antiques could be had for almost nothing. It was all too much to take in, or to talk about so late at night, Lucy said, especially when you must be exhausted and still on funny time.

"Oh, no," Jane said. "Carter was determined to get on your time and he wouldn't let me take a nap that first awful day. We walked all the way from the National Gallery to the Tate in the rain, which had this huge retrospective of this horrid Kitchen Sink school."

"Such fun you make it sound," Lucy said, tucking her plump freckled calves under her on the tired-looking sofa. The living room was rather small, though high-ceilinged. The furniture, which they must have brought here, clustered like a threadbare, expectant audience about the tiny grated fireplace, as it vivaciously consumed chunks of wood too short to be called logs. "We thought we'd be going down to London every other day but there seems so much to do *here*."

The birding was incredible, and Lucy had become, to her own surprise, quite involved with the local church and with village good works. Frank was painting very seriously, and had joined an artists' association in Norwich, and had displayed a number of watercolors in their biannual shows. Some of his new works were hung in the living room: wet gray skies and tiny dark houses in the lee of gloomy groves scrubbed in with purple and green. Having poked the fire, and added more chunks (whose smoke smelled narcotically sweet), Frank pressed drinks upon the Billingses, though, as all agreed, it was already late and tomorrow was a big day. Lucy was going to drive them to the sea while Frank rode in the local hunt. Scotch, brandy, port, Madeira, and several tints of sherry were produced; Carter remembered the Egglestons as abstemious, but English coziness seemed to have teased that out of them. Carter drank port and Jane cream sherry as they gave the American news: Mitch Lothrop and the Jamaican bodybuilder live in Bay Village and have a baby, while Augustina has turned the Weston place into some sort of commune, with a total of five women living in it now. Ken McEvoy is out, having served less than two years, and has been given a job by one of the big Boston banks as an accountant, because he's supposedly an expert on fraudulent bookkeeping. Though he and Molly still drive their old Jaguar and a Volvo station wagon, it's obvious he must have stashed millions away, because they're always flying off now, even just for weekends, to this place they seem to own in the Bahamas. And so on.

Frank and Lucy had grown smilingly silent under this barrage of imported gossip, and when Carter stood and announced, "We're boring you," neither one of them contradicted him. He had lost count of the times Frank had refreshed his port, or poured himself another brandy, and the freckles on Lucy's shins were beginning to swarm; yet he felt he was cutting something short, standing at last. All seemed to feel this—this failure, for all their good will, to remake the old connection—and it was an atmosphere of reluctance that the guests were, sensibly, led up to bed, Lucy showing them the bathroom again and making sure they had towels.

In the night, Carter awoke and needed to go to the bathroom. All that port. A wind was blowing outside. Vague black-on-blue tree shapes were thrashing. Turning on no light, so as not to wake Jane, he found the bedroom door, opened it softly in the dark, and took two firm steps down the hall toward where he remembered the bathroom was. On his second step, there was nothing but air beneath his foot. His sleepy brain was jolted into action; he realized he was falling down the stairs. As he soared through black space, he had time to think what a terrible noise his crashing body would make, and how the Egglestons would be awakened, and how embarrassing and troublesome it would be for them to deal with his broken body. He even had time to reflect how oddly selfless this last thought was. Then something—someone, he felt—hit him a solid blow in the exact center of his chest, right on the sternum, and Carter was standing upright on a landing partway down the stairs. He listened a moment, heard only the wind as it moaned around the strange brick house, and climbed the six or so steps back to the second floor.

He remembered now that the bathroom was reached by turning immediately left out of the bedroom and then right at the bannister that protected the stairwell, and then left again, at the second door. He crept along and pressed this door open. The white toilet and porcelain basin had a glow of their own in the moonless night, so again he did without a light. His legs were trembling and his chest ached slightly, but he felt better for having emptied his bladder. However, emerging again into the dark hall, he couldn't find his way back to his bedroom. Walls as in a funhouse surrounded him. A large smooth plane held a shadowy man who actually touched him, with an abrupt oily touch, and he realized it was himself, reflected in a mirror. On the three other sides of him there were opaque surfaces paneled like doors. Then one of the doors developed a crack of dim blue light and seemed to slide diagonally away; Carter's eyes were adjusted to the dark enough to register wallpaper—faintly abrasive and warm to his touch—and the shiny straight gleam, as of a railroad track, of the bannister. He reversed his direction. There seemed many doors along the hall, but the one he pushed open did indeed reveal his bedroom. The wind was muttering, fidgeting at the stout English window sash, and as Carter drew closer to the bed he could hear Jane breathe. He crept in beside her and fell swiftly asleep.

Next morning, as he examined the site of his adventure, he marveled that he had not been killed. The oval knob of a newel post at the turn in the stairs must have been what struck him on the chest; had he fallen a slightly different way, it would have hit him in the face—smashed in his front teeth, or ripped out an eye—or he could have missed it entirely and broken his neck against the landing wall. He had no memory of grabbing anything, or of righting himself. But how had he regained his feet? Either his memory had a gap or he had been knocked bolt upright. If the latter, it seemed a miracle, but Jane, when he confided the event to her, took the occasion not for marveling, but for showing him, as one would show a stupid child, how to turn on the hall light, with one of those British toggle switches that look like a stumpy rapier with a button in its tip.

Carter felt rebuffed; he had told her of his nocturnal adventure, while they were still in bed, in hushed tones much like hers when, thirty years ago, she would confide a suspicion that she was pregnant. The Egglestons, downstairs at breakfast, responded more appropriately; they expressed amazement and relief that he hadn't been hurt. "You might have been *killed!*" Lucy said, with a rising inflection that in America had never been quite so pert, so boldly birdlike.

"Exactly," Carter said. "And at the time, even as I was in midair, I thought, What a nuisance for the poor Egglestons!"

"Damn white of you," Frank said, lifting his teacup to his face. He was in a hurry to be off to his hunt; he had been up for several hours, doing a painting that needed dawn light, and there were blue and yellow under his fingernails. "Not to pop off on us," he finished.

"It happens," Carter told him. "More and more, you see your contemporaries in the *Globe* obituaries. The Big Guy is getting our range." This outburst of theology was so unexpected that the three others stared at him with a silence in which the chimneys could be heard to moan and the breakfast china to click. Carter felt, however, unembarrassed, and supernaturally serene. The world to which he had awoken, from the English details of the orange-juiceless, marmalade-laden breakfast set before him to the muddy green windswept landscape framed in the thick-sashed and playfully various windows, reminded him of children's books he had read over fifty years ago, and had the charm of the timeless.

He squeezed his feet into Lucy's Wellingtons and walked out with Frank to admire the horses. This Norfolk earth was littered with flint—chalky, sharp-edged pebbles. He picked one up and held it in his hand. A limestone layer, porous like bone, had wrapped itself around a shiny bluish core. He tried to imagine the geological event—some immense vanished ocean—that had precipitated this hail of bonelike fragments. The abundant flint, the tufty grass so bursting with green, the radiant gray sky, the strong smells of horse and leather and feed and hay all bore in upon Carter's revitalized senses with novel force; there seemed a cosmic joke under mundane appearances, and in the air a release of pressure which enabled the trees, the beeches and oaks, to attain the size of thunderheads. The air was raw—rawer than he had expected England in April to be. "Is the wind always like this?" he asked the other man.

"Pretty much. It's been a tardy spring." Frank, in hunting coat and jodhpurs, had saddled a horse in its stall and was fiddling with the bridle, making the long chestnut head of the animal, with its rubbery gray muzzle and rolling gelatinous eyeball, jerk resentfully. The physical fact of a horse—the pungent, assaultive hugeness of the animal and the sense of a tiny spark, a gleam of skittish and limited intelligence, within its monstrous long skull—was not a fact that Carter often confronted in his other life.

"Doesn't it get on your nerves?"

"Does 'em good," Frank said with his acquired brisk bluffness. "Scours you out."

"Yes," Carter said, "I can feel that." He felt delicate, alert, excited. The center of his chest was slightly sore. His toes were numb and scrunched inside Lucy's boots. With a terrible shuffling of hooves and heaving of glossy mass, the horse was led from the barn and suddenly Frank was up on it, transformed, majestic, his pink face crowned by his round black hat, he and the horse a single new creature. The two women came out of the mustard brick house to watch its master ride off, at a stately pace, down the flinty driveway to the path through the wood. The trees not yet in full leaf were stippled all over with leaflets and catkins, like a swathe of dotted swiss. Frank, thus veiled, slowly vanished. "A grand sight," Carter said, feeling that some such entertainment, astonishing yet harmless and intangible, would be his steady diet here. He felt weightless, as if, in that moment of flight headlong down the stairs, he had put on wings.

Lucy asked them which they would like first, the walk to the river or the drive to the sea. Then she decided the two should be combined, and a supply of boots and overshoes was tossed into the car. Carter got in the back of the little Austin—red, though it had looked black at the station last night—and let the two women sit up front together. Jane occupied what in America would have been the driver's seat, so that Carter felt startled and imperiled when she turned her head aside or gestured with both hands. Lucy seemed quite accustomed to the wrong side of the road, and drove with a heedless dash. "Here is the village, these few houses," she said. "And the church just beyond—you can't see it very well because of that huge old chestnut. Incredibly old they say the tree is. The church isn't so old."

On the other side of the road, there were sheep, dusted all over with spots of color and mingled with gamboling lambs. The river was not far off, and they parked by an iron bridge where water poured in

steady cold pleats down the slant face of a concrete weir. Embank-
ments had been built by stacking bags of cement and letting natural
processes dampen and harden them. Lucy led the way along a muddy
path between the riverbank and a field that had been recently plowed;
the pale soil, littered to the horizon with bonelike bits of flint, was visibly lifting into the silvery, tumbling sky. The wind was scouring dark
trails of soil upward, across the plowed miles.

"It's been almost a drought," Lucy said, her voice buffeted, her
kerchief flattened against her freckled cheek. Her squinting eyes were a
pale color between blue and green, and this beryl, beneath this sky,
had an uncanny brilliance. "Oh, look!" she cried, pointing. "A little
marsh tit, doing his acrobatics! Last week, closer to the woods, I saw a
pair of waxwings. They generally go back to the Continent by this
time of year. Am I boring you both? Really, the wind is frightful, but I
want you to see my gray heron. His nest must be in the woods somewhere, but Frank and I have never been able to spot it. We asked
Sedgewick—that's the duke's gamekeeper—where to look for it, and
he said if we got downwind we would *smell* it. They eat meat, you
know—rodents and snakes."

"Oh dear," Jane said, for something to say. Carter couldn't take
his eyes from the distant dark lines of lifting earth, the Texaslike dust
storm. As the three made their way along the river, the little black-
capped tit capered in the air above them, and as they approached the
woods, out flocked starlings, speckled and black and raucous.

"Look—the kingfisher!" Lucy cried. This bird was brilliant,
ruddy-breasted and green-headed, with a steel-blue tail. It flicked the
tail back and forth, then whirred along the river's glittering surface.
But the gray heron was not showing himself, though they trod the
margin of the woods for what seemed half a mile. They could hear tree
trunks groaning as the wind twisted their layered crowns; the tallest
and leafiest trees seemed not merely to heave but to harbor several
small explosions at once, which whitened their tossing branches in
patches. Carter's eyes watered, and Jane held her hands in their fat,
borrowed gloves in front of her face. At last, their hostess halted. She
announced, "We'd better get on with it—what a disappointment," and
led them back to the car.

As they drew close to the glittering, pleated, roaring weir, Carter
had the sudden distinct feeling that he should look behind him. And

there was the heron, sailing out of the woods toward them, against the wind, held, indeed, motionless within the wind, standing in midair with his six-foot wingspread—an angel.

The wind got worse as they drove toward the sea. On the map, it looked a long way off, but Lucy assured them she had often done it and back by teatime. As she whipped along the narrow roads, Carter in the back seat could not distinguish between her tugs on the steering wheel and the tugs of the wind as it buffeted the Austin. A measured, prissy voice on the radio spoke of a gale from the Irish Sea and of conditions that were "near cyclonic," and Jane and Carter laughed, though Lucy merely smiled and said that they often used that expression. In a village especially dear to her, especially historical and picturesque, a group of people were standing on the sidewalk at the crest of a hill, near the wall of a churchyard. The church was Norman, with ornamental arcs and borders of red pebbles worked into the masonry. Lucy drove the car rather slowly past, to see if there had been an accident.

"I think," Carter offered, "they're watching the tree." A tall tree leaning from within the churchyard was swaying in the wind.

"Brother," Lucy said. "I've driven too far—what I wanted to show you was back in the middle of the village." She turned around, and as they drove by again several of the little crowd, recognizing the car, seemed amused. A policeman, wearing a rain cape, was pedaling his bicycle up the hill, very energetically, head down.

What Lucy wanted the Billingses to see in the village was a side street of sixteenth-century houses, all of them half-timbered and no two leaning at the same angle.

"Who lives in them?" Carter wanted to know.

"Oh, people—though I daresay more and more it's trendy younger people who open up shops on the ground floor." Lucy backed around again and this time, coming up the hill, they met a police barricade, and the tree had fallen flat across the road. Just half of the tree, actually; its crotch had been low to the earth, and the other half, with a splintery white wound in its side, still stood.

The three Americans, sealed into their car, shrieked in excitement, understanding now why the villagers had been amused to see them drive past under the tree again. "You'd think *some*body," Jane said, "might have said something to warn us."

"Well, I suppose they thought we had eyes to see as well as they," said Lucy. "That's how they are. They don't give anything away; you have to go to them." And she described, as they bounced between thorny hedgerows and dry-stone walls, her church work, her charity work in the area. It was astonishing, how much incest there was, the drunkenness, and hopelessness. "These people just can't envision any better future for themselves. They would never *dream*, for example, of going to London, even for a day. They're just totally locked into their little world."

Jane asked, "What about television?"

"Oh, they watch it, but don't see that it has anything to do with them. They're taken care of, you see, and compared with their fathers and grandfathers aren't so badly off. The *cru*elty of the old system of hired agricultural labor is almost beyond imagining; they worked people absolutely to death. Picking flint, for instance. Every spring they'd all get out there and pick the flint off the fields."

That didn't seem, to Carter, so very cruel. He had picked up bits of flint on his own, spontaneously. They were porous, pale, intricate, everlasting. His mind wandered as Lucy went on about the Norfolk villagers and Jane chimed in with her own concerns—her wish, now that the children were out of the house, to get out herself and be of some service, not exactly jump into the ghetto with wild-eyed good intentions but do something *use*ful, something with *pe*ople...

Carter had been nodding off, and the emphasized words pierced his doze. He felt he had been useful enough, in his life, and had seen enough people. At work now—he was a lawyer—he was conscious of a curious lag, like the lag built into radio talk shows so that obscenities wouldn't get on the air. Just two or three seconds, between challenge and response, between achievement and gratification, but enough to tell him that something was out of sync. He was going through the motions, and all the younger people around him knew it. When he spoke, his voice sounded dubbed, not quite his own. There were, it had recently come to him, vast areas of the world he no longer cared about—Henry James, for example, and professional ice hockey, and nuclear disarmament. He did not doubt that within these areas much excitement could be generated, but not for him, nevermore. The two women in front of him—Lucy's strawberry-blonde braids twitching as she emphasized a point and Jane's gray-peppered brunette curls softly bouncing as she nodded in eager empathy—seemed alien creatures, like the horse, or the marsh tit with his little black-capped head. The two wives seemed as stirred up and twittery as if their lives had just begun, and courtship and husbands and childbearing were a preamble to some triumphant menopausal ministry among the disenfranchised and incestuous. They loved each other, Carter reflected wearily. Women had the passion of conspirators, the energy of any underground, supplied by hope of seizing power. Lucy seemed hardly to notice, while talking and counseling Jane, that she had more than once steered around the wreckage of limbs that littered the road. Through the speeding car windows Carter watched trees thrash in odd slow motion and overhead wires sway as if the earth itself had lost its moorings.

Then, out of the bruised and scrambled sky, a rain pelted down with such fury that the wipers couldn't keep the windshield clear; it became like frosted glass, and the car roof thrummed. Lucy lifted her voice: "There's a lovely old inn right in the next village. Would this be a good time to have a bite?"

Just in dashing the few yards from the parking lot to the shelter of the inn, the three of them got soaked. Inside, all was idyllic: big old blackened fireplace crackling and hissing and exuding that sweet scent of local woodsmoke, carved beams bowed down almost to Carter's head, buffet of salmon mousse and Scotch eggs and shepherd's pie served by a willing lad and blushing lass, at whose backs the rain beat like a stage effect on the thick bottle panes. They ate, and drank beer and tea, and over Lucy's protests Carter paid.

Next door, an antique shop tempted tourists through a communicating archway, and while the storm continued, Lucy and her visitors browsed among the polished surfaces, the silver and mirrors, the framed prints and marquetry tables. Carter was struck by a lustrous large bureau, veneered in a wood that looked like many blurred paw prints left by a party of golden cats. "Elm burl, early eighteenth century," the ticket said, along with a price in the thousands of pounds. He asked Jane if she would like it—as if one more piece of furniture might keep her at home.

"Darling, it's lovely," she said, "but so expensive, and so big."

"They ship," he responded, after a few seconds' lag. "And if it doesn't fit anywhere we can sell it in town for a profit." His voice didn't sound quite like his own, but only he seemed to notice. The women's conversation in the car had obligated him to show that power, male power, did more than induce weariness in the holder. Elm burl: perhaps that was the charm, the touch of an attractive fantasy. In America, the elms were dead, as dead as the anonymous workman who had laid on this still glamorous veneer.

Lucy, deepening her hint of a British accent, courteously haggled with the manager—a straggly fat woman with a runny red nose and a Gypsyish shawl she held tight around her throat—and got four hundred pounds knocked off the price. Carter's plunge into this purchase frightened him, momentarily, as he realized how big the markup must be to absorb such a discount so casually.

There were forms to sign, and credit cards to authenticate over the telephone. As these transactions were pursued, the storm on the roof abated. The three buyers stepped out into a stunning sunlit lapse in the weather. Raindrops glistened everywhere like a coating of ice, and the sidewalk slates echoed the violet of the near-cyclonic sky.

"Darling, that was so debonair and dashing and untypical of you," Jane said.

"Ever so larky," Lucy agreed.

"Kind of a game," he admitted. "What are the odds we'll ever see that chest again?"

Lucy took mild offense, as if her adopted fellow countrymen were being impugned. "Oh, they're very honest and reputable. We've dealt with these people a few times ourselves."

A miraculous lacquer lay upon everything, beading each roadside twig, each reed of thatch in the cottage roofs, each tiny daisy trembling in the grass by the lichen-stained rough field walls. Then clouds swept in again, and the landscape was dipped in shadow. Many trees were fallen or split. Little clusters of workmen, in raincoats that were pumpkin-colored instead of, as they would have been in America, yellow or Day-Glo orange, buzzed with saws and pulled with ropes at limbs that intruded into the road. Waiting to be signaled past such work parties took time, while the little Austin gently rocked in the wind as if being nudged by a hand. Carter caressed the sensitive center of his chest, under his necktie: his secret, the seal of his nocturnal pact, his passport to this day like no other. It had felt, in the dark, like a father's rough impatient saving blow. "How much farther to the sea?" he asked.

"Well might you ask," Lucy said. "On a day of smooth sailing, we'd be there by now." The cars ahead of them slowed and then stopped entirely. A policeman with a young round face explained that lines were down across the road.

"That does rather tear it," Lucy said. The detour would add fifteen miles at least to their journey. The landscape looked dyed, now, in an ink that rolled across the pale speckled fields in waves of varying intensity. Along a far ridge, skeletal powerline towers marched in a procession, their latticework etched with a ghostly delicacy against the black sky. A band of angels.

Jane consoled Lucy. "Really, dear, if I saw too many more charming villages I might burst."

"And we see the sea all the time when we're on the Cape," Carter added.

"But not *our* sea," Lucy said. "The *North* Sea."

"Isn't it just ugly and cold and full of oil?" asked Jane.

"Not for much longer, they tell us. Full of oil, I mean. Well, if you two don't really mind, I suppose there's nothing to do but go back. Frank *does* like an early supper after he's been on a hunt."

It was growing dark by the time they reached Flinty Dell. Exposing to view a small, drab Victorian church, the ancient chestnut had blown down—a giant shaggy corpse with a tall stump torn like a shriek, pointing at the heavens. The tree had fallen across the churchyard wall and crushed it, the outer courses of sturdy-seeming brick spilling a formless interior of rubble and sand.

Frank came out into the driveway to meet them; in the dusk his face looked white, and his voice was not amused. "My, God, where have you people been? I couldn't believe you'd be out driving around in this! The hunt was called off, the radio's been canceling everything and telling people for Christ's sake to stay off the roads!" He rested a trembling hand on the sill of the rolled-down car window; his little fingernail still bore a yellow fleck.

"In this bit of a breeze?" Lucy asked him, birdlike.

Jane said, "Why, Frank darling, how nice of you to be worried."

And Carter, too, was surprised and amused that Frank didn't know they were beyond all that now.

THE PRESIDENT OF THE ARGENTINE

John Cheever

Coldness falls from the air, she thought, as she carried the white roses up the stairs to the paneled library. That, or: How like sandpipers were the children on the beach, she thought, as she stood by the rusty screen door of their rented house on Nantucket. Zap. Blam. Pow. Here endeth my stab at yesterday's fiction. No one's been reading it for forty years. It went out with easel painting, and by easel painting one means the sort of painting that used to be displayed on easels. Two curates playing checkers by a cockatoo's roost. Painting has cast off its frames, and yet one deeply misses these massive and golden cele-brations—fruit and angels—for their element of ultimate risk. By framing a painting the artist, of course, declared it to be a distillate of his deepest feelings about love and death. By junking the frame he destroyed the risk of a declaration. He may, as he will claim, have opened doors, porticos, gates, and mountain passes onto an unframed infinity of comprehension: or he may merely have displayed his abysmal lack of vitality. The woman climbing the stairs with her white roses is in a sense a frame, a declaration, and my account of putting a hat on a statue is frameless and may indeed not deserve a frame at all.

The statue of Leif Erikson was wearing a necktie that day when I started to walk down Commonwealth Avenue from Kenmore Square to the Boston Public Garden. The statue's tie was a foulard, frayed and stained. It was a cold afternoon but I carried my vicuña over my arm because my father had taught me never to wear a coat unless it was absolutely necessary. If I wore a coat I might be mistaken for an Irishman. I think my knowledge of Boston to be comprehensive and vast but framed entirely in the language of a farewell. I claim to know the cheapness of good-byes—that boyish shrug sent up as a lure for some lover whose face I have never seen although I have seen and tasted everything else. I am not a Bostonian but my provincial credentials will get me over the border. I have no true nostalgia for the city because I remember the aristocracy in my youth as being tragic and cranky. Old C. F. Adams was still challenging anyone—anyone at all—to a sailboat race and Hester Pickman was translating Rilke, but I can remember Jack Wheelwright tossing the sandwiches for tea onto the fire because they were unsuitable. The maid cried. She was a pretty Irish girl. The painting over the mantle was a Tintoretto and Jack had been talking about Henry Adams, his favorite uncle, but when I walked home the night was dark and cold and I, having already read Proust, could recall nothing in his accounts of the fall of Paris that seemed to me so horrible as the smoking sandwiches and the weeping maid. My credentials seem to pass; indeed they take some true knowledge of the situation in order to be assessed. "Oh, do sit down." Mother exclaimed, "do sit down and let me tell you about the funeral of Phillips Brooks! On the day of his funeral there were *trumpets* in Copley Square. Oh so many *trumpets!* I don't remember the time of year but it seems to me that it was cold and brilliant although of course that may have been the loud music of the *trumpets.* Phillips Brooks was a big man, you know. He was a very big man. He used to go right down to the South End and drink beer with strange Irishmen! He was not the sort of skinny clergyman who drank sherry. And speaking of sherry, did I tell you about your father and the sherry last Thursday?"

I knew the story although she counted so on innuendo that one would have had to know the facts in advance to understand what she was talking about. My father was a celebrated drinking companion. He had drunk Robert Ingersoll and James O'Neil under the table at the old Adams House when Frank Locke ran the bar. The story mother was about to hint at had taken place on Thursday morning. This was in the old house on the South Shore. It was eleven. Father wanted a drink. It was Thursday and S. S. Pierce would deliver his potables that afternoon but the delivery wouldn't be until after three. The sherry decanter on the sideboard was full. He unstopped the decanter and drank the sherry. Then, as a precaution—merely a precaution—he pissed the decanter full. The color was exactly right. Everything in the room was as he had found it except that the fireplace was smoking. He gave the logs a poke and, with his spirits greatly renewed, he went upstairs to read the Shakespeare sonnets to his cat as he so often did. Enter the rector, then. Enter Mother, taking off her apron. "Oh, do sit down, Father Frisbee," she said, "do sit down and join me in a glass of sherry and a biscuit." So the poor man of God, sitting in a Windsor chair with half its spokes broken, coughing in the smoke of a fireplace that wouldn't draw, ate moldy pilot crackers and sipped piss. No wonder none of us ever wanted to go to Harvard.

So I banged down Commonwealth Avenue in the cold. The statue of Wm. Lloyd Garrison was wearing a scarf. Statues in parks, I've always thought, have a therapeutic effect on one's posture. Walking among gods and heroes one always keeps one's head up. I saw two women walking dogs. One of the dogs was a Labrador, a line I've bred but when I whistled to the dog and he pulled on his leash, the woman—a good-looking woman—pulled him in the other direction and hurried on to Beacon Street. She seemed in flight and I was hurt. A black man in a sleeping bag lay on a bench saying: "I din' do nothing wrong. I din' do nothing wrong." There were two couples hitchhiking on the avenue. They were ragged and looked dirty. I thought that I had never seen hitchhikers in the city before, not ever in a city that counted so for its strength upon deeply rooted concentric provincialism. Ahead of me I could see the statue of the President of the Argentine. The statue is vulgar and bulky and what in the world was he doing on Commonwealth Avenue? I decided to put my hat on his head. Why should I, a grown man, put a hat on a statue? Men have been putting hats on statues since the beginnings of time. My father read Shakespeare to the cat, my life is impetuous and unorthodox, and I cannot distinguish persiflage from profundity, which may be my undoing. There was a faded ribbon and a handful of wax flowers on the President's pedestal. I decided to make my ascent by his cosmic and Rodinesque tailcoat.

My hat was a Locke hat. My coat is a very, very rare vicuña, left to me by my fourth father-in-law, a Des Moines haberdasher. My coat is thirty-five years old but I have discovered that there are only three clubs left in the world where the age of my coat is respected. Only that afternoon, when I threw it over an empty barstool in the Ritz, the man on the next stool fingered the material and was pleased to think he admired the age, radiance and beauty of the vicuña, but what he was admiring, it seems, were the numerous darns. This put him, in my eyes, into the lower classes and presented me, in his esteem, as a straight thrift-shop type; secondhand rose. I put my folded vicuña on the pedestal and started my ascent. The President is difficult to climb. I would sooner write about my mountain-climbing experiences—coldness, indeed, thought, falls from the summit of the mountain—but that would be some other afternoon. I was struggling up the bronze surface when a man said, *"Ciao, bello."*

He was a good-looking young man who wore a serge middy blouse with three crimson chevrons sewn to the sleeve. No navy in the world, I knew, had ever issued such a costume, and I guessed he had mostly seen the ocean from the summit of some roller coaster. *"Desiderai tu un'amico?"* he asked.

"You've got a terrible accent," I said. "Where did you learn Italian? Bergamo? Someplace like that?"

"From a friend," he said.

"Break it up," shouted a policeman. "You boys break it up." He came running down the walk from a cruise car that was parked on Exeter Street. "Break it up, break it up or I'll throw you both in the lockup. You spoil everything."

The man in the middy blouse headed north, and the policeman's anger seemed so genuine and so despairing that I wanted to explain my purpose but I couldn't do this without sacrificing any chance to be taken seriously. "I'm very old," I said. "I'm really terribly old and I insist upon the prerogatives and eccentricities of my time of life. I can remember when there was an elevated train on Atlantic Avenue. I can remember the Boston Police strike! I can remember when every village, homestead, hill, and pasture in this great land was dominated by a tree called The Elm. There were the English Elms, the Portuguese Elms, the Wineglass and the Penumbra Elms. They were shaped like fountains, columns, and explosions of grace. They were both lachrymose and manly. They were everywhere and now there are none."

"Common's full of elms," he said.

"All right," I said, "then Chestnuts. My father told me he could remember when every hill in New England was crowned with the noble, native Chestnut. In the autumn their leaves turned a deep, rich brown and the nuts they bore were delicious. I've never seen one of these beautiful trees. Not one! My generation was left with the Chestnut Hill Country Club, the Chestnut Grove Tearoom, and quite a few undistinguished streets called Chestnut."

"Please go away," he said. "You spoil everything. Everything."

I went away. I went up to the Exeter Street Theatre and saw a few reels of a Bergman film in which a woman mutilated herself with broken glass. I do not choose to describe the scene but I couldn't anyhow because I shut my eyes. Then I returned to Commonwealth Avenue, determined to put my hat on the President. During my absence the light had changed. The light in Boston, on a good day, I've always thought, has the incandescence of a sea light. Only the alchemy of sea air could have turned the statue of George Washington into the fairest verdigris. So in this fading sea light I returned to the President of the Argentine. A young girl was sitting on a bench near the statue and I sat down beside her. "May I?" I asked.

"Certainly," she said.

"What's your name?"

"Pixie," she said. "That's what they call me. My name is Alice-Mae."

She had marvelous legs and breasts. I don't mean at all that they conformed to any measured beauty but that there was some extraordinary congruence between their proportions and one's desires. The legs were not showgirl legs, they had nothing thrilling, lengthy, or brilliant about them. Their gleam and their shape were modest and youthful.

"Do you live around here?" I asked.

"I live in a dormitory," she said. "We're not allowed to have men visitors."

"What's your university?"

"It's not a university. It's really a college. They call it an academy. It's where my parents wanted me to go."

"What does your father do?"

"He's a funeral director," she said.

Then I knew that she was a student at the embalming school in Kenmore Square. This had happened to me once before. I picked up a very good-looking girl in a hamburger place called The Fatted Calf. At first she said she was studying anatomy but then she came clean, or clean enough to say that her task, her study and vocation, was to beautify death, to make death comprehensible to the cruelly bereaved.

"What do you study?" I asked.

"Well, we don't have regular courses," she said. "I mean we don't study history or arithmetic or things like that."

"You are learning," I asked, "how to beautify death?"

"Oh yes, yes," she exclaimed. "However did you know?"

And so we will end as the movies do when, having exhausted the kiss, the walk-off, the reconciliation, and the boundlessness of faith, hope, and charity, they resort to a downward or falling crawl title giving the facts in the case—usually to the fading music of police sirens. The girl's real name is Alice-Mae Plumber and she has flunked out of embalming school and is afraid to tell her parents. The man in the middy blouse is named Lemuel Howe and he will be arrested three days later for possession of dangerous drugs and sentenced to five years in the Suffolk County Jail. The man who wanted to put his hat on the statue of the President is I.

TYLER AND BRINA

Sue Miller

Tyler loved women. He was in love with women. He saw them in shops, on the subway, at work, and imagined them falling back over and over, laughing, crying, soft, wet. He had a hard-on half the day. He didn't much care what they looked like. The firm young girls with T-shirts ending above their navels, who weighed his fruit at the grocery store. His secretary, with the little rim of fat over her girdle and her sad eyes. He stood, offering a plum, holding out a bill, and he loved them. He wanted to lift the hair out of their eyes, to slide his hand down over the tops of their blue jeans onto their tanned bellies, to push them down—so gently!—to make them smile, open their mouths, to make them cry out softly, to take their pain away.

He had thought this might change when he married Brina. He had hoped it would. But even though he slept around less, he still yearned after women all the time, yearned for their gentleness, their loving response, their sweet dampness.

Now Brina wanted a divorce. She'd moved out and was living in an apartment belonging to a woman from her office who was on vacation. Tyler dropped by nearly every evening after Petey was asleep. He wanted Brina back. He made love to her again and again on the living-room couch where she slept at night often with all his clothes on, Brina's skirt wrinkled into a thick belt at her waist. Something about seeing her like that in the purplish light of the street lamp which flooded into the room drove him on. Even when he couldn't come anymore, he was hard, he wanted her. "Oh, you asshole," she'd moan. "You mother fucker. God, I hate you. I hate you."

Petey was seven years old. He was Brina's son by her first marriage. She wouldn't let Tyler see him anymore. She thought it would be difficult for Petey. It had been difficult for him to get used to Tyler in the first place. It had taken nearly the whole year he and Brina had been married. As recently as a few months before Brina moved out, Petey would take the opportunity, if he and Tyler were wrestling or tickling, to punch or kick Tyler as hard as he could in the groin. Once Tyler had heard Petey actually whisper to himself, "Get him!" before he struck.

The morning of the day that Brina left him, Tyler had taken a shower with Petey. He had squatted down under the spray and let Petey scrub his back. Petey's wiry small body felt strange gliding across Tyler's back and buttocks while Petey scrubbed. Then Tyler felt a short stream of lukewarm water on his back, and Petey said, "I spit on you, Tyler, did you feel it? I spitted right on you." Tyler turned, still squatting, to look at Petey. He was grinning expectantly with his mouth open, the water flattening his blond hair dark against his small, neat head. Tyler felt the sense of uneasiness he often felt with Petey and never felt with women, a sense of not knowing what the next move ought to be.

"Now can I get you?" Tyler asked.

"Yeah!" Petey said. His body jigged in anticipation.

Tyler tipped his head up into the spray and filled his mouth.

He squirted the water onto Petey's chest. Petey laughed, and Tyler laughed with him, partly in relief that he'd chosen the right thing to do.

"I can't even feel it," Petey said. "I can't even feel it because I'm *already* wet."

Tyler had seen Brina smile at them through the clear plastic shower curtain while she put her makeup on. He had felt a sense, suddenly, of the three of them as a family, locked together irrevocably. Something about this rekindled his feelings of uneasiness, and he stood up and turned away from Petey to rinse himself off. But when they had dropped Tyler off at the subway on the way to Petey's school, her work, he had kissed Brina's mouth, had rested his hand briefly on Petey's damp hair.

Tyler was a contractor and a part-time developer. He owned and managed eight small apartment buildings around the city. He'd bought them one by one, including the one he and Brina lived in, and done the renovations on them himself. That night just before he left the office, one of his tenants called, a woman named Meredith. Someone had broken into her apartment, had stolen her television set and stereo. The lock on her door had been broken, and the super was out for the evening—he'd left a note by his buzzer. She was afraid to stay overnight by herself unless someone fixed it. Tyler called Brina and told her he'd be late for supper, not to wait. He took the truck and stopped at the hardware store for a new lock, and a chain because he guessed that the extra protection would reassure his tenant.

When he arrived at her apartment, she was sitting in the entryway with the door swung open, smoking a cigarette and drinking what looked like whiskey. "Oh, thank God you're here," she said. She stood and stubbed out the cigarette. "Look, just look at what these jerks did to my house!" She gestured behind her toward the living room. Tyler could see records in and out of their jackets spilled all over the floor. Papers were strewn everywhere.

"And look in here," she said. She walked down the hall ahead of him. She was wearing heels and a skirt. Tyler watched her legs, the quick shifting gleam of the light on her stockings as she moved in front of him. She stood in her bedroom door. It was worse in here. Her clothes had been dumped from the drawers. The closet yawned open, the empty hangers angled awkwardly this way and that. "It just makes me feel so *violated*," she said.

Tyler had heard it before. Several of his buildings weren't in such great neighborhoods. He was carefully sympathetic, though. He talked to her for a while before he started working on the door. When he'd finished, she offered him a beer and asked him to sit down for a few minutes before he left, just until she calmed down. She had been working in her bedroom, and she'd changed into jeans and a fuzzy pink sweater. Tyler sat on the couch, and she curled up in a large chair opposite him. They talked about insurance, what kinds of coverage they had. Then he asked her about her work. She was a social worker, she said. She worked with juvenile offenders. "In fact," she said, and giggled, "the chances are excellent that some *client* of mine pulled this little number tonight."

Tyler smiled and gently shook his beer can. Almost empty.

"Oh, I'm going to miss my record player," she said abruptly. "I was just thinking how usually when people are over I play music while we talk. Course, I've got a radio. Do you want some music?" She was a little drunk, too serious. Tyler grinned and shrugged. "I'm going to get my radio," she said. "You stay right there." She got up and ran down the hall. When she returned, Tyler noticed she wasn't wearing a bra under the sweater. She looked up from plugging the radio in and caught him staring at her. As she sat down next to him on the couch, they were both smiling as if they already shared some kind of secret.

When he called Brina at her job, about ten the next morning, she said, "Oh, God, you're all right." There was a long silence, and then she said more softly, "I called the hospitals, but you weren't there." He could hear that she was starting to cry.

"No," he said. And then, "I'm sorry."

After a minute, she said in a pinched voice, "How can this be? I don't want this to happen, Tyler."

"I'm sorry," he said.

"But *what*? What do you plan?" she said. "How can this be?" She was crying openly now. He could imagine her in her office, trying to cover her face in case anyone walked in.

"Can we talk about it tonight? Can I come home?" he asked.

"Home?" Her voice soared to an unfamiliar, awkward register on the word. "Home?" she asked, and then she hung up.

One side of Brina's face was dead, injured in a childhood accident. When they made love, Tyler, for some reason, lay more often with his head on that side of hers. Looking at her, he was sometimes startled by the stillness on her face, as though she were in a deep dreamless sleep. "Oh oh, oh God," she would cry in an agonized voice from her blank face as Tyler lowered his head to her shoulder, his body hard at work. When she smiled, half of Brina's face lit up, and the rest lifted only slightly in sympathy, as though, Tyler thought, she knew of some deep sorrow that lay under every fleeting joy.

When Tyler first saw her after he'd slept with Meredith, the live side of her face was distorted with rage, and both eyes were puffy from sleeplessness and tears. He'd gone home first, but she wasn't there. Their apartment looked a little as Meredith's the night before. Brina had pulled things out of drawers and left them all over their bedroom, Petey's bedroom. The suitcases that usually sat on the top shelves of their closet were gone. Tyler felt such a sense of desolation that for a moment he thought of leaving the apartment too, of going somewhere to have a drink. But he didn't. He got out their Rolodex and began to call their friends, Brina's friends, until he found someone who knew where she had gone. In a cold voice, Marietta said, "Well, I suppose you'll find out anyway," and gave him the address.

It was about ten o'clock when Tyler got there. The building was an old triple decker in a run-down part of town where mostly students and blacks lived. Under the stairs in the entrance hall were baby carriages, someone's cross-country skis, heaped-up boots. From the first-floor apartment came laughter and Otis Redding. Tyler mounted the stairs. On the second floor, the name he was looking for, Eliopoulos, was printed on masking tape above the doorbell. He rang and waited. Then he rang again. He could hear Brina blowing her nose. The door opened. She looked at him for a moment, half of her face pulling into hard, angry lines. Tyler tried to look at the other side, her sad eye, her drooping lips. Abruptly she stepped forward and began to hit him. She hit him sharply with her fists, four times, then stepped back and slammed the door. Neither of them had said anything, though Brina had made a little noise of effort with each blow. She had been swinging awkwardly, from the side, and Tyler covered his head as well as he could after the first blow smashed into the side of his nose, but one of his ears was ringing dully as he left, and when he reached up to touch it, his hand came away wet with blood.

He had stopped in a drugstore on the way home to get disinfectant and a styptic pencil. He stood in front of a display of pantyhose thinking about Brina, about what he could do to get her to talk to him. He knew if he could just talk to her, just get his hands on her— he could see his hands slide across the top of her bathrobe onto her breasts—things would be all right. She was all he wanted.

"Can I help you find something?" a girl asked. Tyler looked at her. Freckles, long straight hair. She was wearing a pale blue drugstore smock and very tight jeans. She smelled of Juicy Fruit chewing gum. She smiled at him. A big gap between her two front teeth touched Tyler's heart, and he smiled back. "Yes," he said.

Tyler was careful with Brina. He didn't bring flowers or presents; he didn't call or try to get in touch with Petey. He just kept coming over. At some point, he knew, she would have to take responsibility for his silent presence outside her door. It took a week and a half for her to let him in, and twenty minutes after that, Tyler was making love to her on the couch. He pushed up onto his elbows to look at her. She had her face turned away from him, and her eyes were shut. She seemed trusting, utterly at peace. Tyler's heart welled with remorse and gratitude toward her and he began to weep softly. She turned to him, and he saw that her face was remote, cold, full of hard anger. "Brina," he said, frightened. He couldn't believe she could make love with him without feeling love. He touched her face gently, as though he could change what he saw with a gesture.

"Don't talk to me," she whispered furiously, and pulled him to her.

Now Tyler began to woo Brina. She wouldn't let him in until after nine or so, when Petey was asleep, because she thought that it would be hard for Petey to see him. But every night, Tyler arrived at nine and stayed until midnight or so, when Brina kicked him out. Mostly they made love, although once or twice Brina wouldn't. Then Tyler talked. He talked about how much he loved her, how weak he was. About how his weakness didn't affect his love for her, about how hard he'd tried to be faithful. He talked about how much he wanted her back. Brina seemed to listen; but she still wept or cursed him when they did make love. And she always turned away afterward and hunched over, facing the back of the couch or holding herself as if for comfort.

Sometime in the second week of this strange courtship, Meredith called him at work. She sounded tense. There were some problems at the apartment. Could he stop by after work? She'd be home by five-thirty or so.

Tyler couldn't go to Brina's until after nine anyway, so he told Meredith he'd stop by quickly around six.

He drove over in the truck again. He was driving it home regularly now, so he'd be able to get to Brina's and back easily. Lying on the dashboard was a miniature boot from one of Petey's superhero dolls. Tyler had found it in the glove compartment. He was planning to take it to Brina's later. He'd even thought of a joke he might try on her when he got there, about being a prince looking for the woman who'd fit this shoe. He wasn't sure he would, though, because Brina was several inches taller than he was and so far he'd only imagined two or three tough, sarcastic things she might say in response, having to do with her size.

Meredith had Vivaldi on the radio when he came in. She was wearing jeans and a work shirt, but her makeup was fresh, Tyler could tell. He followed her to the kitchen. She opened the refrigerator and brought out some wine. He watched her lift two glasses down from the shelf. He could see the bumps of her nipples against the light blue shirt. She was thinner than Brina. He took the wine.

She raised her glass. "Cheers," she said, and smiled.

He sipped and set the glass down on the butcher-block counter. He'd installed it three years ago. He couldn't help admiring it for a moment. He turned to her. "What's the problem?" he asked.

"No problem," she said. She stepped closer to him. There was a little nick of lipstick on the corner of one of her front teeth. Tyler felt sorry for her.

"I thought there was something wrong," he said.

"Only that I hadn't heard from you," she said, and looked at him. Tyler felt a shrinking inside. "I had a nice time that night."

"Me too," Tyler said, not meeting her eyes. He drank some wine.

"Well?" she said. She cocked her head and smiled flirtatiously at him.

Tyler took a step or two backward. "Look," he said. "I don't know if you knew it or not the other night. I probably should have said something. But I'm married."

She stood very still, but nodded her head. "I knew."

Then Tyler explained what had happened, how Brina had moved out. She stared at him while he told her, and he watched the determined cheerfulness bleed from her face, the bitter lines creep to the corners of her mouth. She was running her finger again and again around the top of her wineglass. Tyler was telling her how much he loved Brina. Suddenly she smiled at him, a forced, brilliant smile. He fell silent. After a moment she said, "So love her, for Christ's sake." Her upper lip trembled slightly, and a single tear snaked through her makeup. "God knows I wasn't asking you to love *me*."

Tyler's heart squeezed tight with pity. He closed his eyes and reached for her.

When Brina called from her office, she sounded so crisp and efficient that Tyler for a moment thought it was Meredith again. But then she said, "I'm just calling, Tyler, to tell you where we'll be now. Maryanne's back, so we're going to the Lloyds' for a couple of weeks, while they're gone. Do you have their address?"

"I'm not sure," he said. "I might somewhere, but why don't I write it down, to be safe?"

Brina dictated it to him in her secretarial voice. Tyler's hands trembled as he wrote the numbers and letters. He read it back to her because he was so excited that he wasn't sure he'd heard it right. She had called him! She wanted him to know how to get to her. "Thanks, Brina," he said. "Thank you."

The Lloyds had a king-size bed, as Tyler and Brina did at home. The first night Tyler visited Brina there, he slowly and carefully took off all her clothes, then removed his own, and they made love until four in the morning. Before Brina made him leave, he got her to promise to think about moving back home again.

The second night, Tyler brought a bottle of wine and some grass over, but Brina met him at the door wearing an old sweatshirt and jeans. She'd pulled her hair back into a limp ponytail. She told him he couldn't come in. Petey had some stomach bug and was up every half hour or so, vomiting. Tyler wanted to stay, wanted to help with Petey, but Brina was both distracted and absolute.

Driving home, Tyler began to get angry at her rigidity, at the way she insisted that his life should be affected by her principles. He turned out of his way and drove past Meredith's apartment. Her living room lights glowed yellow on the second floor.

She answered the door with the chain on. She was wearing a striped robe and big green puffy slippers. Tyler held up the bottle of wine. "Party time," he said.

She smiled and shut the door. He heard the chain slide off and then she reopened it. She had kicked off the slippers. "I was wondering when you'd get around to coming over again," she said.

Tyler hadn't meant to talk about Brina with her tonight, but after they made love he felt a resurgence of the anger that had brought him to her apartment in the first place. He told her what Brina had done, making it sound as though it had happened several days before. This time, instead of getting tearful or angry, Meredith took a professional tone. Brina, she offered, was projecting her own anger and fragility onto Petey and using him as a way of punishing Tyler. There were several possible reasons for this, psychodynamically speaking, and Meredith offered one or two.

Tyler knew better than to listen to much of anything she had to say, but he liked speaking about Brina with someone else, liked hearing her name out loud. He felt excited and closer to Brina while he and Meredith were talking about her, and he asked questions to keep the conversation going. He supported her theories with intimate details Brina had told him about her first husband, her childhood. Meredith went to the kitchen to get a cigarette. He watched her walk away from him, small and boyish without any clothes on. "I'm sorry," he said, when she was sitting next to him on the bed again. "I shouldn't talk so much about this. About Brina."

"It's all right. People need to talk about the things that are bothering them."

"But it can't be very much fun for you."

"I don't mind. It's all right."

"It's all right for a while. It shouldn't be for very long, though."

Meredith looked at him as though he were making some sort of promise. "I'll let you know when it starts to bother me."

The next night the phone was ringing when he got back from Brina's. He knew it was Meredith and almost didn't answer it, but the thought of her sitting alone at the other end, listening to the phone ring in his empty apartment, swept him as suddenly and forcefully as a pang of self-pity, and he picked up the receiver.

She was cheerful. She invited him over for a nightcap. Tyler tried to say no, but when she persisted, even began to offer to come to his house, he decided it might be the best thing to go over there briefly.

Tyler saw Meredith five or six times in the next two weeks, sometimes at her apartment, sometimes at his, though they never made love in the bed he shared with Brina. There was something about her sexual greediness that excited him, that gave him an appetite for the tenderness and restraint he had to employ with Brina. And she was the only person he could really talk to about what had happened. He felt all right about it all because, as he told himself, he was always honest with Meredith, he never pretended to her that he didn't want Brina back or wasn't seeing her. In the end, he thought of himself as being faithful to both Meredith and Brina during this period, and he was only tempted once, by a girl he met in a bar on the way home from Brina's one night. She told him she was a law student, and claimed she could also tell his fortune. She took his hand and leaned over it a long time. He could feel her breath warm on his palm. But then she said either the light was bad or he was in sad shape, because she couldn't even find his life line, not to mention his love line and all that other stuff.

Brina and Tyler were lying in the Lloyds' big bed. The Lloyds were supposed to get back from their vacation in five days. Tyler and Brina had avoided talking about this, about where Brina and Petey might go next.

Abruptly, Brina asked if he'd come to dinner the next night.

"What time?" Tyler asked.

"About six or so." There was a silence.

Tyler felt his heart thudding as it sometimes did when he'd drunk five or six cups of coffee in one morning. "With Petey," he said.

"He misses you," Brina said. "It just seems dumb, after a while, to keep punishing him because I'm mad at you." Tyler didn't let himself look at Brina, didn't let himself hope. They were lying on their backs, not touching, and he stared intently at the useless, nipple-like fixture on the ceiling above him.

"And I'm not so mad at you anymore, Tyler." She sighed. "I guess I see that you can't help yourself—that you're just going to slip every now and then. And that it doesn't mean much of anything to you and me. Or Petey. To who we are as a family, I mean." She had turned on the bed, and Tyler could tell she was looking at him. "But if I think about it too long or hard, I can literally make myself throw up. And I never want to see it or know about it again. Ever." Her voice was like a threat. Tyler nodded his head, and she relaxed again. The light from the candle on the bedside table flickered on the ceiling with the little rush of air from her movement. Tyler lay absolutely still, full of longing for her but afraid to touch her.

"I don't know," she said. Her voice was softer, almost as though she were talking just for herself. "I feel like it's a terrible compromise. Terrible. One I never thought I could make. Or would even be asked to make. I thought of our bodies as being part of each other. It made me feel . . . injured, or damaged. And Petey too. I felt like you broke something that held us all together." Her voice wavered and she was silent for a while. "But then I saw, I guess I saw, that other things really held us together. Or could. Because I do still love you, Tyler." She had turned toward him again. He felt her breath on his shoulder. "What's loving and generous in you. The stuff Petey misses. I miss it too. And it sort of seems fair to me that in the same way you have to struggle with your nature to stay with me, to stay true to me, that I should struggle with mine, with my . . . inflexibility, I guess, to be with you."

Tyler reached out and touched Brina's hand. She responded quickly, passionately, and for the first time since she'd moved out, she led them through their lovemaking.

Afterward they talked about when she should move back. Tyler persuaded her that there was no reason to wait until the Lloyds returned. He'd come Saturday with the truck, and they could throw everything in and bring her and Petey home. They talked a long time. Tyler fell into a light, then a deep, sleep. Brina didn't wake him until five-thirty. For a moment, opening his eyes in the strange bed, with dawn just outside the windows, Tyler thought he'd stayed too long with some other woman and almost panicked. Then he focused on Brina's half-tender face and his heart slowed down.

Tyler left work early on Friday. He stopped at the five-and-ten and bought a Tonka truck and two new superhero dolls for Petey. Outside Brina's, though, there suddenly seemed something cheap about apologizing to Petey with toys, and he left them in the truck.

He rang the bell. He could hear Petey shout, "It's him!" behind the door. It swung open, and Petey stood there grinning. He was larger than Tyler remembered. He threw himself up and into Tyler's arms. His wiry arms and legs wrapped tightly around Tyler's shoulders and hips. Petey had never embraced Tyler before—no child had—and Tyler was startled and momentarily almost revolted by the animal-like energy in his grip, the sense of his making some claim on Tyler's affection. He realized abruptly how little he'd thought about Petey in the last month or so.

He held Petey awkwardly and patted his narrow, hard back. After a minute, the boy uncoiled himself and dropped from Tyler's body, still smiling up at him, but shyly now, as though he sensed the hesitation in Tyler.

Tyler knew some gesture was required of him. He felt helpless. "My man!" he said, and held out his hands. Petey laughed, and they went through the elaborate hand-slapping routine Tyler had taught him. Then Petey started to tell him about a new game Brina had bought for him. He disappeared down the hall to get it.

Tyler looked up and saw Brina standing in the kitchen doorway. He went to her and held her. Tears were in her eyes and she bowed her head to rest it on Tyler's shoulder for a minute. "I'm so glad you're here," she whispered.

Petey reappeared, carrying a big flat cardboard box. He asked Brina if he and Tyler could play his game before supper. Brina turned back quickly to the sink so that Petey could see only the blank side of her face. "Of course," she said smoothly. Tyler had never realized she might consciously decide which side of her face to show to the world, and he felt a momentary shock, as if of recognition.

The next day, Brina and Petey moved back in with Tyler. As Tyler carried the suitcases, the boxes of Petey's toys up to the apartment, he felt the same sense of hope, the sense that everything could be different, that he'd felt the first time he'd done it. He even tried to carry Brina into the bedroom, but they gave up, laughing, as they had the first time.

That night, while Brina was reading Petey a story, Tyler called Meredith. He'd been nervous all day about the possibility of her telephoning him and Brina's answering, but they'd been out a lot doing errands, getting beer and groceries; and they'd had dinner at a Chinese restaurant, Petey's favorite, to celebrate. Tyler planned to see Meredith sometime Monday, for lunch if he could, and to tell her as gently as possible what had happened.

She sounded glad to hear from him, although there was an edge to her voice. But when he asked her about getting together Monday, she was silent a moment. Then she said, "Monday? That seems suddenly pretty far away. I mean, I haven't seen you for days."

"Well, things have been happening. We need to talk."

"Let's talk right now. I can talk right now. Why don't you come over?"

"No, I think Monday's best," Tyler said.

"Why?"

"Well, see I think what's going to happen is that probably . . . well, it's almost definite that Brina's going to move back in." Tyler wasn't aware of lying to Meredith. He was conscious only of a need to spare her feelings.

"Oh, now wait a minute, Tyler. *Wait* a minute," she said. He recognized her tone with relief. She wasn't hurt. She was going to give him advice. "When did all this happen?" she asked.

"Well, it's sort of happening. I mean, we've been talking about it for a couple of days; that's why I haven't called. And I'm going over there tonight."

"So that's it? That's why you can't see me?"

"Right."

"Have you talked to anyone else about this, Tyler? I mean, to get a sense of perspective about what Brina's doing here?"

"No. Just Brina."

"Jesus!"

"What?"

She paused a moment, as though to think of the best way to break bad news. Then she said, "You are so . . . malleable, Tyler. Or gullible, or something. I've never met anyone like you." He didn't answer. "Look," she said after a moment. "Where are you now?"

"Why?" Tyler asked, suddenly nervous.

"Just, where are you? Are you home?"

"Yes, but I'm leaving. In just a second. I'm due over there."

"She can wait a few more minutes," Meredith said. "You just sit tight. I'm coming over."

"No!" he said sharply. Then, "No. I need to take off now."

"I'll be there in five minutes, Tyler. You just wait." She hung up.

Tyler sat a few minutes by the telephone trying to think what to do. He heard Brina reading the story, her voice full of expression, and Petey's bright laughter. He went to the door of Petey's room. Brina was stretched out on Petey's bed, the book propped up on her stomach. Petey leaned against her breast, rhythmically twirling a strand of his hair. Brina finished a sentence and looked up.

"I'm just going to go out for a minute," he said. He knew his voice sounded evasive.

She stared at him. "Out where?" Petey sat up and looked from one of them to the other, worried by their voices.

Tyler felt a little band of irritation squeeze his stomach. "I'm going to go sit on the front stoop. Okay with you?"

She looked at him a moment more, frowning. Then she lifted her shoulders. "Okay," she said.

Tyler went downstairs and stood on the front steps. It was a warm night and it was still light outside. From the park on the corner he could hear the sounds of a ball game. An old couple three doors down had brought folding chairs outside and were sitting on the sidewalk, talking and surveying the empty street. Tyler put his hands in his pockets and looked first one way down the street and then the other. He sat down. Minutes passed. He felt almost sick. He debated walking to the corner to head Meredith off, but worried that for some reason she might come from the other direction and ring the bell before he could get back. He suddenly recalled her frosted hair, the dark nail polish she wore, things he knew that Brina would think cheap. A window opened and closed above him. Somewhere, someone called a wandering child to a slow rhythm: "D*aaa*vid. *Daaa*vid."

Meredith drove up. She got quickly out of the car, walked around behind it and came to stand in front of him. She smiled. "Hi," she said.

Tyler stood up. "Look, I've gotta get going," he said. "This really isn't a good time for me."

She looked at the old couple, who were watching them. "Let's just go inside for a few minutes, Tyler," she said. "I think I really need to talk to you about this."

Her voice was firm and authoritative, and Tyler felt again the irritation he'd felt before with Brina, more sharply this time. Who were these women, who thought they could run his life?

"Can't swing it," he said. He was startled by the absoluteness of his own voice.

She looked at him. "This isn't like you, Tyler." He shrugged. She shook her head. "I just have to tell you, Tyler, that I think she's done a real number here."

"We're married, Meredith. She doesn't have to do any number for us to live together."

She looked at him, her eyes widening. They were a lighter color than he'd thought. "I really can't believe this," she said. "I just cannot believe it."

Tyler felt as though he were being accused of breaking some promise. "I never told you I was leaving Brina," he said.

"You never said so, no," she said. "But what were all those conversations we had? I mean, someone just doesn't *talk* that way."

He looked at her blankly.

"Tyler," she said. There was pleading in her voice and her lower eyelids suddenly shimmered with tears. Tyler hated this. She saw him weakening and reached up to put her hand on his arm.

Tyler had just begun to pull away gently when he heard the crash behind him. He turned around. Brina stood in the lobby between the building's two glass doors. She stared through the outer glass door at Meredith and Tyler on the stoop. She held an empty tray crookedly, and around her feet on the tiled floor were green shards of broken bottle glass, an overturned bowl, a bubbly pool of what must have been beer. Tyler stared in at her. Slowly he raised his hands and put them on the glass door. She looked back out at him for a long moment, her whole face expressionless. Then her lips parted, moved a little as though she were whispering something; and the muscles began to pull and shift in the live side of her face. Tyler stepped closer to the door. But as he stared through the glass wall at her, she turned away from him. Now all he could see in Brina's face was her vacant serenity as she looked down at the mess that lay around her feet.

STAND

David Michael Kaplan

Some things you just couldn't seem to say good-bye to, Frank thought, as he drove up the dirt road to the summer house. His father had sold it three years earlier, after his mother died, and Frank hadn't been back since helping him close it for the last time. That was also the last time he'd seen his father: each time his father had called, suggesting they get together, Frank had put him off. Now his father was dead, these past six months; he had died suddenly, of a stroke. At age thirty-nine, Frank was alone—mother and father dead, Jena gone, no children. Sometimes he felt this solitude as freedom. He could go anywhere, do anything. As if to prove this to himself, he bought an old Triumph TR3 and began driving on weekends into the New England countryside. These trips had no real destination. They usually ended with his drinking beer in some over-air-conditioned motel lounge and then driving back to Boston with the radio turned up loud on an oldies station. Now, on this Fourth of July weekend, he had come back here to the Berkshires, to the summer house by the lake.

The new owners, whoever they were, were gone—strange, on a holiday weekend. The door was locked, the deck chairs neatly stacked. Frank peered through the porch window, but the sun's slant was wrong and he could see nothing. He walked down to the dock and looked at the rope swing hanging over the water. As a child, he had jumped from it, his skin as pimply as a chicken's in anticipation of the lake's coldness. Frank sat on the edge of the dock and looked up at the house. Everyone he'd thought he loved had been here with him: his parents, Jena, a woman before her, one after. All were gone. He should be too.

He was alone, he told himself, but he was free.

Still—the early evening was fine and musky, and Frank had no desire to return yet to Boston. He'd seen posters at a gas station announcing a fireworks display at the lake. He glanced at his watch—in a few hours the show would start. He could drive back to Boston afterward, or get a motel room along the way. He drove down the road to the Mini-Mart and bought chicken-salad sandwiches, potato chips, and a six-pack. On a display rack he saw a Yankees baseball cap much like one he'd had as a boy. He bought that, too.

The beach was crowded with sunbathers and barbecuers and volleyballers. Frank wanted to be more alone. A quarter mile past the beach the asphalt turned into a narrow dirt road that threaded through thick pines, which hid the shore and prevented parking. Frank was about to back up when he came upon an unexpected clearing, with picnic tables and a dock that jutted into the lake. He heard voices and smelled charcoal. Two pickups, a Ford and a Chevy, were parked off the road. He pulled up beside them: at least this would be quieter than down at the beach. From the dock he'd have a good view of the fireworks.

Four men shared the clearing with him. One was turning hamburgers and hot dogs on a hugely smoking grill while a friend solemnly watched. The other two lazily passed a football, catching with one hand and holding beer with the other. Except for one of the football throwers, who was clean-shaven and long-haired and seemed younger than the rest, they were all bearded and thick-set, their T-shirts hanging loosely over their bellies. Local boys, Frank thought. He took a beer from his six-pack and walked down to the dock to sit apart from them. The grill tender nodded as Frank passed, and his friend belched. The football players ignored him.

Frank sat on the dock and drank his beer. The lowering sun scattered thin rays through the trees on the opposite shore. He shaded his eyes and searched for the summer house but couldn't find it. He raised his beer in a farewell salute and felt strangely guilty, as if he were abandoning the house, leaving it to chance and ruin. It's not mine at all, he reminded himself. It was nothing he had to care for.

A breeze raked the water. Frank crushed his beer can and walked back to the car for the sandwiches. The two men who'd been throwing the football were inspecting the Triumph. The heavyset one had a puffy, bearded face that seemed not to have settled right that day. He nodded at Frank, while his friend, the clean-shaven one, grinned. Up close he wasn't as young as he'd seemed—the long hair contributed to the illusion—and the corners of his eyes were crinkled, as if he'd been squinting for a long time.

"Nice car." He rubbed his thumb along the fender, so that it squeaked.

"Thanks," Frank said.

"You sure don't see too many of these. Old Porsches, MGs, you see a lot of. Not these."

"I've noticed that," Frank said. He opened the car door and took out the sandwich bag. He had no real desire to talk.

"Ride nice?"

"It's okay."

"I always wanted to have one of these, didn't you, Polk?" His friend grunted. "It's really something." He patted the Triumph's fender. "'Course I'd never give up my little beauty." He nodded toward the Ford pickup. "You need a truck around here more than a sports car."

"Where you from?" the other man asked Frank. His voice was thick and tarry.

"Boston."

"What brings you up here?"

"The fireworks," Frank said lightly.

"Shit, man—you come all the way here for fireworks? Don't they got fireworks in Boston?"

"I was visiting," Frank said. "My folks used to have a summer house here."

"Did they, now." The clean-shaven man seemed amused. "Well, that almost makes you a home boy, then, don't it?" He pointed to his friend. "That's Polk. I'm Eddie."

"Frank." He offered his hand, but Eddie was already pointing to the men at the grill.

"Over there's Teal and Mace." He shouted, "Teal! Mace! This here's Frank."

The barbecuer waved his hamburger turner, and Frank nodded. "Well," he said to Eddie, "I think I'll go sit—"

"You still got that house, Frank?" Polk asked.

Frank shook his head. "My father sold it a few years ago."

"So who were you visiting?"

"Well, nobody, really."

"So why'd you come back?"

"He told you, Polk," Eddie said. "He came for the fireworks."

"Oh, right."

"Polk's a little slow," Eddie said. "Don't mind him. Have a beer with us, Frank?"

"That's okay. I brought my own."

"Something wrong with our hospitality?"

"No, I just—"

"What you got there anyway, Frank?" Eddie pointed to the paper bag.

"Sandwiches."

"No shit? Let me see." Frank hesitated and then handed him the bag. Eddie pulled out a sandwich. "Chicken." He held it up for Polk to see. "And chicken. Two chicken sandwiches."

"Huh," Polk said.

"Polk, why don't you get our friend here a beer?" Eddie put the sandwiches back, carefully folded the bag, and handed it to Frank, who resigned himself to having a beer with them.

Eddie leaned against the Triumph. "So you say you used to come up here summers?"

"We had a house about a half mile off Lake Road. Up from where that Mini-Mart is now."

"That's not the place burned down?"

"No, no."

Polk returned with the beers, accompanied by one of the men from the grill.

"Mace, what's that place burned down off Lake Road?" Eddie asked the newcomer.

"Brenner place," Mace said.

"Why, I knew them," Frank said. "Mr. Brenner used to go fishing with my dad. They had a daughter who got killed in a car crash."

"That's them."

"Their place burned down?"

"About five years ago."

"Jesus."

"Hard-luck family," Eddie said.

"Brenner got into a little fight with some boys down at the marina about some repair work on his boat," Polk said. "Place burned down over the winter."

"You mean they burned it?" Frank asked.

"No, I don't mean that."

"Things happen sometimes, Frank," Eddie said. "Coincidences. It's spooky. You think there's a connection, but there ain't none. It's just the way things happen."

"Those poor people," Frank said.

"Yeah, they don't come here no more," Polk said.

The four men were silent for a moment.

"Where you from, Frank?" Mace asked.

"Boston."

"Hey—one thing Boston's got that we don't is spooks," Polk said. "You got a lot of them there, don't you?"

"I don't know," Frank said uneasily.

"What—can't see them?" Polk laughed, and Mace did too.

"Come on, Polk," Eddie said. "Don't act ignorant." He winked at Frank. "He don't bother you, does he?"

Frank shook his head.

"Just don't mind him. Some of his best friends are spooks, you know."

"Hell they are," Polk muttered.

Frank took a deep swig of his beer.

"Why're you here anyway, Frank?" Mace asked.

"Damn—" Polk said. "How many times we gotta hear this? He's here for the goddamn fireworks."

"You come all the way up here just to see fireworks?"

"Jesus," Polk groaned.

"I wanted to look around a bit," Frank said. "My folks used to—"

"I hope we don't have to go through all this again just for you, Mace," Eddie said.

"Well, up yours," Mace said.

Frank finished his beer and crumpled the can. "Well—I guess I'll be taking off."

Eddie looked surprised. "I thought you were staying for the fireworks."

"Well, I—"

"Polk didn't offend you, now, did he?"

"Oh, no. No."

"So why're you running off, then?"

"I'm not. I just—"

"You don't mind our company, do you?"

"No, no."

"Well, hell—" Eddie said affably. "Sit awhile. Have another beer."

Frank didn't know what to do.

"Hey, let me see that." Eddie pointed to Frank's cap. "Come on, come on," he urged. Frank handed it to him. Eddie put it on, squared it. "You know," he said to Polk, "I always wanted to have me one of these Yankees caps."

"You're a Yankees fan?" Frank asked.

"Hell, no. I hate that team."

Mace raised his beer. "Red Sox all the way."

"I just always wanted to have one," Eddie said. "It's like wearing your enemy's ears or balls or something. The Hottentots or Genghis Khan or somebody used to do that."

"Niggers," Polk snorted.

"Polk," Eddie said patiently, "Genghis Khan wasn't no nigger." He looked at Frank and shook his head, as if to say, What can you do? He tipped up the Triumph's sideview mirror and stared into it. "Yankees," he murmured. For a moment Eddie seemed absorbed in his reflection. Then he looked up, and his grin was quick and knifelike. "You married, Frank?"

"No—divorced."

"I thought so. I could tell that about you. Any kids?"

"No."

"Footloose and fancy-free, huh?"

"Sure. I guess." Eddie's questions made him uncomfortable. He'd get his cap back; then he'd go.

"Hey, Frank—" Mace had walked to the rear of the Triumph. "Do you know you got a SAVE THE WHALES bumper sticker back here?"

"Save the whales?" Eddie said.

"Sure enough."

"Screw the whales," Polk said.

"Hey—come on, Polk," Eddie said. "Whales are beautiful." He winked again at Frank. "It's all right. I can relate."

"I seen one at Rockport once," Polk said. "Big, sorry dude. Just threw himself up on that beach there. Just wheezing away. Got himself a real big crowd."

"They say they're pretty smart animals," Mace said.

"Well, what that whale did was real dumb-ass, that's for sure."

"Here's to whales," Eddie said. Except for Frank, who had none, they all raised their beers. "Hey, Frank, you sure you don't want another?"

"No—really, I've got to get going." He waited for Eddie to give him back his cap.

"You know, Frank, I've got a sense about you." Eddie tapped the bill of the cap. "Let me guess—I think you're the kind of guy who had a McGovern bumper sticker a few years back, right?"

"That's right," Frank said. "I did."

"And maybe a—who was it?—a McCarthy sticker before that."

"Well, no—"

"Or maybe a GET OUT OF VIETNAM sticker, then. Am I right?"

"No," Frank lied. "I didn't."

"You serve in Vietnam, Frank?" Polk asked.

Frank shook his head.

"How come? You weren't a damn hippie, now, were you?" Polk grinned for the first time, a grin that vanished almost as soon as it came.

"I—had a deferment."

"What for? Got bad feet or something?"

"No." Frank hesitated. "It was an occupational deferment."

"What the hell's that?"

"I had a job the draft board thought was in the national interest."

Polk and Eddie exchanged glances.

"Well, what was this job, Frank?" Eddie asked. "That was so important and all?"

"I was an educator," Frank said.

"A teacher?"

"Well, I—I didn't teach, exactly. I worked for a company that made up tests." Frank saw their puzzled expressions. "You know, standardized tests in reading and math and so on. For young kids. I helped make up test questions."

"They let you out of Vietnam for *that?*" Polk said.

"It wasn't me. It was their decision."

"But you had to ask them for that deferment," Eddie said. "Didn't you?"

Frank was silent.

"Hey, you guys!" Teal shouted from the grill. "Food's on."

"You weren't scared to go, were you, Frank?" Eddie asked.

"Nobody wanted to go to that war."

"That's not what I asked. I asked, were *you* scared?"

"No, I—I—of course not."

"Well, you're a brave man, Frank." Eddie raised his beer in another toast. "I sure was scared."

"You were over there?"

Eddie nodded. "Me and Teal."

"You tell him, Eddie," Polk said. He was smiling again.

Eddie counted on his fingers. "Ben Hu, Qui Duc, the Delta—one lousy place after another."

"Huh," Frank said.

"You know," Eddie said, "a lot of guys over there didn't much care for the guys who got to stay home. I mean, there you were, getting your ass zinged, eating those rotten peaches, and some guy back home was eating a chili dog, screwing your sister—"

"You don't got a sister," Mace said.

"I didn't say this was me, Mace. I'm talking about guys in general. Now, don't worry, Frank. Me—I didn't hate that guy at all. Hell, no—more power to him. He was smarter than me. He got out."

"He got a deferment," Polk said.

"I even *admired* him," Eddie said. "I'd think about the absolute good times he was having, and I just admired him. He was smarter than me. I thought, When I go home, I'm going to shake his hand. And Frank—I'd like to do it." He thrust out his hand. Frank dumbly, automatically, extended his, and Eddie grasped it and shook it once, twice, and let it fall. "There, now."

Polk laughed, and Frank reddened.

Eddie glanced again in the side-view mirror. "Hell, look at me, guys." He fingered a clump of long hair, and laughed. "I'm the one who looks like a hippie now." He tipped Frank's cap back on his head. "You know, I just love this cap."

"Maybe Frank'll give it to you," Polk said.

"Hey—that'd be real nice." Eddie looked at him, and Frank was startled by the challenge in his eyes. They were all looking at him.

"Sure," Frank said. "You can have it."

"Why, that's real nice of you, Frank." Eddie grinned broadly. "Hey, Teal!" he shouted. "Frank here gave me his Yankees cap."

"You guys ever gonna come eat?" Teal shouted back.

"C'mon, Frank," Eddie said. "Let's get us something to eat."

"I should get going," Frank said.

"Oh, come on, now," Eddie clapped him on the shoulder, held him. "You're not scared of our cooking, now, are you?" He guided Frank toward the grill. "You gave me this nice cap, now I've got to give you something. We've got to break bread together, like the old Israelites." Eddie speared a hot dog, put it on a burnt bun, and shoved it into Frank's hand. "We'll eat and have us another beer and then we'll all watch the fireworks, right? Now, you just get yourself some beans and stuff and come sit with us." He turned and walked back to his pickup. Polk and Mace fixed their hot dogs and hamburgers and went over to sit with him on the tailgate.

Frank lingered at the grill. He bit into his hot dog.

Why, why had he given Eddie his cap? He felt stupid. If they hadn't all been standing around, making him nervous—

"Don't let him get to you," Teal said. "Eddie's okay. He just likes to needle folks."

Frank hadn't realized he'd overheard. "I don't think he cares much for me," he said.

Teal flipped over a hamburger. "Eddie don't care much for nobody. That's Eddie."

"Were you in Vietnam together?"

Teal looked puzzled. "What do you mean? Eddie wasn't over there at all. Did he say that?"

"Yes."

Teal grinned. "That crap artist. *I* was over there, but he wasn't. He was in the army, but they stopped sending new guys by then."

"But why'd he—"

"He was just kidding you."

Frank looked at the three men eating by the truck. Eddie was saying something to Polk and Mace, and they all laughed. *Just kidding me.* Frank felt foolish but also relieved. Okay, fine. He'd play the fool, he'd lost his cap. So what? Let Eddie have it. He'd just go.

The sun had disappeared behind the trees and the sky was streaked with fire. Frank finished his hot dog. "Well, I better get going," he said.

"Take care," Teal said.

"Hey, Frank," Eddie called as he passed by them. "You're not leaving, are you? The fireworks'll be starting soon."

"No, I've got to go."

"Why? No one's expecting you, are they?"

"I'm a little tired. It's a long drive back."

"Well, it's up to you."

And I'm gone, Frank thought. He'd go down to the beach and watch the fireworks with everyone else.

"Hey, Frank—" Eddie jumped off the tailgate and walked over. "Look, before you go—I was wondering—I got a favor to ask." He seemed hesitant, almost shy. "Could I—you know—take your car for a little spin? Just down the road a ways?"

"I wouldn't let him do that," Mace yelled.

"I can't," Frank said.

Eddie seemed surprised. "Why not?"

"I—" Frank searched for a reason. "My insurance."

"Oh, the hell with that," Eddie said. "Come on—I'll just take a quick spin."

"No, really, I can't."

"You surely don't think something's gonna happen on this little old road, do you?"

"No, I—"

"Well, what are you scared of, then?"

"I'm not scared. I just—"

"You don't have something against *me* driving your car, do you?"

"No, no—"

Eddie spread his hands. "Well?"

Frank didn't know what to say or do. He couldn't argue with

Eddie, and he couldn't just get in his car and go. Again they were all looking at him.

"Come on, now," Eddie said, softly, so that only Frank could hear. "I told Polk and Mace you'd probably let me 'cause you're a good guy." He grinned.

"Okay," Frank said. "Just a short ride."

"Hey, Polk," Eddie yelled. "Frank here says we can take his car for a spin."

"Whoee!"

"You're a brave man, mister," Mace called out.

Frank handed him the keys, and Eddie and Polk got in. Eddie revved the engine. Pine needles scattered under the exhaust. He jammed the gearshift forward and the Triumph lurched toward the lake, barely missing Frank's leg.

"Whooee!" Polk yelled.

Ten yards from the bank Eddie braked, glanced back, and ground the car into reverse. Kicking up pine needles and dust, it shot up the slope straight toward a tree stump. He will see it, Frank thought, he will swerve—but Eddie didn't, and the Triumph slammed dully into it.

Frank ran over. Eddie and Polk were already out, inspecting the damage. The rear bumper was dented like a piece of bad fruit.

"Sorry about this," Eddie shook his head. "I don't know where that damn stump came from."

"You saw it!" Frank cried. "Jesus—"

"Sure didn't."

"You rammed it on purpose!"

"Hey, now—" Eddie held up his hand.

"Did you see?" Frank appealed to Mace and Teal, who had just arrived.

"Wasn't watching," Mace said. Teal shook his head.

"It's no big thing," Polk said. "Car'll still run."

"Damn it, why'd you do it?"

"I told you," Eddie said. "It just happened."

"It's just a little bump," Polk said. "You can get a hammer and pound that right out."

"Frank—look here." Eddie pulled two five-dollar bills from his wallet. "Here's ten dollars. That ought to be plenty for getting it pounded out."

"You can't just pound it out! They're going to have to replace the whole damn bumper."

"Here's my ten dollars," Eddie repeated.

"Look at this—" Frank gestured helplessly.

"Real, real sorry."

"Who's your insurance company?"

"Oh, come on, Frank." Eddie looked disgusted. "We don't want to get them involved, now, do we?"

"Somebody's got to pay for this!"

Eddie waved the bills.

"Who's your insurance company?" Frank asked again.

Eddie sighed. "I don't really recall offhand, Frank. It's back there with my papers."

"You can call your agent."

"Don't remember him either." Eddie rocked slightly on the balls of his feet.

"Hey, mister," Polk said. "Are you a lawyer or something?"

"You know who your agent is, don't you?" Frank said.

Eddie's eyes narrowed. "You calling me a liar now too, Frank?"

"Look, I just—"

"Are you?" Eddie's voice rose.

"Look, friend," Mace said reasonably. "Why don't you just take the man's money and go? No trouble. Nothing to get excited about."

"He don't want my ten dollars, Mace," Eddie said. He put the bills in his pocket. "My money's not good enough for him."

"He sure does bitch and moan a lot," Polk said.

"Don't he, though," Eddie said.

"Look—" Frank said. "You smashed my bumper. You—"

"I'm getting real tired of you accusing me of things, Frank," Eddie said angrily. "You know that? Maybe you'd best just get out of here."

Frank looked desperately to Teal. Almost imperceptibly, he shook his head.

"Go on," Eddie said. He came toward Frank. "Get the hell out of here."

Frank stepped back to the car door.

"Get!" Eddie hissed.

Frank opened the door. "I'll call the police," he said, his voice cracking slightly.

"You do that," Eddie said. "Go cry to them."

Frank started to get in. "I need the keys," he said.

Eddie reached into his shirt pocket and threw the keys on the ground between them. His face burning, Frank walked over, stooped down, and picked them up. Someone snickered.

His ears were ringing, and Frank wasn't even aware of driving until he was through the pines, almost to the beach, and then the ringing lessened and he felt only humiliation and the acid taste of shame. He stopped at the end of the road across from the Mini-Mart.

"Bastards!" He hit his palm against the steering wheel. "Goddamn bastards."

He got out and looked at the dented bumper.

"Ten dollars," he muttered. "Ten lousy dollars."

Frank crossed the road to the outdoor phone. He was agitated and couldn't decide whether to call the highway patrol or the local police, and when he decided on the police, he couldn't remember the name of the community he was in. He found a police emergency number in the front of the directory, started to dial, and then hesitated. Even if he could get a cop out here on a Fourth of July evening for a dented bumper, wouldn't Eddie and the others be long gone by the time he arrived? And if they weren't, wouldn't they all stick up for Eddie anyway?

He sure does bitch and moan a lot, Polk had said. He could see them all looking at him with contempt: he'd gone and cried to the police after all.

He hung up. Just go, he thought. Forget it, get out of here.

Frank crossed the road again and got back in the car. He turned on the engine but didn't pull away. Instead he stared out the windshield.

They humiliated me, he thought. And I let them. His face burned as he remembered. But what else could he have done? He'd been outnumbered. Eddie was crazy; the bumper, after all, wasn't that big a deal. And besides—

You weren't scared, were you? Eddie had asked.

Frank turned off the engine.

I was scared, he thought.

When he'd run from them, he'd been scared. When he'd let Eddie drive the car, when he'd given him the cap, he'd been scared.

And he was scared now.

I got a sense about you, Eddie had said, grinning. And behind him was Polk, and behind Polk, Mace and Teal. And behind them, still others—his father and Jena and the children they'd never had, that he'd never wanted and he'd been scared of them, too, had run from them just as surely as he was running now.

I've always been scared, Frank thought.

He closed his eyes, and when he opened them, the images were gone except for Eddie. Frank's cap perched mockingly on his head.

Frank started the car and turned back toward the pines.

They were sitting at the picnic table now passing a joint. Polk raised his arm in a half wave, as if Frank had just gone out for some beer. He parked beside Eddie's truck and walked toward them. They sat in silence, like kings in judgment.

"I want my cap back," he said to Eddie.

Eddie took a deep hit off the joint, held the smoke, and then expelled it harshly. "I thought you gave me this cap, Frank."

"He did, Eddie," Polk said.

"I didn't mean to," Frank said.

"Here, have a hit." Eddie offered him the joint. Frank shook his head. Eddie shrugged and passed it to Mace.

"I'd just like it back," Frank said. His heart was pounding—he was sure they could hear.

Eddie sighed. "That sort of makes you an Indian giver, don't it?"

"He's still hot about the car, Eddie," Polk said.

"I don't care about the car."

Eddie folded his arms. "Why do you want it now, Frank?"

"It—it's mine. I didn't mean to give it away."

Eddie pursed his lips and pulled the cap lower on his head. "How much you want it, Frank?" In the deepening twilight, his face was a mask. Polk laughed sharply.

"You want to fight," Frank said. "That's what you want, isn't it?"

"Hey, now," Mace said.

"Nobody said nothing about fighting," Eddie said. He took off the cap and twirled it on his finger.

"Oh, give him the damn hat, Eddie," Teal said. "Quit kidding around."

Eddie carefully put it back on. Frank flushed. As if they were the words of a stranger, he heard himself saying, "Okay, I'll fight you, if that's what you want. I'll fight you."

"You really want to fight for it, Frank?" Eddie seemed amused. "For this little old hat?" He slowly rose, crossed in front of the table, and stood not more than ten yards away.

"Watch out, now," Polk said.

"Eddie—" Teal said.

"Well, he wants to fight, Teal." Eddie looked at Frank. "Don't you?" Frank felt a lightness in his stomach, as if he were falling. He didn't know what to do. He knew nothing about fighting.

Eddie spread his arms. "Don't you?"

"What—what are the rules?"

Polk groaned. "I told you he was a lawyer, Eddie."

Eddie reached into his jeans and pulled out a knife. "Hey—these are the rules, Frank—" The blade snicked open.

"Eddie—" Teal said, and Mace whistled softly.

Absurdly, Frank said, "That's not fair."

"That's right—it's not. It's just the way things are."

"Eddie, put that damn thing away," Teal ordered. He rose from the table, but made no further move.

"Hey—" Frank said. "Come on."

"Come on where, Frank?" Eddie poked the air between them. "Where do you want to go now?"

"This is crazy!"

"Oh, I am crazy." He began circling Frank. "I'm the craziest thing you've ever dreamed of."

"Eddie," Teal said, "quit dicking around."

Further down the lake a string of firecrackers pop-popped. Frank heard shouts and laughter, impossibly far away. In all the world he was alone.

"You better take off, mister," Mace said.

Eddie circled him but came no closer. And Frank realized that Eddie was going to let him run, that he could if he wanted to—he would be allowed that final humiliation. It was, after all, what was expected of him.

"These are Vietnam jungle rules, Frank," Eddie said, brandishing the knife. "See what you missed?"

"You didn't go to Vietnam!" Frank cried.

Eddie cocked his head. "What's that, Frank?"

"You didn't go to Vietnam either. I know you."

Eddie stared at him, knife at arm's length. He glanced back at the table. "You didn't, Eddie," Teal said.

Eddie grinned. "Well, you sure can't put one over on old Frank, can you?"

"He's a lawyer, Eddie," Polk said.

Something searing, neither rage nor shame but of them both, passed through Frank then, and he yelled, "I'm not a lawyer, goddamn you! You don't know a goddamn thing about me!" He shook his fists at Eddie. "I'll fight you, you son of a bitch! I'll fight you."

"Don't be a fool, mister," Mace said. "Take off."

"No, goddamn it!"

Eddie stood as if frozen, knife extended, the lines of his face tight. "Don't be crazy," he said.

"I don't care," Frank cried. "Come on!"

Eddie squinted, as if trying to see him better in the fading light. The knife blade wavered slightly.

"Come on," Frank said. "You've got the knife."

Eddie didn't move.

"Damn you!" Frank cried. "All your damn talk—" He took a step toward Eddie.

"You're crazy, man." Eddie folded the knife and put it in his pocket. He spread his empty hands and grinned. "I can't fight anybody crazier than me."

He took off the Yankees cap and tossed it at Frank's feet. For a moment Frank couldn't move, couldn't stop watching him. Slowly he unclenched his fists. He picked up the cap and turned it over.

"Happy now?" Eddie said.

Frank put it on.

"Maybe you'd best go now," Teal said.

"I'm not going anywhere." Frank said. His voice seemed to come from far away. "I'm going to watch the fireworks." He walked past them, down the slope to the lake.

Frank sat on the dock's edge: it was dark now, and the lake smelled deep and mossy. His hands shook, lightly at first, then harder, and he hugged himself, as if that might contain the shaking. A first rocket flared and fell, followed by another that opened like a rose. "I won," he said softly.

Frank looked across the lake to the summer house, and, yes, in the rocket's light he could see it. They were all there—his mother and father and Jena, waiting to receive him, to bind his wounds. "I'm not going anywhere," he told them as they opened the door. "I'm staying right here."

The rocket faded; it was gone. He had won, but no one was there to tell, no one to care.

Three more rockets, red and white and yellow, burst over the lake. In their light Frank saw Teal and Polk and Mace and Eddie, faces turned skyward, almost reverent.

"I'm not going anywhere!" he shouted to them, but the men gave no sign of having heard. The rockets faded, they disappeared, and he was alone once more. "I'm not going anywhere," he murmured. "I'm not going anywhere at all."

THE BLACK HAND GIRL

Blanche McCrary Boyd

My mother hadn't wanted me to go to Harvard Summer School because of the Boston Strangler. "I just hate to think of you like that," she kept saying, "with your face all purple and your tongue hanging out. Why can't you be a normal girl and get a tan?"

The Dean at Duke University probably had not wanted me to go to Harvard either. At Duke I was viewed as a troublemaker, partly because of hypnosis.

When I was in high school I had learned to hypnotize people by accident. "Look deep into my eyes," I said to my cousin Sister-Girl one night when we'd been watching an evil hypnotist in a B movie on television. I said this with great conviction, and Sister-Girl looked at me in great fun. Then something peculiar happened: Sister-Girl seemed to drift toward my eyes. "I'm going to count to five," I whispered, "and when I get to five you'll be in a deep trance." I whispered because I was afraid. There was a current between us as certain as the electricity in a doorbell I'd once touched.

Sister-Girl's eyelids fluttered. She was a sweet, lumpish girl everyone loved. I counted to five and her eyes closed. "Can you bark?" I asked.

"Yes," she said.

"Will you do it?"

"Yes."

"Be a dog, then. Bark."

Her eyes remained closed, but Sister-Girl's lips pulled back from her teeth. She began to make little yipping noises. I recognized our neighbor's Pomeranian.

I counted backward from five and Sister-Girl woke up. "I don't think we ought to tell Momma or Aunt Rose about this," I said.

During my senior year in high school I developed a different technique, no longer hypnotizing through eye contact, which scared me too much, but with a lighted cigarette in a semi-dark room. My favorite trick remained making people bark. Sometimes I asked, after they were barking, "What kind of dog are you?" The answer might be, "I'm a German shepherd," or "I'm a Lhasa apso." I knew I shouldn't be doing hypnosis, especially at parties, but at Duke it made me popular and feared.

College caused me authority problems. There were rules against women wearing pants to classes or to the dining room, and rules against wearing curlers in public; there was even a "suggestion" against women smoking cigarettes standing up. Soon there was a new regulation concerning hypnosis.

The Dean's note came right after second semester began. For my audience I wore a madras wraparound skirt, a Gant button-down shirt, and a cardigan that had leather patches on the elbows. I even wore a panty girdle and hose. The Dean would see that I was a normal, healthy sorority girl, not a troublemaker.

Dean Pottle was at least forty years old. Her hair was brown and she was wearing a brown tailored suit. Her skin was pocked, as if she'd once had acne. She was smoking a cigarette and seemed quite friendly as she invited me to sit down across from her.

"Ellen," she said comfortingly, "we have had a report that you went to Dr. Hillyer's class in the medical school wearing nothing but a bathing suit and carrying a bottle of champagne on a silver tray."

I tried to think of how best to reply. "I'm not in the medical school," I said, "so I didn't think the regular rules would apply. Anyway, it was Dr. Hillyer's birthday, and some of his students asked me to deliver the champagne. It seemed harmless enough. I would never have agreed to do it if I'd known the class was at eight-thirty in the morning. I can assure you of that."

When the Dean said nothing, I continued with less confidence. "I wore my trench coat over my bathing suit until I got to the door of the classroom, and I put it right back on as soon as I gave him the champagne."

Her eyes seemed less affable. "The same trench coat you've been wearing to your regular classes?"

I nodded.

"Is it true you've been wearing your trench coat to classes with nothing under it?"

"It certainly is not true, Dean Pottle. I wear a slip and a bra. I even wear hose."

"Ellen, you do know about the dress code, don't you?"

"I'm within the dress code, Dean Pottle. It just says you can't wear pants, it doesn't say you have to wear skirts. Also, a slip is a kind of skirt, isn't it?"

The Dean was trying to look stern, but I began to suspect she might like me. "Do you think of yourself as an unusual girl?"

I nodded miserably. "Listen, Dean Pottle, would you mind if I smoked too? I'm very nervous."

"Go ahead. You have a tendency to bend the rules a bit, don't you think, Ellen?"

I lit a Winston. "I don't know."

"Let's start with the hypnosis."

"There was no rule against hypnosis."

The Dean took a final meditative drag on her own cigarette and crushed it out in a brown glass ashtray.

"Anyway, there's not much to it," I said. "To hypnosis. I saw it on TV one night. I say corny stuff like 'Look only at the tip of my cigarette, your eyelids are getting heavy.' Most people are just dying to go into a trance."

The Dean was staring at the smoke curling from my cigarette.

"Hello?"

With effort she looked up at me. When she didn't speak I continued, "I tell them, look at the glowing ember of the cigarette. Let your mind relax."

The Dean looked back at my cigarette. She seemed like a nice enough person. She probably thought the rules were dumb too.

"Your eyelids will close by themselves."

Her eyelids lowered quietly, like dancers bowing.

I counted slowly to ten. "That's good. You're feeling very good. Just rest now."

A manila folder with my name on it was lying on her desk. In it were my college application, my board scores, and a handwritten report on the hypnosis incidents. The conclusion said I had difficulty accepting discipline and was on academic probation for poor grades.

I replaced the folder and said in my most soothing voice, "When you wake up, you'll feel great. You won't have any memory of this trance. No memory of it at all. You'll think Ellen Burns is a nice, interesting girl with no problems. Nod your head if you understand me."

The Dean nodded.

I was curious to know what kind of dog she might be, but someone could walk in, and I wanted to put this unexpected opportunity to use. Several acquaintances of mine were going to Harvard for the summer.

"When you wake up, I'm going to ask you about recommending me for Harvard Summer School, and you're going to think that's a wonderful idea, in spite of my academic record. You'll say that Harvard is going to help me with my authority problems. Do you understand?"

She nodded again.

I counted slowly backwards from ten to one, then said, "Wake up now."

The Dean's eyes opened. "I feel great. You're a wonderful girl, Ellen, with no serious problems."

I put out my cigarette in her brown glass ashtray. "Dean Pottle, I wanted to ask you about Harvard Summer School."

I had made several unsuccessful attempts to lose my virginity at Duke, and Harvard had begun to seem like a possible solution.

My roommate at Duke was named Darlene. Darlene was an angular, good-looking girl with sharp cheekbones and black hair cut in a smooth pageboy that swayed when she moved.

She had been coaching me on the loss of my virginity. In high school I had read an article that said sperm could swim right through your underpants, so whenever I got close to intercourse with a boy, I imagined microscopic tadpoles swimming desperately through cotton fibers the size of the columns at Stonehenge. And I was distracted by other thoughts: germs swim back and forth between mouths; the tongue is a muscle and disappears down the back of the throat, so what is it attached to?

"I want to be normal," I kept saying to Darlene. "I want to lose my normal virginity. Normally."

"I'll fix you up with Don. He doesn't have any experience either. You can learn together."

"Darlene, how could that be a good idea?"

"Trust me, it's a good idea."

Darlene arranged for Don to take me to dinner at a restaurant called Chicken in the Rough. The restaurant's logo was a long-legged chicken in a tam-o'-shanter swinging a golf club. Sitting in one of the dark red booths, I felt as if I were in a dentist's waiting room.

Don was a melancholy boy with dark, dramatic looks. His thick black eyebrows moved when he chewed. When he bit into a chicken leg I pointed at the tiny string of meat hanging from the bone. "That's a ligament. In the fourth grade they told us that you could see what ligaments were when you ate fried chicken."

He looked uncertain.

"I only eat white meat," I said.

"Why are you telling me this?"

"Once the top of my mouth started getting loose. I could move the skin with my tongue. So I went to the dentist and said, 'The roof of my mouth is rotting off. I have some terrible disease.' He looked in my mouth and said, 'Do you eat soup?' So I said of course I eat soup. 'Do you drink coffee?' Yes I drink, coffee. 'Well, you're drinking it too hot.' I was kind of disappointed, you know? I thought I had some rare disease."

Don put down his chicken leg. "I don't know what Darlene said to you, but we don't have to do anything. We really don't."

"Can we drink some beer?" I said.

So, while the fried chicken and fried potatoes congealed in their grease and the salad wilted in its pool of dressing, Don and I drank a pitcher of beer, and I began to relax. Don was a good enough looking boy, although he lacked the wildness I found compelling in Darlene's boyfriend, who had taken the mike away from a singer of a black blues band at a fraternity party and sung a version of "Put Your Head on My Shoulder" called "Put Your Legs Round My Shoulders."

Don had been raised by his grandmother in Greensboro, North

Carolina. When he graduated he wanted to be a newspaper reporter in a small Southern town. His grandmother's lifelong wish was to meet Lawrence Welk, and someday Don hoped to arrange that for her.

"I have to go to the bathroom," I said.

In the bathroom I confronted the most serious obstacle to the loss of my virginity: under my skirt I was wearing a panty girdle. I hadn't meant to wear the girdle, but when I was dressing, I kept hearing my mother's voice saying *Any woman looks better in a girdle,* so I'd put it on experimentally, and it felt so secure, so bracing, I'd left it on. Now I didn't know what to do about it. I considered taking it off, but it was too bulky for the pocket of my trench coat.

What I did have in the pocket of my trench coat was a Norform vaginal suppository that Darlene had given me to insert "just before intercourse." It was supposed to lubricate me, a word which made me feel like a car. But when was "just before intercourse"? After I peed, I inserted the suppository and pulled the girdle back into place, feeling deeply relieved: the girdle meant I couldn't make love, but the suppository meant I sincerely wanted to.

On the way out of Chicken in the Rough I stopped at the bar in the front room and downed a double shot of bourbon, neat. "I never met anybody like you," Don said.

"I'm just normal," I said, feeling a rush of love for the shot glass. "I'm normal for me. Really."

The November night was inky blue, the air clean and brisk. Don put his arm around me as we walked. The bourbon warmed my blood and the Norform melting made me feel odd. I stopped Don on the street and kissed him on the mouth the way I thought someone in a movie might kiss.

Soon we were in the dormitory parking lot, leaning against a stranger's empty car, still kissing cinematically. Then we were in the back seat of the same car, half lying down. Just when the kissing was getting boring, Don put his hand up my skirt. I had never had anyone's hand up my skirt before.

His fingers moved tentatively up my legs. "My God, what's this?" he said, encountering the girdle.

I wanted to explain, but I felt too dizzy.

His hand wandered around the flesh of my thigh, then moved inward and upward. The dissolved Norform was all over the crotch of the girdle. "My God, you're wet," he said.

I tried to hold still.

"Okay," he mumbled, sliding two fingers awkwardly up the leg of the panty girdle. When he touched me something flashed in my head, and my hips pushed hard against his hand.

"Oh my God, oh my God," he said, pulling his hand free.

"I'll take it off," I said. "No problem. No problem, really."

Don was still crouched over his hand. His fingers glistened in the darkness. A lump appeared behind his knuckle and swelled while I watched.

"It's . . . it's growing," I said.

"It's sprained," he said.

Don's hand was not sprained, but he had broken a blood vessel behind his knuckle. Overnight the blood spread under his skin, turning it puffy and greenish. By the end of the week his hand had turned black, with a dark red palm.

Apparently Don told no one about the girdle, perhaps out of kindness, perhaps to save face, but he did admit to Darlene's boyfriend that his injury was "sort of sexual."

"*Sort of* sexual," Darlene's boyfriend kept saying to her. "*Sort of* sexual."

I became famous almost overnight. Boys I had never heard of called me, and Don followed me to several classes. "We'll try it again. We've got to try it again." He looked vulnerable, stunned by love, extending his black hand.

I never wanted to see Don again in my whole life, so when my mother telephoned and said, "Why don't you fly home this weekend and get measured for your hand-sewn human hair wig?" I felt relieved at the chance to leave school.

My mother met me at the airport in Charleston, just before midnight on a Friday. She was wearing purple toreador pants, a gold lamé shirt, gold lamé slippers, a stroller-length mink coat, and large dark glasses. "I don't want anyone to *recognize* me," she whispered, looking uneasily around the deserted airport. "That's why I have on these *glasses*."

For two years my mother had been addicted to diet pills. "*Ambars*," she would say in a singsongy voice, "I was a different person before I found *Ambars*! The *am* stands for amphetamine and the *bar* stands for barbiturate! The amphetamine speeds you *up*, and the barbiturate slows you *down!* You don't have any *ap*petite, but you're not *ner*vous!"

Before my mother had found diet pills, she did not speak in italics and exclamations, and she was not wiry and loud. Before she found diet pills, she was heavy and depressed. Now she liked to scrub the tiles in the bathroom with a toothbrush, and she had fired the maid because she said it felt so good to push the vacuum cleaner around and polish the silverware herself. She liked to get down between the tines of the forks. "It takes *patience,*" she said. "I have lots of *patience!*"

Her arms vibrated as she embraced me. "Doesn't it look real?" she whispered. "Isn't it *astounding?*" She patted her French twist.

Her hair was so smoothly arranged that no false scalp showed, but the elegant twist looked odd: my mother's real hair is naturally curly.

The next day I was staring at myself in the beautician's mirror. "Thank you, Momma." Like Momma's wig, Aunt Rose's wig, and Sister-Girl's wig, mine was set in a French twist.

The four of us were standing around the beauty parlor. We had a monolithic look, like a gang. "The French Twist Gang," Sister-Girl said quietly, meeting my eyes in the mirror.

Sister-Girl had become large and statuesque, a natural blonde with a sweet smile and a quiet manner. A year older than me, she had declined college graciously, as if she were not hungry for dessert.

Her mother, Rose, was my mother's sister. "We all look alike in these wigs," Rose said, "but I'm the inflated version." Rose didn't care for the diet pills because they made her heart hurt.

Rose was built square, "like a refrigerator," she said cheerfully, and she wheezed almost all the time. "There's just not much room for air in there," Sister-Girl had once remarked.

After my wig fitting, we all went shopping, and I bought a garter belt. "I'm not wearing girdles anymore, Momma," I said. "Don't ask. I'm just not, no matter what."

The wig not only changed how I looked, it changed how I felt about myself. When I got back to school, boys stopped pursuing me. Perhaps they no longer recognized the black hand girl. I abandoned not only the hypnosis but parties, and my study habits improved. By the time I went to Harvard Summer School, I had been taken off academic probation. Dean Pottle thought it was her confidence in me that had "turned me around."

At Harvard Summer School I met the man I would eventually marry. On a sticky Saturday night in a drugstore in Harvard Square I was buying a new copy of *Peyton Place* because the pages of my copy were falling out. Nicky Sommers was buying a book called *Thinking About the Unthinkable,* which I assumed was pornographic. It turned out to be about nuclear war.

My copy of *Peyton Place* was worn out because, in the long afternoons in my apartment in the Back Bay, while my roommate, Dottie Plant, was out waitressing, I had discovered masturbation.

When I was wearing the wig, I dressed like a Duke sorority girl and studied calmly, but when I was not wearing the wig a certain wildness seemed to overtake me. So I wore my French twist almost every day and I was making very good grades. Dean Pottle was going to be proud.

My wig got gummy with dirt, and I had to give it up for six days to have it professionally cleaned. Without the wig I began to wear white lipstick. I combed my hair out straight, drank Scotch on the rocks while I studied, and imagined I was a beatnik like the ones I'd seen in *Time* magazine. I was at Harvard and no one in the South need ever know I was behaving this way.

Sexually, I began to experiment. I read the sex scenes in *Peyton Place* and drifted into them like hypnosis, my old teddy bear clutched tight between my legs. I felt bad about my teddy bear, who was not holding up well under this assault, but as long as I didn't touch myself directly, I was sure I couldn't be doing anything wrong. Then, one afternoon when it was too hot in the apartment to wear a lot of clothes, the situation got out of hand, so to speak. I bled and it wasn't my period. The word masturbation came to me. I realized I had deflowered myself.

I was getting my wig back on Monday. On Saturday night, since I was ruined anyway, I went to a drugstore in Harvard Square in my white lipstick, my black jersey and tight black jeans, to buy a new copy of *Peyton Place.* I was standing furtively behind the paperback rack when this greasy, stringy-haired boy in Levi's that looked like they hadn't been washed in weeks said to me, "Are you from down home?" He had an unmistakable southern drawl.

I didn't answer, of course. My mother's warning about the Boston Strangler had made a vivid impression on me, so vivid, in fact, that when I tried to swear off *Peyton Place*, fantasies about the Boston Strangler had drifted in to replace them.

"Southerners look different," the boy continued. I looked at him out of the corner of my eye. "We walk different, or something."

It seemed unlikely that the Boston Strangler was a Southerner, so I looked him full in the face. "Where are you from?"

"Texas." He had a nice smile and crooked teeth.

"Texas isn't the South," I said. "Texas is the West."

If I hadn't agreed to go drink beer with Nicky Sommers, I wouldn't have told him funny stories about Sister-Girl and Aunt Rose, and if he hadn't laughed so much at my stories, I wouldn't have drunk so much, I wouldn't have ended up back at my apartment with him. When he kissed me I put my hands on my throat. "Squeeze just a little bit," I said. "I want to see how it feels." If Dottie Plant had been home, I wouldn't have ended up on the sofa with him, and if he hadn't been lying with his skinny hip jammed against my tight black jeans, I wouldn't have drifted into *Peyton Place*.

Your nipples are as hard as diamonds, the irresistible man in *Peyton Place* had whispered.

Do it to me, the woman whispered back.

Nicky unbuttoned my shirt and cupped his whole hand over my breast.

"Diamonds!" I shouted, and we both began to shudder. I was extremely embarrassed and shut my eyes tight.

"Hey," Nicky kept saying, "hey," only it wasn't as if he expected an answer.

I was breathing like I'd been running.

"Wow," Nicky whispered. "You had an orgasm."

"I certainly did not." I was trying not to cry.

"Wow. I never gave a girl an orgasm. Hey. Wow."

When Nicky arrived at my apartment for our first real date on Monday night, he had cut his hair and shaved so close his jaw looked raw and scraped. We were going to dinner at a restaurant where, Nicky had promised, the menu would be written in French.

Nicky was wearing a suit and tie, and on his feet were grownup, lace-up men's shoes. In his hand was a bouquet of daisies.

I had picked up my wig from the cleaners. I was wearing a blue dress, a garter belt, hose and high heels.

"Your hair looks great that way," Nicky said.

We stared dumbly at each other, like people who have fallen in love.

LIES

Ethan Canin

What my father said was, "You pays your dime, you takes your choice," which, if you don't understand it, boils down to him saying one thing to me: Get out. He had a right to say it, though. I had it coming and he's not a man who says excuse me and pardon me. He's a man who tells the truth. Some guys my age are kids, but I'm eighteen and getting married and that's a big difference. It's a tough thing to get squeezed from your own house, but my father's done all right because he's tough. He runs a steam press in Roxbury. When the deodorant commercials come on the set he turns the TV off. That's the way he is. There's no second chance with him. Anyway, I'll do all right. Getting out of the house is what I wanted, so it's no hair off my head. You can't get everything you want. This summer two things I wanted were to get out of the house finally and to go up to Fountain Lake with Katy, and I got both. You don't have that happen to you very often, so I'm not doing so bad.

It's summer and I'm out of High. That's a relief. Some guys don't make it through, but they're the ones I was talking about—the kids. Part of the reason I made it is that my folks pushed me. Until I was too old to believe it my mother used to tell me the lie that anybody can be what you want to. "Anybody can rise up to be President of the United States," she used to say. Somewhere along the line you find out that's not true and that you're either fixed from the start or fixed by something you do without really thinking about it. I guess I was fixed by both. My mother, though, she doesn't give up. She got up twenty minutes early to make me provolone on rye for four years solid and cried when I was handed my diploma.

After graduation is when I got the job at Able's. Able's is the movie theater—a two-hundred-fifty-seat, one-aisle house on South Huntington. *Able's, where the service is friendly and the popcorn is fresh.* The bathrooms are cold-water-only though, and Mr. Able spends Monday mornings sewing the ripped seat upholstery himself because he won't let loose a few grand to re-cover the loges, which for some reason are coming apart faster than the standard seats. I don't know why that is. I sell maybe one-third loge tickets and that clientele doesn't carry penknives to go at the fabric with. The ones who carry knives are the ones who hang out in front. They wouldn't cut anybody but they might take the sidewall off your tire. They're the ones who stopped at tenth grade, when the law says the state doesn't care anymore. They hang out in front, drinking usually, only they almost never actually come in to see the movie.

I work inside, half the time selling tickets and the other half as the projectionist. It's not a bad job. I memorize most movies. But one thing about a movie theater is that it's always dark inside, even in the lobby because of the tinted glass. (You've seen that, the way the light explodes in when someone opens the exit door.) But when you work in the ticket booth you're looking outside to where it's bright daylight, and you're looking through the metal bars, and sometimes that makes you think. On a hot afternoon when I see the wives coming indoors for the matinee, I want to push their money back under the slot. I want to ask them what in the world are they doing that for, trading away the light and the space outside for a seat here.

The projectionist half of the job isn't so bad, even though most people don't even know what one is. They don't realize some clown is sitting up in the room where the projectors are and changing the reels when it's time. Actually, most of the time the guy's just smoking, which he's not supposed to do, or he has a girl in there, which is what I did sometimes with Katy. All there is to do is watch for the yellow dot that comes on in the corner of the screen when it's time to change the reel. When I see that yellow dot there's five seconds before I have to have the other projector running. It's not hard, and after you do it a while you develop a sense. You get good enough so you can walk out to the lobby, maybe have popcorn or a medium drink, then sit on the stairs for a while before you go back to the booth, perfectly timed to catch the yellow spot and get the next reel going.

Anyway, it's pretty easy. But once I was in the booth with Katy when she told me something that made me forget to change the reel. The movie stopped and the theater was dark, and then everybody starts to boo and I hear Mr. Able's voice right up next to the wall. "Get on the ball, Jack," he says, and I have the other projector on before he even has time to open the door. If he knew Katy was in there he'd have canned me. Later he tells me it's my last warning.

What Katy told me was that she loved me. Nobody ever told me they loved me before except my mother, which is obvious, and I remember it exactly because suddenly I knew how old I was and how old I was getting. After she said that, getting older wasn't what I wanted so much. It's the way you feel after you get your first job. I remember exactly what she said. She said, "I love you, Jack. I thought about it and I know what I mean. I'm in love with you."

At the time the thing to do was kiss her, which I did. I wanted to tell her that I loved her too, but I couldn't say it. I don't mind lying, but not about that. Anyway, we're up there in the booth together, and it's while we have our tongues in each other's mouths that the reel runs out.

The first time I met Katy was at the theater. She's a pretty girl, all eyes, hair that's not quite blond. It falls a certain way. It was the thing I noticed first, the way it sat there on her shoulders. But it more than just sat; it touched her shoulders like a pair of hands, went in around the collar of her shirt and touched her neck. She was three rows in front. I wasn't working at the theater yet. It was end of senior year and I was sitting in two seats and had a box of popcorn in my lap. My friend LeFranc was next to me. We both saw Katy when she came in. LeFranc lit a match. "Put me out," he said, "before we all burn." LeFranc plays trumpet. He doesn't know what to say to a girl.

During the bright parts of the movie I keep looking at her neck. She's with three other girls we don't recognize. It turns out they go to Catholic school, which is why we don't know them. Then about halfway through she gets up by herself and heads back up the aisle. LeFranc breathes out and lights another match. I smile and think about following her back to the candy counter, where I might say something, but there's always the chance that she's gone out to the ladies' room instead and then where would I be? Time is on my side, so I decide to wait. The movie is *The Right Stuff*. They're taking up the supersonic planes when this is happening. They're talking about the envelope, and I don't know what that means, and then suddenly Katy's sitting next to me. I don't know where she came from. "Can I have some popcorn?" she says.

"You can have the whole box," I answer. I don't know where this comes from either, but it's the perfect thing to say and I feel a little bit of my life happening. On the other side LeFranc is still as an Indian. I push the bucket toward Katy. Her hands are milk.

She takes a few pieces and holds them with her palm flat up. Already I'm thinking. That's something I would never do—the way she holds the little popped kernels like that. Then she chews them slowly, one by one, while I pretend to watch the movie. Things come into my head.

After the movie I talk to her a little and so we go on a few dates. In the meantime I get the theater job and in August she invites me to her sister's wedding. Her sister's marrying a guy twenty years older named Hank. It's at a big church in Saugus. By this time Katy and I've kissed maybe two hours total. She always bites a piece of Juicy Fruit in two when we're done and gives me half.

Anyway, at the wedding I walk in wearing a coat and tie and have to meet her parents. Her father's got something wrong with one of his eyes. I'm not sure which one's the bad one, and I'm worried he's thinking I'm shifty because I'm not sure which one to look at. We shake hands and he doesn't say anything. We put our hands down and he still doesn't say anything.

"I've been at work," I say. It's a line I've thought about.

"I don't know what the hell you kids want," he says then. That's exactly what he says. I look at him. I realize he's drunk or been drinking, and then in a second Katy's mother's all over him. At practically the same time she's also kissing me on the cheek and telling me I look good in my suit and pulling Katy over from where she's talking with a couple of her girlfriends.

For the ceremony we sit in the pews. I'm on the aisle, with her mother one row in front and a couple of seats over so that I can see all the pleats and hems and miniature flowers sewn into her dress. I can hear her breathing. The father, who's paid for the whole bagful, is pacing behind the nave door waiting to give away the bride. Katy's back there too, with the other maids. They're wearing these dresses that stay up without straps. The wedding starts and the maids come up the aisle finally, ahead of the bride, in those dresses that remind you all the time. Katy's at the front, and when they pass me, stepping slowly, she leans over and gives me half a piece of Juicy Fruit.

So anyway, we've already been to a wedding together and maybe thanks to that I'm not so scared of our own, which is coming up. It's going to be in November. A fall wedding. Though actually it's not going to be a wedding at all but just something done by a justice of the peace. It's better that way. I had enough the first time, seeing Katy's father pace. He had loose skin on his face and a tired look and I don't want that at our wedding.

And besides, things are changing. I'm not sure who I'd want to come to a big wedding. I'm eighteen in two months and so is Katy, and to tell the truth I'm starting to get tired of my friends. It's another phase I'm coming into, probably. My friends are Hadley and Mike and LeFranc. LeFranc is my best friend. Katy doesn't like Hadley or Mike and she thinks LeFranc is okay mostly because he was there when we met. But LeFranc plays amazing trumpet, and if there's a way for him to play at the justice-of-the-peace wedding I'm going to get him to do it. I want him to play because sometimes I think about how this bit with Katy started and how fast it's gone, and it kind of stuns me that this is what happened, that of all the ways a life can turn out this is the way mine is going to.

We didn't get up to Fountain Lake until a couple of months after her sister's wedding. It's a Sunday and I'm sitting on the red-and-black carpet of Able's lobby steps eating a medium popcorn and waiting for the reel change to come. Able himself is upstairs in the office, so I'm just sitting there, watching the sun outside through the ticket window, thinking this is the kind of day I'd rather be doing something else. The clowns out front have their shirts off. They're hanging around out there and I'm sitting in the lobby when a car honks and then honks again. I look over and I'm so surprised I think the sun's doing something to my eyes. It's Katy in a red Cadillac. It's got whitewalls and chrome and she's honking at me. I don't even know where she learned to drive. But she honks again and the guys out front start to laugh and point inside the theater. What's funny is that I know they can't see inside because of the tint, but they're pointing right at me anyway.

There's certain times in your life when you do things and then have to stick to them later, and nobody likes to do that. But this was one of them, and Katy was going to honk again if I didn't do something. My father has a saying about it being like getting caught between two rocks, but if you knew Mr. Able and you knew Katy, you'd know it wasn't really like two rocks. It was more like one rock, and then Katy sitting in a Cadillac. So I get up and set the popcorn down on the snack bar, then walk over and look through the door. I stand there maybe half a minute. All the while I'm counting off the time in my head until I've got to be back in to change the reel. I think of my father. He's worked everyday of his life. I think of Mr. Able, sewing on the loge upholstery with fishing line. They're banking on me, and I know it, and I start to feel kind of bad, but outside there's Katy in a red Fleetwood. "King of the Cadillac line," I say to myself. It's a blazing afternoon, and as soon as I open the door and step outside I know I'm not coming back.

On the street the sun's thrashing around off the fenders and the white shirts, and it's like walking into a wall. But I cross the street without really knowing what I'm doing and get into the car on the driver's side. All the time I'm crossing the street I know everybody's looking, but nobody says anything. When I get into the car I slip the seat back a little.

"How'd you get this?"

"It's Hank's," she says. "It's new. Where should we go?"

I don't know what she's doing with Hank's car, but my foot's pushing up and down on the gas and the clowns out front are looking, so I have to do something and I say, "The lake, let's go up to Fountain Lake." I put it in drive and the tires squeal a second before we're gone.

The windows are up and I swear the car's so quiet I'm not sure there's an engine. I push the gas and don't hear anything but just feel the leather seats pushing up under our backs. The leather's cool and has this buttered look. The windshield is tinted at the top. After about three blocks I start thinking to myself, I'm out, and I wheel the Cadillac out Jamaicaway toward the river. I really don't know the way up to Fountain Lake. Katy doesn't either, though, so I don't ask her.

We cross over the river at BU and head up Memorial Drive, past all the college students on the lawns throwing Frisbees and plastic footballs. Over by Harvard they're pulling rowing sculls out of the water. They're all wearing their red jackets and holding big glasses of beer while they work. The grass is so green it hurts my eyes.

On the long stretch past Boylston I put down the electric window and hold my arm out so that the air picks it up like a wing when we speed up, and then, just before we get out to the highway, something clicks in my head and I know it's time to change the reel. I touch the brakes for a second. I count to five and imagine the theater going dark, then one of the wives in the audience saying something out loud, real irate. I see Mr. Able opening the door to the projection booth, the expression on his face just like one my father has. It's a certain look, half like he's hit somebody and half like somebody's hit him. But then as we come out onto Route 2 and I hit the gas hard one of my father's sayings comes to me, that it's all water over the bridge, and it's like inside my head another reel suddenly runs out. Just like that, that part of my life is gone.

By the time we're out past Lincoln I'm really not thinking anything except Wow, we're out of here. The car feels good. You get a feeling sometimes right after you do something. Katy's next to me with her real tight body and the soft way girls look, and I'm no kid anymore. I think about how nice it would be to be able to take the car whenever you want and go up to the lake. I'm thinking all this and floating the car around big wide turns, and I can see the hills now way up the road in front of us. I look over at Katy, and then at the long yellow line sliding under the front of the car, and it seems to me that I'm doing something big. All the time Katy's just sitting there. Then she says, "I can't believe it."

She's right. I'm on the way to Fountain Lake, going fast in a car, the red arrow shivering around seventy-five in the dial, a girl next to me, pretty, smelling the nice way girls do. And I turn to her and I don't know why except you get a feeling when you finally bust out, and I say, "I love you, Katy," in a certain kind of voice, my foot crushing the accelerator and the car booming along the straightaways like it's some kind of rocket.

WAY TO THE DUMP

E.S. Goldman

Zuerner was breaking away from the Boston meeting to come to the Cape, but surely not because of a casual invitation extended in a passing encounter with Elligott a year ago. The two men disliked each other for no particular reason, the most incurable kind of aversion; Elligott's invitation emerged for want of something better to say; neither he nor Zuerner had expected it to be taken up. Even so, Zuerner had telephoned and asked if it would be convenient if he came by.

Was the merger on again? Did they want his stock?

"Stay for lunch," Elligott had said, impulsively, and immediately regretted this sign of weakness. He never managed to get the tone right with Zuerner. He hadn't even had the presence of mind to say, "Let me look at the calendar." Not even "Let me see if Daisy can make it for lunch."

Elligott moved the slider and stepped out onto his terrace. Unlike early settlers' houses, placed with buffers between themselves and the wind, his house had been a summer shack before the alterations and had been built right there on the low bluff above the beach. Its prospect was across the steaming bay toward an awesome pink dawn. On the way out the tide had trapped his skiff in shore grass; returning, it mirrored the forested dune. Some day! Some scene! Elligott felt the exhilaration of a discoverer. He wondered what he'd have to pay to commission this view from the fellow who did the Indian marsh paintings in Derek's gallery. It would be worth a thousand dollars. First a strong week in the market, and now a day like this!

He shrugged comfortably in his new Bean sweater; it was just the thing for this chill Sunday morning in October. October—so soon. Quarter to six. Dowling would be open in . . . now fourteen minutes.

Nobody was on the water. Nobody was anywhere. Not a bird. The only sound came from a ratcheting cricket, augmented in Elligott's hearing aid. Fat with good luck, the cricket tensed toward cover, but the man's foot was too quick. Elligott felt a small startle at the confrontation, not enough to call fear—afraid of a cricket?—but it would have read on an instrument. Perhaps a blood admonition not to kill easily. He kicked the squash over the edge into the sand, leaving a stain and a twitching leg on the mortar joint. In an impulse of compassion or guilt he stepped out the twitch.

He stood for another moment at the terrace edge, bothered slightly that the new sun-room, in the nature of all new things, had estranged the house from its environment. It had happened before, and he knew now that in a few years the rugosa, creeper, poison ivy, catbrier, fox grape, beach plum, and innumerable unidentifiable wind- and bird-brought weeds fleeing upward from the salt would blur the margins of the foundation into the land, and the shingles would darken. The house would then come fully into its destiny. It was an extraordinary house.

He thought of a small boat going by and somebody looking up and saying to himself, That's Elligott, a noticeable man. You would trust your widow to Elligott. Perhaps not your wife; look at the bush of hair for a man his age and the athletic way he carries his weight. The house is suitable to the commanding view, what you would expect of a man like Elligott.

The hydrangea that he had cleverly placed below the terrace, so that its enormous plates of bloom could be seen from above, was at its fullest. The branch he had layered stood erect in full leaf, surely rooted. He had never imagined that gardening could be so pleasurable, and that he had such a hand for it. Farther below, in the narrow courses veining the grassy marsh, blue crabs fed; they were most big this time of year, no chicks; big as mitts, swimming to the rotten-meat bag and taking alarm too late to escape the sneaking net.

Wait till Zuerner began to net crabs down there for his lunch. That would get to him, all right. That would open his face! That would balance all accounts.

The irritation at his forced retirement which Elligott frequently waked with before they came to the Cape had been diminishing all year, and this morning it gave way completely to the anticipation of how boggling it would be to Zuerner to see, on this best of all possible days, how well he and Daisy lived.

Gone were the clubs and restaurants, the church and duty boards, where men who knew he had been pushed aside observed him. He had made known that resigning to become a consultant was his idea, but McGlynn, Andrewes, Draveau, Thompson, Zuerner—all of them and their wives—had known that his résumé circulated. He felt himself become transparent. To distance himself from his telephone he had the building agent's girl record that she was Mr. Elligott's office, and if you waited for the tone you could leave a message of any length. After an interval Elligott called back insurance agents he had never before heard of; the *Wall Street Journal* offered a trial subscription; business papers wanted ads for Consultant Service Indexes; somebody wanted his cousin Lewis Elligott.

And one day Daisy had said, "Why don't we fix up the cottage and see what living on the Cape would be like?"

A steadying wife—what a blessing.

From that came days like this. Today he wouldn't mind comparing lives with Andrewes, Zuerner, with McGlynn himself—any of them. Most of all Zuerner.

An odd feeling of emptiness seeped into him. He felt as he had after eagling the fifth at the Heights Club, a mixture of triumph and loss. He had been playing alone; nobody was there to see the two iron drop, nobody to take the burden of telling from him. The not quite convincing story was one he could slip into a conversation but couldn't *tell*. Zuerner was the man to sign your card. Zuerner's authority would authenticate Elligott's life to McGlynn, Andrewes, all of them at Elligott Barge & Dredge.

He decided to take the wagon. It hadn't been turned over all week; it would do the old girl good to have hot oil in her cylinders and valves. He punched the garage-door button and got in while the door complained to the top and the control panel nattered at him to put on his galoshes, comb his hair, brush his teeth, stop squinting. At The Pharmacy the *Times* would be shuffled by six. Dowling's wouldn't be busy yet; he would be able to open the paper on the counter. Be back before Daisy was even up.

The driveway crackled through the allowed disorder of scratch pines and pin oaks, bayberry and blueberry bushes, rising from the rust of pine needles. He regretted mildly that for thirty years he had let the native growth have its way when for a few dollars he could have set seedlings of better breeds that by now would have been huge, towering, elegant. You could truck in hand-split shakes for the roof and Andersen windows with instant Colonial mullions and eighteen-dollar-a-square-foot tiles, but only God could make a tree. Only time marketed tall white pines. And rhododendrons like Pauley's.

He bobbed along the stony humpbacked lane kept up by the Association—PRIVATE 15 MPH PLEASE OBSERVE—and onto the state blacktop that forked at WAY TO THE DUMP, taking him toward town by the back road past Pauley's rhododendrons.

Development had not yet made progress here. The small properties were held by owners who frugally fought mortgages every percent of the way and counted on thirty bags of December scallops to help with the fuel bills. The houses had no views. The families used to grow cranberries in adjacent bogs. Cut off by barrier roads, the bogs were reduced to wetland unbuildable by law and some years away from the sort of new owners who could see the interesting tax consequences of a gift to the Conservation Fund.

But here ancestors and young marrieds had seen thickened hedges prefigured in a few sticks. He slowed while he envied the maturities. Cedars spiked in a grove of pines; lilacs that, come spring, would bear trusses above a man's reach; Pauley's rhododendrons.

Elligott knew Pauley the way he knew half a dozen building tradesmen around town; he had assumed the driver to be the man whose name was on the truck. He had called Pauley once and asked if he would work up a price on a new shower.

I'll stop next week and look at it. You near Haseley?

Elligott explained how one could easily find his place from Haseley's. He never heard from Pauley again. Par for the trades. Meanwhile, out of courtesy, Elligott waited three weeks, lost all that time before calling another plumber.

In June the rhododendrons between the road and Pauley's house had been amazing, a jungle. Maybe the bogland accounted for it. Purples, whites, reds, creams shot with yellow, ink and blood spatters. Like a park. Fifty or sixty plants must be in there, some of them giraffe-high, twenty or forty thousand dollars' worth if you had to truck them at that size and set them, and all from a few sticks. Imagining the plumber's rhododendrons transported to border his own driveway, Elligott regretted and went on.

Not a soul on the road. Not a car. Not a fisherman. Not a mass-bound Catholic.

He swung into the business-center block and parked at The Pharmacy. The business had been sold recently by heirs of the original owner, four brothers, each more famous than the next for surliness. No one had ever been said good morning to by one of these men. Downcast or elevated, each was on his way to transact troubling business; taking inventory; looking for dropped quarters, spider webs. They had sold out to a chain whose owners—some said from Worcester, some said Quincy—could distance themselves from light-bulb specials, jewelry deals, ad tabloids, senior-citizen discounts, and generic-drug propaganda. The first act of the new owners after opening Days of Bargains was to add a dime to the price of the Sunday *Times*.

As a businessman, Elligott conceded that combination was the order of the day and that somebody had to make up the premium paid for the Going Concern—but not necessarily Paul D. Elligott. He would have taken his trade elsewhere except that The Pharmacy still employed at its cash counter a pleasant man named Len who had overheard his name and very nearly remembered it. It was worth a dime to have Len say, "It's Mr. Elliott. Good morning, Mr. Elliott."

"How are you today, Len?"

"Gonna make it. Will that be it? One seventy-five out of two bills. Have a nice day, Mr. Elliott."

Twice Elligott had spelled his name in full for the *Times* reservation list, but Len's memory scan rejected such an improbable reading. Elligott forgave him. Had he thought about it at the time, Elligott would have written "Len" in the space on the Board of Trade questionnaire that asked for reasons he liked to shop in town: Good selections. Good prices. Good parking. Convenience. Other . . ."Len."

Nevertheless, Elligott's acknowledging smile was of measured width. He recognized in himself a tendency to overcordiality. One of the images of Zuerner that dripped in him like a malfunctioning gland was the recollection of the day Zuerner had come aboard and had been introduced around by McGlynn. Elligott had gone out to him, welcomed him warmly, braced his arm, and gotten back—what would you call it: reserve? civility? The face made interesting by the scarred cheek had barely ticked.

"I look forward to working with you, Elligott."

He might have been talking to a bookkeeper instead of the vice president for corporate relations.

Zuerner's disfigurement conveyed the idea that something extraordinary had formed him and implied that the distinction was not only external.

Since that meeting Elligott had become increasingly aware of a recompensing phenomenon that in time brought forward men who had certain kinds of injury, handicap, unhandsomeness, names—asymmetries that when they were young had kept them down. Elligott had occasionally pointed out to people whom he suspected of thinking he lacked independent weight that the advantage of being the namesake of the founder, even in a collateral line, might get you in at first, but in the long run it was hardship. Elligott sensed he would have difficulty being taken seriously compared with a man like Zuerner, with a mark on his cheek and a bearing rehearsed to imply that he knew how to make up his mind.

In most matters whatever decision was taken, even a decision to do nothing, worked out all right if firmly asserted. Zuerner's function was to make one decision seem better than another and to identify himself in this circular way as the cause of what he was in truth an effect. McGlynn had been taken in, but not Elligott.

He thought himself wiser than Zuerner by virtue of having understood him and the power cards he played. His way of holding back to conceal his limits. His strategic unwillingness to speak early in meetings. Never answering a question if it could be turned back on the asker.

"You've given it thought. What is *your* feeling?"

"Come on, Walter," Elligott had once said, "stop the crap. Just answer the question. I'm not asking you to invest in it."

He had been certain Zuerner would retreat from such a frank challenge. But Zuerner had maintained a steady silence that made Elligott seem petulant even to himself. Involuntarily, his face repeated its recollection of Zuerner's at their first meeting, the moment watched by McGlynn, when Zuerner gained ascendancy.

At other times, when he reflected with the candor he was pleased to note in himself, Elligott conceded that the ascendancy also derived from a magical emanation from the man. He remembered from his days at Colgate an upperclassman who had the same mysterious ascendancy. For no particular reason this Clybairne occasionally appeared in Elligott's thoughts, and Elligott felt himself back down, as he had with Zuerner.

In consideration of his move to the Cape, where he could live the personality he chose, he resolved to contain himself so that nobody would ever again observe his limits in the sincerity of his smile, and have ascendancy over him.

Pleased by the exchange with Len, and enjoying the additional insight that he had risen a notch toward the status of old-timer, now that the heirs were gone, Elligott carried his newspaper the few steps to Dowling's.

As usual, others were there before him. He never managed to be the coffee shop's first customer. Even when he arrived at the opening minute and the door was unlocked for him, locals were already there, having coffee; these were insiders, friends of Dowling's who came through the kitchen door or grew in the chairs, fungus.

Two of these insiders were at a table. He recognized them and assumed they recognized him, although they were not acquaintances, not even the order of acquaintance he would have crossed a room in a distant city to greet as compatriots; at most he might in, say, Milan have widened his eyes more generously and nodded less curtly. They returned his signal in a way that indicated they might not know him even in Nairobi.

Nobody was sitting at the counter, but someone had cluttered what Elligott thought of as his regular place, at the kitchen end, with a half-finished cup of milky coffee and a cigarette burning in an ashtray. They would belong to a waitress. He disliked having to choose a stool in unfamiliar territory. He felt exposed, diminished in well-being. He was happy, however, to see that the doughnut tray had arrived from the bakery and he would not have to eat one of Dowling's double-sweet bran muffins. Brewed coffee dripped into the Silex. On the stool he arranged the *Times* in the order he would get to it: sports, business, front news, the rest.

Small tremors of alienation continued to assail him. He was still not entirely used to having breakfast in a coffee shop. Men of his rank had breakfast at home. Unless they were traveling, or early meetings required them, they never entered restaurants, let alone coffee shops, before lunch. It seemed illicit, a step over the threshold to hell, a date with Sistie Evans. It took some getting used to that among carpenters, telephone repairers, real estate agents, and insurance men were authentic businessmen, retired like himself. They, too, had discovered late in life the pleasure of coffee and a bakery doughnut that was neither staling nor slippery, not one of those mouse-skinned packaged doughnuts.

Where was the waitress?

With the Gabberts last night the subject of best-remembered meals had come up, which led to choices of what you would order if you were on Death Row. When his turn came, he said coffee and fresh cinnamon doughnuts.

They wouldn't accept a frivolous answer. He withdrew it. He asked Daisy to refresh him on what had been served that night at the governor's, still believing in the doughnuts and knowing in his soul that he mentioned dinner at the governor's only to tell the Gabberts he had been to such an event. Daisy did not remember the frogs' legs as all that remarkable.

A profile appeared in the window of the kitchen door, like a character on TV. A new blonde pushed in, not the dark girl with a dancer's tendony legs whom Elligott had expected.

While she hesitated, considering whether her first duty was to her coffee and burning cigarette or to the customer, he read her marked-down face and slightly funhouse-mirror figure, the fullness to be made marvelously compact throughout her life by tights, belts, bras, girdles, pantyhose, and the shiny, sanctifying nurse's uniform Dowling provided for his staff. She would smell like an hour in a motel.

"Coffee?"

"Black. Is there a cinnamon doughnut left?"

She assembled the order, remembering at the last moment what Dowling had told her about picking up pastry with a waxed square. She filled the cup two-thirds full, placed the spoon with the bowl toward him. The tag read LINDA, in Mrs. Dowling's childish cursive. The blonde reached for two cream cups and showed a tunnel between her breasts. Sexuality is whatever implies more. Elligott drifted forward to fall within her odor, but couldn't find it. Without drawing back from the counter she tilted her head to him, intimately; the gesture may have been something she picked up from her mother.

"Will that be all?"

Their eyes met precisely. She was no longer furniture of the establishment; she had come forward and was isolated with him.

"For now."

She closed her order book, stuffed it in the apron pocket, and walked away, around the end of the counter to take up again her cigarette and milky coffee. He felt that he had opened a conversation and had been rejected. When they picked up again, he would not be so subtle. He could ask her where she came from, what she did before, what schedule she worked.

He scanned the newspaper with an inattention that would have enraged the editor. He found nothing about why Pitt hadn't scored with all that first-half possession he had caught a mention of on the ten-o'clock news, only junk that came in before the paper went to bed: the weather and highlights from the first few series of downs, and nothing on Colgate other than the losing score. Unimportant golf and tennis this week. Horses. He didn't know anybody who paid attention to horses beyond the Derby-to-Belmont sequence in the spring, and the steeplechase, on account of Rolling Rock and Dick Mellon. Hockey was Catholic, a real Massachusetts sport for you. Basketball was black. Nobody he knew followed those sports until the playoffs. From yesterday's paper he already knew what his stocks had done. He scanned the section all the way back to the engineering jobs and didn't see anything about Interways making a new offer for Elligott Barge. He could see her in the back-counter mirror, poking at the falling-apart bundle of her hair.

He shifted the paper and looked around column one into the tunnel of her armpit. The girl was seamed with tunnels. Her raised arms drew her back erect, giving an inviting thrust to her figure. He mused that women could come off while looking you in the eye and combing their hair, while talking about flowers, money, baked potatoes, anything, just squeezing; the hidden agenda of mothers who told their little girls to keep their legs crossed. He willed the girl onto his wavelength: right guard not that many years ago at Colgate. A girl with a figure like hers wouldn't mind a little mature fattening. He watched for a sign, an eye flicker, that she was heating with him, but she finished with her hair and slumped into her mass. She seemed to have no spine. She subsided into wasted time, dribbling smoke.

He folded with a motion that caught her eye. He raised a hand to bring her to him to fill his cup, to try again to fall within her odor of cheap powder or sweat, it made no difference, and to tell her that all he wanted was an hour of the thousands she had to give carelessly away. Why should he have to look for a new way to say God's first truth? In the Beginning was no more or less than this moment. It wasn't as though he had nothing to bring to the transaction; he would give more than he asked—more want, more skill, more risk. Elligott, husband, father, grandfather, retired vice president of corporate relations, elder, member of duty boards. More risk.

He thought of her going back to the kitchen and asking Dowling what kind of creeps he had for customers. Linda and Dowling talking about him and laughing while they challenged each other in the narrow aisle in front of the work table. He couldn't find her odor. He imagined it from Sistie Evans forty-one years ago.

"I'll take a check."

She put it in front of him and wished him a nice day. He nodded briefly, as Zuerner would have. He put the paper together again, left her a quarter more than the usual change from the dollar so that she would remember him. Who was he? What did he do?

Walking out, he saw that the plumber Pauley had joined the two at the table. That reminded him to go home again by WAY TO THE DUMP. The girl ceased to exist for him.

Car key poised at the lock, he was suddenly disoriented. *How did I get here? Where am I going? Am I shopping, or about to start? Everything is too quiet for the amount of light.* As if it were an hour ago, people weren't coming and going to get the day moving. The purity of the air and the stillness were like the moment before a tornado; everyone had taken shelter. But, of course, it was Sunday, the hours were displaced. He started up and drove out of the lot.

Having grown up in the city, where nature was the lawn, the hedge, and the golf course, he had been slow to accept the grosser performances of nature, the turning seasons and rotation of flowers. Now he saw the texture of light, predicted weather from sunsets and fuzzy moons, identified the velvet red on the roadside as poison ivy, and leaves speckled like worm-infested apples as shrub cherries. He supposed he should have gone into the landscape-gardening business early.

Like two daring girls back just in time from an all-night party, an apricot maple and a maple more golden stood in the respectable green row that shaded the Pilgrim School. He rolled the window down far enough to get a better look at them, and then at the Betty Prior roses, the ones with a pale splash, piled along the fences. A great rose, out early and still holding; next spring he would put in a couple.

At Pauley's he slowed as he had when coming to town. He was driving so slowly that he might as well stop a moment and really look at the rhododendrons. He pulled onto the shoulder, dropped the keys on the floor, as was his habit, and went over.

Every finger of leaf had the thick look of health; none were browned or curled in distress. Buds were packed so tightly that they seemed ready to explode before wintering. But they would hold until spring, when great holiday bursts would show on the big broad-leafed plants, and the crisp varieties with small clustered leaves would light up like Christmas trees. No rain had fallen since early July—where did they get their well-being? Pauley seemed unlikely to water stock this fat.

Elligott bent to the ground and scratched with a forefinger. Sandy black stuff, hard and dry as his own dirt. Did the old bog leach up here to wet the roots? Elligott didn't have a bog, but he had a hose, and the town water bill didn't amount to much. He looked for the angle of the sun and saw that it got in there a few hours every day, over the oaks, beyond where the wagon was stopped. His plantings at the Association got that much sun.

He noticed young plants a foot or two high scattered through the hedge. Probably grown from cuttings to replace the older stock. Maybe layered off the big stock. He felt for a branch that might loop into the ground and come up as a new plant. He found no connections, and decided the young plants must be cuttings.

Bent and reaching, Elligott now had an idea whose enormity tightened his chest. He pivoted to look both ways along the road. Carefully he opened the hedge to see the house. The shades were down.

Pauley owed him something for the time he had wasted waiting for the shower. Elligott grasped a plant by the throat and felt it break free of the top crust so easily that he reached for another and slung it under his arm. He looked again both ways on the road and quickly crossed.

Unlocking the tailgate delicately, to avoid a loud click, he laid the plants on the carpet. He was going around to the driver's door at the accelerated pace of someone not wanting to look pushy but nevertheless determined to get to the head of the line when he sensed an action at the house—a door or window opening—and somebody hollered, "What the hell are you doing there?"

Pauley's son.

He jumped into the seat while the voice pursued him; he dragged the door closed, found the key ring on the floor, stabbed at the ignition. The lock rejected the upside down key. He fumbled it home, jerk-started and stalled, and rammed his foot on the pedal to clear the flooded carburetor, thinking *Calm! Calm! Breathe!*, terrified that he had done himself in. He fought the key, and the engine caught at the moment frost sprang on the window lip, and he was struck on the side of the neck by what he experienced as hard-thrown gravel. He ducked and fell away from the blow and straightened again to control the careening wagon. *Get away from here fast!*

In seconds he was over a low rise and curve that distanced him from Pauley's place. He realized he was locked at mach 2, rigid arms and legs shoving him hard against the seat back. He relaxed a turn and took in air. As the tension eased from his shoulder and back, he became aware that his neck ached.

He put his hand to it and it came away wet. Blood. Blood thin as water defined the creases and whorls of his palm. He was not prepared for blood. So much.

He wiped his hand on his new sweater and felt the wound with his fingertips. It felt like no more than an open boil, but the amount of blood scared him. He rolled his head to feel if the injury went deep. It seemed to stop at the surface. A spread of light shot? Had the man been lunatic enough to shoot because someone was poking in his bushes? What if the target had been some poor bastard with bad kidneys?

Christ, look at the blood! He eased the speed and held the wheel with his bloody hand while he reached around with the other for a handkerchief, but he hadn't put one in his pocket that morning. With his knees he held the wagon in line, though falling toward the berm, unbuttoned his sweater, and ripped open his shirt to get enough cloth to plaster against the wound. He hunched up his neck to cramp the cloth tight. His mind set changed from *Get away!* to *Where to?* and he couldn't deal with the options.

Home was four minutes away, the hospital emergency branch was twelve by the shortcut past Pauley's, but he couldn't even think of going back that way. The other road around the rotary was long, very long, and he was so very bloody, his neck cramped awkwardly against his shoulder. He tried to remember the name of the doctor, and what kind of doctor he was, who had a shingle at the lane going off after the next right—or should he try for a paramedic on rescue-squad duty at the firehouse? He would have to do so much explaining. Had the wagon been identified? Just an old Chevy wagon. Who would believe it was his? His head felt enlarged, packed with engine noise and a mossy texture that resisted intelligence. It was only partly from the blow: his mind blurred in a crisis; he was not at his best at such times, he knew it, and there had never been a time quite like this.

The corner came at him faster than he could steady himself for it. The wagon waited for direction until the last instant before lunging over-steered toward the doctor, the Association, and home almost out of habit—his hands grabbing for control of the slippery wheel. The wagon bolted across the eroded center line; the tires washboarded, skidded, and sprayed berm. His neck jarred loose from the bandage. He got back in lane while blood poured from the shoulder and sleeve of his sweater as if pumped.

As if pumped! It was more than he could get his mind around. He had just gotten up and gone for a cup of coffee and a doughnut, and his blood was slopping out down his arm into his lap. He stuffed the wad of makeshift bandage back in place and pressed hard against the wound; this is what you were supposed to do to an artery wound— press hard, and not too long, or you would black out. An *artery?* He refused the word, absorbed it into the moss of his head.

Dr. Albert F. Bernhardt's sign came out of the brush like a cue card to remind him that Daisy, joking, had said a psychiatrist lived there, if they ever needed one. He raced past the psychiatrist who wouldn't know anything about blood, about *arteries,* not as much as an Eagle Scout, in a wagon full of blood and stolen plants, and Zuerner on the way. A scrim of weakness fell. He wanted to let his eyes close. He sobbed to suppress the perception that he could be dying and didn't know what to do about Zuerner's coming just in time to find out that he stole plants in the neighborhood.

A small gray car, the first traffic on the road that morning, closed toward him, and he roused to the thought of something better than sleep: obliteration. A smashup jumbling and concealing everything, everything wiped out, blood explained in bashed rolling metal and fire.

The small car came on as innocent of danger and terror as he himself had been a short while ago. Catholics going to church. It would be easy, fast, over.

At the moment, the only moment he had, he was incapable of aiming. He felt a blurt of nobility as the small gray car went by. Did they see the blood? Did they think he held his head this way because he was sleepy? Did they know he held their lives in his hand for a moment and was merciful? He was a merciful man with no possession in the world but mercy, toward strangers, and nobody was there to sign his card.

The wagon was at the fork where the Association road came in. Barely driven, it was taking him home to tell Daisy to protect him from Zuerner. Daisy would clean up everything and think of a plausible story. He found the least strength necessary to guide onto the sudden rough and sounding surface.

He couldn't bother to steer around potholes. He went down the crown of the dirt road, jouncing and pounding the shocks, slack hand on the wheel like a dozing passenger. At the turnoff to his own driveway he knew he wasn't going to get to Daisy. He was gone, he didn't have time to tell Daisy what she had to do. He was going to pass out. In a gravel-scattering skid he entered his own long, curving drive at forty, forty-five, fifty, toward the open garage door that waited to swallow him against the far wall and create a mystery (heart attack? pedal stuck?), his name intact.

Elligott now had his last great idea of the morning.

Alongside the garage the land sloped to the cove through an insubstantial hedge of nursery plants—forsythia, hydrangea, cinquefoil, and the like—and, lower down, wild honeysuckle, briar, and saplings that had volunteered to try again where the city people had cleared. At the foot the returning tide infiltrated the bordering marsh grass.

The possibility came to him almost too late to act on. With nothing measurable to spare he veered past the corner of the garage and over the sunk railroad tie that defined the hedge line, trashed the honeysuckle, flailed through a berserk car wash of saplings, briar, rugosas, grapevines, forcing all the momentum he could into the wagon to scar through the soft wetland and on into the cove where the thrust ended almost gently, like a boat with a sail dropped or an engine cut.

The wagon tilted on a rock and stopped.

He would have to stay in motion to keep from blacking out. He pulled the latch; his weight pushed the door open and he slumped with it clumsily into a tide that took him at the knee. By noon it would be chest high. He steadied on the door. Everything was quiet after the last tearing minutes. *Forget the plants. Can't lift the door. Not unusual to carry plants in the wagon. Water will make a slop back there, mix everything up. Keep moving.*

He staggered around the drowning wagon, slipping on bottom rocks greasy with eelgrass. He glanced up at his house. Through sagging eyelids he saw that it was handsome in the early sun. He started to take his hand from the bloody bundle at his neck so he could look at his watch and verify the time, but he knew at once that the gesture was too foolish to complete. If only Daisy would appear, they could wave goodbye to each other.

Crouched, balancing with his free arm like a remembered sepia picture of a farmer scattering grain, he lurched against the heavy purpose of the tide, toward no vision of a further life or of beings natural or supernatural intended to be called up by ten thousand Sunday-morning mumblings. That and all love, error, and regret; all papers on his desk, all letters, all unkempt plantings, all things unsaid to Daisy and Margie and the grandchildren and the judge in the traffic court: gone, irretrievable. His last mercy dispensed. His last desire a girl in a doughnut shop. His last act theft. Only honor was now left to him.

His new sweater sucked up a weight of water. He swayed and stumbled over the unstable bottom. His eyes closed to a minimum blur of light and form. His head hung forward. The hand that held the blood-wet cloth failed to his side. He dragged one more step, and another, and another toward the obscure channel hidden in the grass over there where an hour ago he had imagined sneaking the net under big blue crabs so that Zuerner would sign his card. Elligott, a man whose name had decided his work and chosen his wife; and she had brought him to this place where a stranger with a gun decided when he was to die.

Or was it Zuerner, who would follow him everywhere, who had decided? Caving to his knees, fainting, falling toward drowning, his impression (the vapor of exhaustion could no longer be called something as coherent as thought)—his impression was that to die this worthily was an act of transcendent honor; beyond the comprehension of a man like Zuerner. And yet, the vapor formed, faded; what is Zuerner to me that I give him my life?

APACHE

David Huddle

She was a blue-eyed blonde, her name was Apache, and if you didn't like it, you could kiss her ass. Worked at the Pussy Cat, not the Naked Cabaret, which she and the other Pussy Cat girls considered tacky, though more than a few had worked there, too. Not Apache. When she came in from New York, she went straight to work for the Pussy Cat. Had the job before she even got there.

Up at the Naked they had one of those peach-skinned girls with silicone tits and light-brown hair, and her name was Miss Cheyenne, but anybody could tell that was bullshit. Apache was called Apache because she had a temper. "I'll jerk a knot in your ass," Apache said in a friendly voice to a clean-scrubbed M.I.T. sophomore if he ran a hand up her thigh. He stopped, too, because there was something back there, something that boy could tell from how she said it or how she looked.

Up on the bar Apache was damn sure no squaw. She started out with what looked like one of those old-fashioned two-piece bathing suits, the kind that just barely showed your navel. The bottom had zippers at each hip, the top had a zipper that came up in the middle. Apache did the zips up to the top first pass up and down the bar. By the end of "Nasty Girl," she was down to a pretty little white-crotched G-string. Blond hair was one of her best features, Apache knew that, and she didn't care if some of the other girls thought she showed it maybe a little too soon. Apache was twenty-nine and said she was twenty-five, but she still had some to spare. If you had style, you could work without resorting to implants.

But Apache knew that what got Lola and the Tucson Twister was the white peignoir and the bridal business. "I'll swear to God, girl, you look like a Barbie Doll up there," Tucson said, but Apache ignored her because her real name was Ida and God knew Apache didn't have to take anything from somebody named Ida.

"Barbie Doll that wants to fuck," murmured Lola, who was black and slinky as a hungry cat. Now that was true, but it didn't bother Apache because she had put some thought into looking kind of bride-like, even down to how she smiled when there was that long pause in the music and she opened the white peignoir and ran two fingers over her best feature.

Apache had been married and divorced three times, starting with when she was sixteen, and for all she knew, she was married a fourth time, too. At least the Chinaman said she was. And she said she was sometimes, when one of the shitheads who bought her a drink asked her. "Yeah, I'm married to a Chinese man," she said, ruefully or hate-fully, depending on how she felt and how much more the shithead was likely to spend on her. It didn't make a damn to her whether she was married or not, and the white peignoir struck her as funny.

"You feeding those little boys' dreams, honey. You jacking off twelve-year-olds," said Lola, and Apache turned on her.

"So what if I am?" said Apache, and she walked right up to Lola even though Lola was the one of all of them who scared her. Apache and Lola stared at each other, and then Apache laughed and said, "I'm a jack off all ages." And Lola laughed, too, and said she was, too, and the Tucson Twister sniffed and went on out to find herself what she in her ignorance called "a sweet thing."

Apache met this real bullshit guy who said that he was an Indian of the Osage tribe. This was on a rainy Tuesday night in June when it looked like nobody and all nobody's cousins was going to come into the Zone. There were five girls for every man who came through the Pussy Cat door, there were empty spaces around the bar, and Apache felt spooked by the place when it was that way. She figured she'd do her ten o'clock number and ask Paulie if she could go home. He'd say yes. Paulie liked her. Apache never complained about anything, even about the night that West Virginia girl, the Coalminer's Daughter, puked all over Apache's locker. And Paulie had caught Apache's number a couple of nights when she's set that place on fire, had them stamping their feet and whistling. But on this particular night Apache was just sitting there having a vodka martini and telling Albert how she was going to leave early and go over and spend some time with the Chinaman, and Albert was telling her how maybe she ought to give the Chinaman a call first, when this guy in a pony-tail and a poncho sat down beside her and started wiping the rain off his glasses.

The guy told Albert he wanted coffee, and Albert of course enjoyed telling him he wasn't going to get no god damn cup of coffee at the Pussy Cat, maybe he ought to try up the street at the Naked. So the guy got his glasses on and ordered a coke, for which Albert charged him three bucks. Apache saw him eyeing her through those gold-rimmed spectacles of his, his poncho still dripping on the floor and on the bar. What the hell, she asked him if he wanted to buy her a drink. He said yes and told Albert to bring this lady a coke. Albert guffawed and walked on down the bar while Apache explained the system to him: he could buy her a "beer," which was a bottle of champagne that cost twenty-one bucks, or he could buy her a "drink," which cost seven bucks. The guy smiled at her, rustled around in his poncho, pulled out his wallet again, opened it, and showed it to her like some kind of rare treasure. It had an old raggedy-assed five in it, that's all, and the guy looked just pleased as could be. Albert came back up the bar and asked them if they'd got it worked out yet, which situation embarrassed Apache. So she said to Albert to bring her another vodka martini, she'd pay for it herself. She jerked her head toward the man in the poncho and said, "This guy's lost, he don't know where the fuck he is."

But the man didn't shrivel up and die just because she insulted him. He grinned at her and admitted that it was true, he was trying to walk back to Cambridge and took a wrong turn, he said. Apache was starting to get up and walk away because it ruins your reputation to sit with somebody who isn't spending money on you. But it was this rainy, dead-assed night, and it made sense to her right then just to keep her badelias parked on that bar-stool where at least she was safe and out of trouble. The guy asked her her name, and she told him Apache, but she didn't look at him any more. Who the fuck needed to look at some lost son of a bitch with a pony-tail who was dripping all over the bar and who couldn't buy her a drink, who was walking around with nothing but a five in his pocket? She damn sure didn't ask him his name, but he told her then anyway, it was John Chapman. Apache hardly ever asked anybody their name; even if they told her, she forgot it. Then John Chapman told her that bullshit about the Osage Indians in Kansas and Missouri.

Apache didn't listen. She was in a trance.

"Apache, you about to nod off there," said Lola, walking behind her, putting a bony hand on Apache's shoulder. "Somebody slip you some shit, honey?" she murmured close to Apache's ear, and when Apache blinked at her, Lola smiled and sauntered on down the bar a few places, Lola in her spike heels and fish-net stockings.

John Chapman pulled the poncho up over his head in a grand crinkling of heavy plastic, bashed that thing into a semi-folded state, and dropped it on the floor between himself and Apache. "I also have an Osage name," he told her, leaning in her direction to get her attention. The man obviously intended to carry on a conversation as long as she sat there.

"Hey, Apache!" Albert shouted at her from way down at the other end of the bar. "Paulie wants to know if you're going on welfare tomorrow or what?"

Apache sighed and stood up and walked back to do her number.

"Another time, and maybe we'll talk," Chapman murmured, watching her when she walked past him even though she kept her eyes on the floor.

"Hell of a night to get married," said Lola when Apache walked past her, and Apache wished she could give Lola a grin, but she didn't have one available.

Sometimes Apache was pretty fabulous. It didn't have anything to do with anything. Or else it did. She could be high and happy, step out there, and then start feeling sleazy and old for no reason. Those times she hated even to look at the shitheads at the bar, gaping at her like a bunch of retards at a retard convention. Or it could happen like tonight when she felt lower than whale shit and dreaded putting a foot through that curtain, and all of a sudden she was flying. She was energy and muscles, and her body was the music, the Pointer Sisters singing, "I'm so excited . . . " Even the few men who sat around the bar seemed acceptable to Apache, and she smiled at them in sweet romance, let her body make its moves. Just before the lights went down for her to twirl in the white peignoir under the silver strobe light, she saw Mr. John Chapman in his poncho, raising a hand to wave to her before he went out the door. The strobe divided her into a thousand spinning Apaches, and one or two of them said aloud into the blast of music, "Go get rained on, Indian. Go get your ass wet."

When she was out working through the tables and around the bar, Apache wore a red velveteen jacket, a black one-piece bathing suit split down to below her navel, smoke-colored tights, and heels. She never had trouble getting somebody to buy her a drink, and she usually had more "beer" tickets to turn in at the end of the evening than any of the other girls. Trouble was, Apache did have difficulty with her vision and her footwork before the evening was over. There weren't more than a few drops of rum in each drink, but she went through fifty or sixty drinks on a good night. She danced a lot of it out of her system, but even so, she usually felt pretty floaty by around midnight.

Which was about the time John Chapman came in, wearing a tie and a three-piece khaki suit. Just to wear that with a pony-tail took a lot of nerve, but to wear it into the Zone and then to wear it into the Pussy Cat on a Thursday at midnight meant the son of a bitch was from another planet. Apache was sitting close enough to the door when he came in to see that the suit was brand new. He'd washed that long black hair of his and tied up his pony-tail in a small silver and turquoise clip. But she was damned if she was going to talk with him. People seemed to be clearing a path for him to one empty seat at the bar, and you could see every girl's eye on him when he took the stool, looked straight at Albert who was waiting in front of him, and ordered a coke.

"Money just walked in and sat down over there," said the Teenage Queen, moving through the crowd behind Apache.

"Ain't gonna spend none of it on you, bitch," whispered Lola moving briskly that way, too, just behind the Teenage Queen.

Apache had to laugh. This place was like something nobody could even dream of. Chapman was strafed in rapid succession by Tina, Erica Mahoney, Coco, Wonder Woman, Patsy Jones, the Teenage Queen, Sweet Anabel, Lola, Nurse Goodbody, and Gladys Garrett. The Teenage Queen tried to pick up one of his hands and lay it on her titty, which was one of several undignified things the Queen did all the time that Apache wouldn't stoop to. John Chapman shook off the Queen, told all of them no, he didn't want any company, and no, he wasn't lonely, and smiled at them to keep them happy and moving on down the bar away from him.

"Wants you," said Wonder Woman, circling back the other way around the bar, passing behind Apache. Apache shrugged, but Wonder Woman wasn't watching to catch her response.

"I'm up," said Apache to nobody. It wasn't even true. She had a while before she was up, but she walked back to the dressing room anyway. It was better to sit around back there than to have to watch the meat show.

Then she was up, and goddammit, she was too sober to get anything going. Everything all around her was so ridiculous it was all she could do not to stop dancing and just stand there giving them the finger, those god damn stupid open-mouthed faces around that bar, a stink rising from the floor of thirty years of spilled draft beer half mopped up every night. "I'm so excited! I'm so excited!" She was bored with the song. The strobe light split her up while she tried to make herself spin. She wished she could just dissolve that way, and when they turned up the lights there would be no more Apache.

"You auditioning for a nursing home?" asked Paulie when she came off. He was sitting on his stool just inside the door. She walked past him, the peignoir, the bathing suit, and the G-string all wadded up in one hand because she didn't give a damn.

"Fuck you, Paulie." She tried to sound friendly, but she really didn't want to talk to anybody right then.

"Man out there wants to talk to you," Paulie told her softly. Paulie was always doing isometrics, pushing one arm against another, flexing his legs, going up on the tips of his toes, and Apache didn't like to look at him, but she knew better than to ignore him.

"Nothing new about that," she murmured, standing there and waiting. "Well?" she said. She turned enough to see past Paulie through the two-way mirror, like a television screen, to where John Chapman sat with a little space around him in that crowded bar, as if everybody knew he didn't belong there.

"Lola's saving you a seat," Paulie said. Sure enough, she could see Lola sitting one seat down from Chapman, talking to somebody who hadn't bought her a drink, Apache could tell that even from that far away.

"I don't need it," Apache said.

"Talk to him or hit the street," Paulie told her and sighed and stood up and stretched.

Apache walked over and threw her clothes at her locker and sat down to take off her white heels. "I was gonna talk to him anyway," she muttered.

"Can I buy you a drink, Apache?" John Chapman asked her when she was walking toward him, before she'd even reached the empty seat beside him.

Apache shrugged and sat down. "Sure you can," she said. "Buy me a beer?" She didn't look at him. She hoped he'd say no. Albert was standing right there in front of them, waiting for the definite signal from one or the other of them. When John Chapman nodded at him, Albert was setting that little bottle of champagne up in front of Apache in ten seconds flat. Chapman put a fifty on the bar, and Albert hustled to make the change.

"So how come you're so dressed up?" Apache made herself sound like a lady who could kick some ass when she wanted to.

Chapman smiled at her but wouldn't say anything. Under the knot of his tie there was a gold pin that made it stand up from his collar; Apache looked at that while she talked to him. "I thought you said you were an Indian?" she said, still making a point of not giving him a smile. She tossed off the first glass of the champagne with Albert right there filling up her glass again when she set it down.

"An Indian can't dress up?" Chapman asked her.

"He teaches up at Harvard, Apache," said Albert, so polite she could have slapped his face.

"You talking to a professor, girl," said Lola on the other side of her.

Apache shook her head. What the hell do I care if he sells ice to the Eskimos? Apache started to say, but then she held her tongue because she could feel Paulie watching her from back behind the mirror.

"I've been trying to talk Albert here into enrolling in some night courses," John Chapman said. "He's thinking about changing jobs."

"Yeah," Albert said, hitching up his trousers and standing up straight, "I want to get into a field where I can screw a lot of women." Chapman grinned at him appreciatively, and Albert burst out laughing.

"You got some customers up that way," Apache told Albert and watched him hustle his silly ass up the bar. "So what do you teach?" She hated asking anybody any kind of question, but she wanted to get this over with fast.

"Para-Sociology."

"Para what?" she said.

"Pair o' what? Pair o' what?" echoed Patsy Jones gliding along the dark wall behind them. Apache reached back there and tried to swat her ass, but she was gone.

"It's one of the social sciences," John Chapman told her. "It's very new."

"Never heard of it," said Apache. She looked all around the bar, getting ready to move away.

"She's just moody," Lola told Chapman, leaning around Apache to catch his eye. "You got to make an impression on her."

Apache grimly tossed off the last of her champagne. "Buy me another beer?" She knew he wasn't going to. When Apache didn't want to see somebody she had a trick of putting her eyes on him but focusing behind him.

"I have a suggestion," said Chapman, folding his hand on the bar and leaning toward Apache.

She cut him off. "I don't go out with anybody."

Albert had been standing in front of them, ready to serve Apache another drink but now he sidled back down the bar to the end where he and Paulie could talk with each other through the curtained doorway.

"This is special," Chapman told her. "I know a nice place. It's quiet. We can talk Indian to Indian, Apache to Osage. By the way, my Osage name is . . ."

Apache stood up and was starting to move away when Albert reached across the bar and caught her wrist.

"You're going out," Albert told her softly, grinning. "Paulie says for you to have a good time.

Apache let her arm go limp and wouldn't look at Albert. She stood there making her eyes blaze at Chapman. "I guess we have a date," she said.

"You don't have to go," Chapman told her. "I don't want you to make her go," he told Albert, and Albert raised his hands, palms open, smiling and shaking his head.

"Let's go," said Apache making for the door. She could get this over with in less than half an hour, even if they were going to make it tough on her.

"Wait," said Chapman behind her.

"What's wrong?"

"Don't you need to change clothes?" He was smiling.

"You want me to wear the G-string?"

"No." He was still smiling at her. "Your regular clothes. What you wore when you came to work."

"A denim skirt?"

"That's fine."

"Christ."

A room like that, shag-carpet-two-double-beds-sliding-glass-doors-to-the-balcony, Apache didn't need to see, and she told Chapman she thought the place sucked. Speaking of which, she said, "If you've got another one of those fifties, you can get out of your clothes, lie back there and relax, and I'll stop wasting your time and mine. How much did you pay Paulie?" she asked him, letting the denim skirt drop, pulling the little cotton sweater up over her head.

Chapman made a slight waving motion with his hand. She couldn't believe him. She hadn't seen a man yet who wouldn't turn his eyes toward a woman taking off a bra, but this one here had turned into a statue. "Traditionally," he said, "the Osage and the Apache nations were never able to agree on any terms of trade. It would have seemed, since the former were farmers and the latter hunters and warriors, that . . ."

"Jesus Christ!" Apache said. She refastened the bra, put the sweater back on, and wrapped the skirt around her waist. She dug a cigarette out of her purse, lit it, plumped up the pillows on one bed, and lay back to smoke and wait him out. Chapman stood, posed, at the far end of the room, his hands in his pockets.

"I don't actually teach at Harvard," he told her, folding his arms in front of him now and staring at her, "but I don't think that ought to matter."

Apache gave him a look, a snort, a sneer, some kind of noise she meant to let him know she could give less of a rat's ass what he did. There weren't many things she hated worse than being out of the bar during working hours, and this was useless, what was going on now.

Chapman took off his glasses, breathed on them, and rubbed them carefully on his vest. "I'm a research assistant," he said, holding the glasses up to the light.

Apache let the smoke from her cigarette curl around her face while she watched him. He kept looking at her as if he expected her to ask him a favor any minute.

"I work for a guy who's writing up pieces on working people in the city," he said. "I told him I wanted you to have an interview." He made it sound like he was giving her something.

Apache let some silence fall between them before she asked him how much he would pay her.

"I don't need a great deal of information," Chapman told her. "Just the standard background kind of thing, your hometown, your family, where you went to school . . ."

Apache asked him how much he would pay her.

"Preliminary expenses were higher than I estimated," he told her, smiling and walking toward her. "I got a deal on this room, but Paulie's fee was substantial. Albert's tip, that drink I bought for Lola, the cab, this suit . . ." He turned a little, modeling the suit for her.

"How much?"

Chapman stood next to her and pulled a ten and two ones out of his wallet, then showed her it was empty. He continued to smile at her, though she could see it was costing him some effort. Digging up two quarters and a nickel, he let change, bills, and wallet fall on the bed beside her. When she laughed at him, he turned away and walked over to pull the drapes and stare through the glass doors. The more Apache looked at his silly pony-tail and the back of his expensive suit, the more she had to laugh.

"You've got some nerve," she said. "I need some air." She walked over to the doors, too, unlatched one of them, and slipped out onto the balcony. It was high and cool and dark out there. She liked it immediately and didn't give a damn if Chapman did come out behind her.

"Mr. Bigshot Indian," she said. She wanted to laugh out loud again, into that open space off the balcony, but it seemed like all she could do was chuckle to herself.

"Ten minutes' worth of talk," Chapman said softly. The man was still coming on like he was doing something nice for her. "Easy Questions. What's your name? What are your hobbies?" He forced a laugh.

Apache glanced straight down from the balcony. She wasn't ready for all that space of darkness that fell away from the railing down to the lighted streets below. She felt her stomach go queasy. Then she shook her head and accepted Chapman's offer of his jacket—he was putting it around her shoulders before she even thought to herself that he was doing it to manipulate her. For a moment she understood what he must feel like being too broke to make her a decent offer and too full of pride to beg her. She shook her head again, to get rid of that understanding. "Make it all up," she told him. "Use any name. What difference does it make?"

A noise swelling around her kept Apache from hearing what he said and made her look up to her left where a huge jet was coasting in across the harbor to Logan Airport. Chapman shouted something, and then he came closer to her. "I have to have some facts," he said.

Apache hated how his face looked now, his mouth shaping the words so carefully and then drawing down into a thin little grimace. She stepped toward the door, and he stepped in front of her. "I spent all that money," he said.

They stood staring at each other, Apache getting madder by the second. All of a sudden she pulled his jacket off her shoulders and flung it out into the air, off the balcony. She didn't know she was going to do that until she'd done it, and neither one of them watched it drop. She started toward him, meaning to scratch his face until he moved out of her way.

Chapman caught one of her hands and then the other. It wasn't that he seemed to know what he was doing, it was just protecting himself, she could tell that, but it was like a dance of when she moved, he moved, too. Then he had her. His left arm was hooked around her neck, not choking but holding her steady, his right hand holding her right hand back up behind her shoulder-blades, and there was such a pain in her right shoulder she thought she was going to black out. In spite of that, she felt herself breathing and sort of crying. She could hear him breathing hard, too, behind her.

Chapman pushed her to the railing where he bent her forward so that she had to look straight down the side of the building. "What's your name?" he rasped into her ear. Apache closed her eyes and wouldn't say a god damn word. "Do you want me to let you drop?" he asked her.

Apache felt herself pissing. She couldn't tell what she was seeing down the side of that building, but she couldn't keep her eyes closed, and her whole body hurt her. She was crying, and she didn't know if she could speak a word in any kind of language. But she tried. "Yes," she got out of herself. "Yes, let me drop."

Chapman let her go.

"Bitch!" he said. He turned away from her, put his hands against the glass door and leaned against it, panting, as if he'd been the one dangled over the edge.

"I pissed in my pants," Apache said. There was one reasonable thing to do, and she did that, took her wet underwear off. She didn't even think about what to do with them, she just flung those underpants right over the side where she'd sent Chapman's jacket. "Tell you what, Mr. Motherfucker Indian," she told his back. "You come with me. I'll give you a god damn interview."

In the taxi Apache told the driver, "Fourteen Ping On Street," and when Chapman raised his eyebrows at her, she told him that they were going to the Chinaman's. No need to go back to the Pussy Cat; it was past closing time. She had a plan now. She made up her mind to be a little more friendly to Chapman. "I go to fix the Chinaman his breakfast when I get off from work. He's my old man." She laughed at how startled Chapman looked.

"You're married?" he said.

She shrugged. "The Chinaman says we are. I can't remember it. He says we did it one morning a couple of years ago when we were both shitfaced."

"Did you?"

"I don't know. I remember drinking a lot, but I don't remember any wedding. He and I both get to laughing when we talk about it. You can ask him and see what he says." Apache felt o.k. now that she knew what she was going to do, but tiredness was coming down on her. She leaned back in the seat and closed her eyes, hugging herself to keep warm.

The sky was lightening when the cab let them out down at the end of a dead-end street, a little pocket of Chinatown. "Original, huh?" Apache stifled a yawn and cast her eyes up at the restaurant sign that blinked feebly, "The Golden Dragon." "The Chinaman says he's owned a dozen restaurants, and he's named every one of them 'The Golden Dragon.'" She had a key to a door at the side of the restaurant, which she opened and locked behind them. She led Chapman down a steep, dimly-lit staircase. At the bottom of the steps she used another key to open the first door in the hallway. The Chinaman was sitting, just as she knew he would be, there at his kitchen table, facing the door.

"Apache," he shouted, "where the hell have you been?" He laughed. He was a short, stocky man, wearing a plain white shirt and an old Cleveland Indians baseball cap tipped back on his head. His kitchen was so brightly lit with fluorescent tubes in the ceiling that even Apache, who was used to it, blinked at the light. Chapman took off his glasses and rubbed his eyes. "You gonna make me sit here and starve, woman?" said the Chinaman.

"The little shit-ass would sit here all day if I didn't come and fry up his breakfast for him," Apache said proudly. She knew the Chinaman was showing off for Chapman. He liked it when she brought him somebody to talk to. "Bill Po, this is John Chapman. Mr. Chapman is a . . . ?" She let it trail off just to see what Chapman would say.

"I do research," said Chapman. Apache could tell he was using his dignified tones. He and the Chinaman shook hands across the kitchen table, Bill Po rising slightly from his chair. "I work up at Harvard."

Apache watched Bill Po give a little bow of his head to express his reverence for Harvard, and it was all she could do to keep from laughing out loud. There were no windows in the Chinaman's kitchen, the walls were bare, and the door that led to the other rooms of the apartment was shut. But Apache still found the place comfortable. She hummed while she set out eggs and bacon and butter on the counter, keeping one eye on the men.

She savored the dignity with which Chapman accepted the chair the Chinaman scooted out for him with his foot. "So you're Apache's husband," he said. "I've heard a lot about you."

Apache couldn't help but snort, and Bill Po grinned at Chapman.

"That god damn Apache," he said, shaking his head. "I don't think she knows anything about me. She don't ask me questions, and if I tell her something, she forgets it the next day. Wish somebody would tell me why I married that woman." He laughed up toward the kitchen ceiling.

"Blonde hair," Apache said and smacked the Chinaman's hat off with her spatula. "Come on, Bill," she said. "I told him about all your 'Golden Dragons.'" She turned back to her cooking, poking at the strips of bacon to make them lie evenly in the frying pan. "Why don't you tell Mr. Chapman about our wedding, Bill."

The Chinaman guffawed. Apache saw Chapman start to set his elbows on the blue and white checked tablecloth, then pull back when he noticed jelly drippings on it. "We had champagne," said the Chinaman. "And everybody sang." He and Apache broke up. Apache held on to Bill Po's shoulder. She could tell Chapman was trying to look casual while he sat there, but he wasn't succeeding at all.

She had to pay attention to the bacon because she liked to cook it at a high heat. The Chinaman had sworn she wanted to set the kitchen on fire, but Apache knew he didn't really care. She did things the way she wanted to, not like a god damn housewife, and she knew he liked that. "Oh, Bill! I gotta tell you this," she said. "Look at this," she said, turning to face him, pulling up her apron and skirt to her waist and holding them while Bill Po took a look. He raised his eyebrows at the sight and turned to Chapman. Apache saw Chapman glance back at the door, as if measuring the distance to it from where he sat.

"She, ah . . . ," said Chapman.

"See, he doesn't have a jacket on," explained Apache. She broke eggs into the sputtering grease.

"Yes?" said Bill Po.

"Apache is the subject of an interview I've been commissioned to conduct," Chapman said. He was straining for poise. She was going to fix his ass.

"Yes?" said Bill Po, looking from one to the other of them.

"We were up in his hotel room," Apache said, setting two slices of bread into the Chinaman's toaster and slapping the handle down. "And Mr. Chapman here offered me twelve dollars to tell him about my life. I walked out on the balcony, and Mr. Chapman followed me out there and gave me his jacket, the gentleman, you know, trying to keep me warm and get me to answer his questions. I wouldn't talk, and he wouldn't let me leave. So I threw his jacket over the side. He grabbed me and held me over the edge, asked me if I wanted him to drop me off the side of that building. He scared me so bad I pissed in my pants, and then he let me go and called me a bitch. I threw my underwear over the side, too." She and Bill Po both stared at Chapman.

"These interviews will be published . . ." Chapman began, but he trailed off, and Apache was satisfied to see him squirming in his chair, facing the Chinaman with nothing to say for himself. She turned and scooped the eggs out of the skillet, laid the bacon on the plate beside the eggs and nudged the toaster handle until it popped. This was the one moment she liked best at the Chinaman's every morning, when she produced that breakfast like a magic trick and set the plate down in front of Bill Po.

"Thanks, Apache." Bill took off his hat and set it beside his plate. Then he reached behind him to a drawer in a kitchen cabinet. She watched him shuffle a batch of tools out of the way before he got hold of what he was looking for, his army-issue forty-five. It looked huge in his thin hands. He kept groping around in the drawer, tossing aside a screwdriver and some pliers and some wire and wrenches. "Apache, have you seen my . . . ," he said. But then he dug out the clip and whispered to himself as if he were alone in the room, "Here you are." He checked the cartridges, popped the clip into the handle, chambered a round and pointed that thing across the table at Chapman's face.

"Bill," said Apache softly. She knew she had to be careful not to provoke him too much.

"All right," Bill told her. He held the pistol steady while Chapman eased himself back down into his chair. Apache watched him open and then close his mouth. The forty-five was three feet from Chapman's forehead. "Mr. Chapman," Bill said, "Apache has left all that shit behind." Bill Po's diction was very precise. "She don't have a background any more. If she did, it would cost you more than twelve dollars. Do you understand?"

"Yes sir," said Chapman, except that he said it with just his mouth, so that you could see what he was saying, but you couldn't hear it.

The Chinaman raised the barrel and squeezed off a round into the transom behind Chapman, shattering glass down onto the floor outside in the hallway.

"Jesus fucking God, Billy!" said Apache, holding both hands over her ringing ears. "Did you have to pull the god damn trigger? Now you're gonna have the cops over here."

Bill Po gave her a quick grin and brought the pistol down. Chapman sat shivering. Apache went over beside him and shouted at him. "You haven't been shot, John! You're all right!" She patted him on the shoulder, but she couldn't get him to look at her.

The Chinaman dropped the clip out of the forty-five and cleared the chamber. He reached behind him and tossed both the clip and the pistol into the tool drawer. He shoved the drawer closed, turned, and picked up his fork. "Nobody in the whole building but us," he said. He took a couple of quick bites of his breakfast while Chapman and Apache watched him. "Check him out, Apache," he said. "See if he pissed in his pants."

Apache peered into Chapman's lap. "Don't think so," she said. She put a hand lightly on his crotch. "Nope."

"Too bad," said the Chinaman. He ate with astonishing speed. Then he put his cap back on and pushed his chair away from the table. He reached behind him into another drawer, at this time, without looking, he pulled out a toothpick. "Do you have any questions?" he asked Chapman.

"No sir," said Chapman with just his lips.

"Apache, you going over to your place now?" Bill Po asked her. Apache nodded and gave him enough of a smile to let him know she appreciated what he'd done for her. Bill Po examined the results of the preliminary pickings of his teeth. "Why don't you walk the man back upstairs?"

Apache took off her apron, retrieved her purse, and with her hands on his arms and back, she directed Chapman back out into the hallway. She couldn't hate him any more now, but she did want to get him on his way. She waved to Bill Po, who had a leg up on the table, digging with the toothpick at a molar far back in his jaw. He winked at Apache just as she closed the door.

Apache steered Chapman up the steps. He seemed willing enough to move as she directed him. "Wasn't that the loudest god damn thing you ever heard in your life?" she asked, giving his elbow a little shake.

Chapman tried to say something, but she couldn't get it.

Apache rattled the key in the door at the top of the steps. The damn lock was half-busted, but the Chinaman had refused to do anything about it when she complained to him. And when she finally did get the door open, Chapman just stood still, looking at the street and the people walking along in the sunshine, but he didn't look like he was planing to go out there any time soon.

"What's wrong?" she asked him.

"I don't know . . ." His voice was feeble, but she could hear him now.

Apache stared at him. "Move out, John," she said softly.

But Chapman just stared at the floor, his hands shoved down into his pockets. His clothes drooped. His pony-tail was snarled and skewed to one side. He really did look like somebody who didn't have but twelve dollars and change to his name. Apache thought for a moment, then pulled the door closed again. A little roughly she tugged him toward her and leaned back against the wall there in the hallway. "Where are you from anyway, John?" she asked him. She was untucking the little pullover from her skirt, reaching up under it behind herself and arching her back. "What's your hometown?"

"Parmalee, South Dakota," Chapman told her. She pulled at his hands and put them where she wanted them, up under her sweater. His glasses were smudged, but it interested her to watch his eyes while she made him touch her. She undid his pony-tail and impatiently combed through its snarls with her fingers. "Did you say you had an Osage name?" she asked him.

"Little Cougar," he whispered, his voice like a hypnotized man's. "I don't know if I want this," he said.

Bending, she unzipped and unbuckled him. "Go down one step, John," she instructed. She moved him down where she wanted him. "There we go," she said. It took a good bit more adjusting of how they were standing and how she leaned against the wall. Chapman wasn't making it easy for her either, but she was determined to make it work.

"Tell you what," she said, softly now that they were so close. "You just relax and tell me what your hobbies are. One at a time." She felt a little jolt of surprise run through his shoulders, but then he really did brace up, and she knew she could make it work now.

"Give me a hobby, John," she rasped into his ear.

"Hiking," he responded.

They each inhaled sharply.

"Yes," she said. "Yes, keep going."

"Horseback riding," he plunged on.

"Good, John," she urged him. "That's good."

"Archery!" he blurted, as if he were running out of time.

"Oh God! Little Cougar!" Apache sang. "That's exactly right!"

IN A FATHER'S PLACE

Christopher Tilghman

Dan had fallen asleep waiting for Nick and this Patty Keith, fallen deep into the lapping rhythm of a muggy Chesapeake evening, and when he heard the slam of car doors the sound came first from a dream. In the hushed amber light of the foyer Dan offered Nick a dazed and disoriented father's hug. Crickets seemed to have come in with them out of the silken night, the trill of crickets and honeysuckle pollen sharp as ammonia. Dan finally asked about the trip down, and Nick answered that the heat in New York had forced whole families onto mattresses in the streets. It looked like New Delhi, he said. Then they turned to meet Patty. She stood there in her Bermuda shorts and shirt, her brown hair in a bun, smelling of sweat and powder and looking impatient. She fixed Dan in her eyes as she shook his hand, and she said, I'm so glad to meet *you*. Maybe she was just talking about the father of her boyfriend, and maybe no new lover ever walked into fair ground in this house, but Dan could not help thinking Patty meant the steward of this family's ground, the signer of the will.

"Nick has told me so much about this place," she said. Her look ran up the winding Georgian staircase, counted off the low, wide doorways, took note of a single ball-and-claw leg visible in the dining room, and rested on the highboy.

"Yes," said Dan. "It's marvelous." He could claim no personal credit for what Patty saw, no collector's eye, not even a decorator's hand.

Rachel had arrived from Wilmington earlier in the evening, and she appeared on the landing in her nightgown. She looked especially large up there after Dan had taken in Patty's compact, tight features; Rachel was a big girl, once a lacrosse defenseman. "Hey, honey," she yelled. There had been no other greeting for her younger brother since they were teenagers. Nick returned a rather subdued hello. Tired, thought Dan, he's tired from the trip and he's got this girl to think about. Rachel came down the stairs; Patty took her hand with the awkwardness young women often show when shaking hands with other young women, or was it, Dan wondered as he watched these children meet in the breathless hall, a kind of guardedness?

Dan said, "You'll be on the third floor." He remembered his own father standing in this very place, saying these same words to polite tired girls; he remembered the underarms and collar of his father's starched shirt, yellowed and brushed with salt. But it was different now: when Dan offered the third floor—and he had done so for some years now—he meant that Rachel or Nick could arrange themselves and their dates in the three bedrooms however they wished.

"The third floor?" said Patty. "Isn't your room on the second floor looking out on the water?" She appealed to Nick with her eyes.

"Actually, Dad . . ." he said.

Dan was still not alert enough to handle conversation, especially with this response that came from a place outside family tradition. "Of course," he said after a long pause. "Wherever you feel comfortable." She wants a room with a view, that's all, he cautioned himself. They had moved deeper into the hall, into a mildewed stillness that smelled of English linen and straw mats. They listened to the grandfather clock on the landing sounding eleven in an unhurried bass.

Dan turned to Patty. "It just means you'll have to share a bathroom with Ray, and she'll fight you to the last drop on earth."

But Patty did not respond to this attempt at charm, and fortunately did not notice Rachel's skeptical look. It was an old joke, or, at least, old for them. Dan remained standing in the hall, slowly recovering from his dense, inflamed sleep as Nick and Patty took their things to the room. Patty seemed pleased, in the end, with the arrangements, and after Dan had said good night and retired to his room, he heard them touring the house, stopping at the portrait of Edward, the reputed family ghost, and admiring the letters from General Washington in gratitude for service to the cause. Theirs wasn't a family of influence anymore, not even of social standing to those few who cared, but the artifacts in the house bracketed whole epochs in American history, with plenty of years and generations left over. He heard Patty saying "Wow" in her low but quite clear-timbred voice. Then he heard the door openings and closings, the run of toilets, a brief, muffled conversation in the hall, and then a calm that returned the house to its creaks and groans, to sounds either real or imagined, a cry across the fields, the thud of a plastic trash can outside being knocked over by raccoons, the pulse of the tree toads, the hollow splash of rockfish and rays still feeding in the sleepless waters of the bay.

A few years ago Dan had taken to saying that Rachel and Nick were his best friends, and even if he saw Nick rarely these days, he hoped it was largely the truth. He'd married young enough never to learn the art of adult friendship, and then Helen had died young enough for it to seem fate, though it was just a hit-and-run on the main street of Easton. Lucille Jackson had raised the kids. Since Helen died there had been three or four women in his life, depending on whether he counted the first, women he'd known all his life who had become free again one by one, girls he'd grown up with and had then discovered as he masturbated in his teens, or who had appeared with their young husbands at lawn parties in sheer cotton sundresses that heedlessly brushed those young thighs, or who now sat alone and distracted on bleachers in a biting fall wind and watched their sons play football. At some point Dan realized if you stayed in a small town all your life, you could end up making love with every woman you had ever known and truly desired. Sheila Frederick had been there year after year in his dreams, at the lawn parties, and at football games, almost, it seemed to Dan later, as if she were stalking him through time. When they actually came together Dan stepped freely into the fulfillment of his teenage fantasies, and then stood by helplessly as she ripped a jagged hole eight years wide out of the heart of his life. There had been one more woman since then, but it was almost as if he had lost his will, if not his lust; the first time he brought her to the house she asked him where he kept the soup bowls, and in that moment he could barely withstand the fatigue, the unbearable temptation to throw it all in, that this innocent question caused him.

He undressed in the heat and turned the fan to hit him squarely on the bed. The air it brought into the room was damp but no cooler, the fecund heat of greenhouses. He felt soft and pasty, flesh that had lost its tone, more spent than tired. He tried to remember if he had put a fan in Nick's room, knowing that Nick would not look for one but would blame him in the morning for the oversight; Rachel, in a similar place, would simply barge in and steal his. Dan knew better than to compare the two of them, and during adolescence boys and girls were incomparable anyway. But they were adults now, three years apart in their mid-twenties, and noticing their differences was something he did all the time. Rachel welcomed being judged among men; and her lovers, like the current Henry, were invariably cheerful, willing bores. This tough, assertive Patty Keith with those distrustful sharp eyes, there was something of Nick's other girls there, spiky, nursing some kind of damage, expecting fear. Patty would do better in the morning. They always did. As he fell asleep finally, he was drifting back into history and memory, and it was not Patty Keith, and not even Helen meeting his father, but generations of young Eastern Shore women he saw, coming to this house to meet and be married, the ones who were pretty and eager for sex, the ones who were silent, the ones the parents loved much too soon, and the ones who broke their children's hearts.

In the morning Dan and Rachel ate breakfast together in the dining room, under the scrutiny of cousin Oswald, who had last threatened his sinful parishioners in 1681. The portraitist had caught a thoroughly unpleasant scowl, a look the family had often compared to Lucille on off days. She had prepared a full meal with eggs, fried green tomatoes, and grits, a service reserved as a reward when they were all in the house. When Nick and the new girl did not come down, Lucille cleared their places so roughly that Dan was afraid she would chip the china.

"I'm done with mothering," she said, when Dan asked if she wasn't curious to meet Patty.

Dan and Rachel looked at each other and held their breath.

"I got six of my own to think about," she said. And then, as she had done for years, a kind of rebuke when Nick and Rachel were fighting or generally disobeying her iron commands, she listed their names in a single word. "LonFredMaryHennyTykeDerek."

"And you'd have six more if you could, besides Nick and me," said Rachel.

"And you better get started, *Miss* Rachel," she said.

"How about a walk," said Dan quickly.

August weather had settled in like a member of the family, part of the week's plans. The thick haze lowered a scorching dust onto the trees and fields, a blanched air that made the open pastures pitiless for the Holsteins, each of them solitary in the heat except for the white specks of cowbirds perched on their withers. Dan was following Rachel down a narrow alley of brittle, dried-out box bushes. She was wearing a short Mexican shift and her legs looked just as solid now as they did when she cut upfield in her Princeton tunic. He would not imagine calling her manly, because hers was a big female form in the most classic sense, but he could understand that colleagues and clients, predominantly men, would find her unthreatening. She gave off no impression that she was prone to periodic weaknesses; they could count on her stamina, which, the older he got, Dan recognized as the single key to business. Nick was slight and not very athletic, just like Helen.

"So what do you think?" she asked over her shoulder.

"If you're talking about Patty I'm not going to answer, I don't think anything."

She gave him an uncompromising shrug.

They came out of the box bush on the lower lawn at the edge of the water and fanned out to stand side by side. "The truth is," said Dan, "what I'm thinking about these days is Nick. I think I've made a hash of Nick."

"That's ridiculous." She stooped to pick a four-leaf clover out of an expanse of grass; she could do the same with arrowheads on the beach. They stood silently for a moment looking at the sailboat resting slack on its mooring. It was a heavy boat, a nineteen-foot fiberglass sloop with a high bow, which Dan had bought after a winter's deliberation, balancing safety and speed the way a father must. When it arrived Nick hadn't even bothered to be polite. He wanted a "racing machine," something slender and unforgiving and not another "beamy scow." He was maybe ten at the time, old enough to know he could charm or hurt anytime he chose. Rachel didn't care much one way or the other—life was all horses for her—and Dan was so disappointed and angry with them both that he went behind the toolshed and wept.

"It's not. I really don't communicate with him at all. I don't even know what his book is about. Do you?"

"Well, I guess what it's really about is you. Not really you, but a father, and this place."

"Just what I was afraid of," said Dan.

"I don't think any of it will hurt your feelings, at least not the pieces I've read."

"Stop being so reassuring. A kiss-and-tell is not my idea of family fun." But Dan was already primed to be hurt. He'd been to a cocktail party recently where a woman he hardly knew forced him to read a letter from her daughter. It was a kind of retold family history, shaped by contempt, a letter filled with the word "never." This woman was not alone. It seemed so many of the people he knew were just now learning that their children would never forgive things, momentary failures of affection and pride, mistakes made in the barren ground between trying to keep hands off and the sin of intruding too much, things that seemed so trivial compared to a parent's embracing love. And even at the time Dan had never been sure what kind of father Nick wanted, what kind of man Nick needed in his life. Instead, Dan remembered confusion, such as the telephone calls he made when he still traveled, before Helen died. Rachel came to the phone terse and quick—she really was a kind of disagreeable girl, but so easy to read. Nick never had the gift of summarizing; his earnest tales of friends and school went on and on, until Dan, tired, sitting in a hotel room in Chicago, could not help but drop his coaxing, nurturing tone and urge him to wrap it up. Too often, in those few short years, calls with Nick ended with the agreement that they'd talk about it more when he got home, which they rarely did.

"But that's really my point," said Dan after Rachel found nothing truly reassuring to say. "This has been going on for quite a while. I'm losing him. Maybe since your mother died, for all I know."

"Oh, give him time."

"He's changed. You can't deny that. He's lost the joy."

"No one wants to go through life grinning for everyone. It's like being a greeter in Atlantic City."

"I don't think he would have come at all this week if you weren't here." It felt good to say these things, even if he knew Rachel was about to tell him to stop feeling sorry for himself.

But Rachel cleared her throat, just the way her mother did when she had something important to say. "See," she said, "that's the thing.

I've been waiting to tell you. I've got a job offer from a firm in Seattle, and I think I'm going to take it."

Dan stopped dead; the locusts were buzzing overhead like taut wires through the treetops. "What?"

"It's really a better job for me. It's general corporate practice, not just contracts."

"But you'll have to start all over again," he whined. "I'd really hate to see you go so far away."

"Well, that's the tough part."

Dan nodded, still standing in his footsteps. "I keep thinking, 'She can't do this, she's a girl.' I'm sorry."

He forced himself to resume walking, and then to continue the conversation with the right kinds of questions—the new firm, how many attorneys, prospects for making partner—the questions of a father who has taught his children to live their own lives. They didn't touch on why she wanted to go to Seattle; three thousand miles seemed its own reason for the move, to be taken well or badly, just like Nick's novel. Dan pictured Seattle as a wholesome and athletic place, as if the business community all left work on Fridays in canoes across Puget Sound. It sounded right for Rachel. They kept walking up toward the stable, and Dan hung back while Rachel went in for a peek at a loved, but now empty, place. When she came back she stood before him and gave him a long hug.

"I'm sorry, but you'll have to humor the old guy," he said.

She did her best; Dan and Lucille had raised a kind woman. But there was nothing further to say and they continued the wide arc along the hayfield fences heavy with honeysuckle, and back out onto the white road paved with oyster shells. They approached the house from the land side, past the old toolsheds and outbuildings, and Dan suddenly remembered the time, Rachel was ten, when they were taking down storm windows and she had insisted on carrying them around for storage in the chicken coop. He was up on the ladder and heard a shattering of glass, and jumped from too high to find her covered in blood. Dr. Stout pulled the shards from her head without permanent damage or visible scar before turning to Dan's ankle, which was broken. Helen was furious. But the next time Dan saw Dr. Stout was in the emergency room at Easton Hospital, and they were both covered with Helen's blood, and she was dead.

Patty and Nick had come down while they were gone, and Dan found her alone on the screened porch that had been once, and was still called, the summer kitchen. It was open on three sides, separated from the old smokehouse on the far end by a small open space, where Raymond, Lucille's old uncle, used to slaughter chickens and ducks. The yellow brick floor was hollowed by cooks' feet where the chimney and hearth had been; Dan could imagine the heat even in this broad, airy place. Patty was sitting on a wicker chair with her legs curled under her, wearing a men's strap undershirt and blue jogging shorts. She was reading a book, held so high that he could not fail to notice that it was by Jacques Derrida, a writer of some sort whose name Dan had begun to notice in the Sunday *New York Times*. Perhaps she had really not heard his approach, because she put the book down sharply when he called a good morning.

"Actually we've been up for hours," she said.

"Ah. Where's Nick?"

"He's working," she said with a protective edge on it.

Again, all Dan could find to say was "Ah." She smiled obscurely—her smiles, he observed, seemed to be directed inward—and he stood for a few more seconds before asking her if she would like anything from the kitchen. There was no question in his mind now: he was going to have to work with this one.

Rachel had just broken her news to Lucille, and the wiry, brusque lady who was "done mothering" at breakfast was crying soundlessly into a paper towel.

"I don't know what it is about you children, moving so far away," she said finally. Dan knew at least one of her sons had moved to Salisbury, and she had daughters who had married and were gone even farther.

"We've gotten by, by ourselves," said Dan.

"But that was just for schooling, for training," she answered; training, if Dan understood her right, for coming back and assuming their proper places in the family tethers. She was leaning against the sink, a vantage point on her terrain, like Dan's desk chair in his Queensville office, the places where both of them were putting in their allotted time. Rachel was sitting at the kitchen table and she stayed there, much as she might have liked to come closer to Lucille and reach out to her.

Dan went back to the summer kitchen and sat beside the girl. "You'll have to excuse us. Rachel's just dropped a bit of a bombshell and we're all a little shaky."

"You mean about her moving to Seattle."

"Well, yes. That's right." He waited for her to offer some kind of vague sympathies, but she did not; it was asking too much of a young person to understand how much this news hurt.

"So," he said finally, "I hope you're comfortable here."

At this she brightened noticeably and put her book face-down on the table. "It's a museum! Nick was going to set up his computer on that pie crust table. Can you imagine?"

Dan could picture it well and he supposed it would be no worse than the time Nick had ascended the highboy, climbing from pull to pull, leaving deep sneaker scuffs on the mahogany burl as he struggled for purchase. But she was right, of course, and she had known enough to notice and identify a pie crust table. "You know antiques, then?"

Yes, she said, her mother was a corporate art consultant and her father, as long as Dan had asked, was a doctor who lived on the West Coast. She mentioned a few more pieces of furniture that caught her eye.

"My mother thinks Chippendales and Queen Anne have peaked, maybe for a long time."

"I wouldn't know," said Dan.

"But the graveyard!" she exclaimed at the end.

Dan was relieved that she had finally listed something of no monetary value, peak or valley, something that couldn't be sold by her mother to Exxon. "As they say in town," he answered, "when most people die they go to heaven; if you're a Williams you just walk across the lawn."

"That's funny."

"I guess," he said. It was all of it crap, he reflected, if he became the generation that lost its children. He'd be just as dead now as later.

"They're the essential past."

Essential past? Whatever could she mean, with her Derrida at her side, her antiques? "I'm not sure I understand what you mean, but to tell you the truth," he said, "I often think the greatest gift I could bestow on the kids is to bulldoze the place and relieve them of the burden."

"I think that's something for the two of them to decide."

"I suppose coming to terms with all this is what Nick is up to in his novel." The girl had begun to annoy him terribly and he could not resist this statement, even as he regretted opening himself to her answer.

"Oh," she said coyly, "I wouldn't say 'coming to terms.' No, I think just looking at it more reflexively. He's trying to deconstruct this family."

"Deconstruct? You mean destroy?" he said quickly, trying not to sound genuinely alarmed.

Patty gave him a patronizing look. "No. It's a critical term. It's very complicated."

Fortunately Nick walked in on this last line. It was Dan's first chance to get a look at him and he saw the full enthusiasm—and the smug satisfaction—of one who has worked a long morning while others took aimless walks. Nick was gangly, he would always be even if he gained weight, but surprisingly quick. As unathletic as he was, he had been the kind of kid who could master inconsequential games of dexterity; he once hit a pong paddle ball a thousand times without missing, and could balance on a teeter-totter until he quit out of boredom. All his gestures, even his expressions, came on like compressed air. And while Dan had to work not to speculate on what part of himself had been "deconstructed" today, this tall, pacing, energetic man was the boy he treasured in his heart.

"The Squire has been surveying the grounds?" said Nick.

"Someone has to work for a living," said Dan, quickly worrying that Nick might miss the irony.

"I was wondering what you called it," he answered.

Patty watched this exchange with a confused look. Any kind of humor, even very bad humor, seemed utterly to escape her. "Did you finish the chapter?" she asked.

"No, but I broke through. I'm just a scene away. Maybe two."

"Well," she said with a deliberate pause, "wasn't that what you said yesterday?"

Good God, thought Dan, the girl wants to marry a published novelist, a novelist with antiques. He said quickly, "But it seems you had a great"—too much accent on the great—"a really very productive morning of work."

Nick's face darkened slightly, as fine a change as a razor cut. "It's kind of a crucial chapter. It has to be right."

"Were you tired?" she asked.

"No. It's just slow, that's all."

During his conversation Rachel had shouted down that lunch was ready, and Dan hung back for the kids to go first, and he repeated this short conversation to himself. It was not such a large moment, he reflected, but nervous-making just the same, and during lunch Nick sat quietly while Patty filled the air with questions, questions about the family, about Lord Baltimore and the Calverts. They took turns answering her questions, but finally it fell back to Nick to unlace the strands of the family, to place ancestors prominently at the Battle of Yorktown. He looked now and again to Dan for confirmation, and Dan knew how he felt reciting these facts that, even if true, could only sound like family puffery. Dan wanted to do better by his son and did try to engage himself back into the conversation, but by the time Lucille had cleared the plates he felt full of despair, gummy with some kind of sadness for all of them, for himself, for Rachel now off to Seattle in a place where maybe no one would marry her, for Nick with this girl, for Lucille so much older than she looked, and hiding, Dan knew it, her husband's bad health from everyone.

Patty ended the meal by offering flatteries all around the table, including compliments to Lucille that sent her back to the kitchen angrily—but loud enough only for Dan's practiced ear—mimicking the girl's awkward phrase, "So pleasant to have eaten such a good lunch." As they left the table finally, Dan announced he had to spend the afternoon in his office. At this point, he wasn't sure what he would less rather do. He changed quickly and left for town with the three of them discussing the afternoon in the summer kitchen, and he could hear Rachel laboring for every word.

He was so distracted as he drove to town that he nearly ran the single stoplight. Driving mistakes, of any kind, went right to his living memory; once he slightly rear-ended a car on Route 301, and he bolted to the bushes and threw up in front of the kids, in front of a very startled carload of hunters. He crawled to Lawyers' Row and came in the door pale enough for Mrs. McCready—it had always been *Mrs.* McCready—to comment on the heat and ask him if his car air conditioner was working properly. His client was waiting for him, Bobbie Perlee, one of those heavy, fleshy teenagers in Gimme caps and net football jerseys, with greasy long hair. The smell of frying oil and cigarettes filled his office. Whenever he had thought of Rachel joining his practice, he had reminded himself that she would spend her time with clients like this one, court-appointed, Bobbie Perlee in trouble with the law again, assaulting his friend Aldene McSwain with a broken fishing pole. McSwain could lose the eye yet. But Dan couldn't blame a thousand Perlees on anyone but himself; he had made the choice to practice in Queensville when it became clear that the kids needed him closer to home and not working late night after night across the bay in Washington. If she had lived, Helen would have insisted anyway.

"What do you have to say this time, Bobbie?"

Bobbie responded with the round twangy O's of the Eastern Shore, a sound that for so long had spelled ignorance to Dan, living here on a parallel track. He said nothing in response to Bobbie's description of the events; he didn't really hear them. Bobbie Perlee pawed his fat feet into Dan's worn-out Persian rug. For a moment it all seemed so accidental to Dan; sitting in this office with the likes of Bobbie Perlee seemed both frighteningly new and endlessly rehearsed. He could only barely remember the time when escape from the Eastern Shore gave meaning and guided everything he did. It was there when he refused to play with the Baileys and the Pacas, children of family and history like himself. It was there when he refused to go to "the University," which, in the case of Maryland gentry, meant the University of Pennsylvania. It was there even the night he first made love, because it was with his childhood playmate, Molly Tobin. They had escaped north side by side for college, and came together out of loneliness, and went to bed as if breaking her hymen would shatter the last ring that circled them both on these monotonous farmlands and tepid waters.

But he'd come back anyway when his father was dying, and brought Helen with him, a Jew and a midwesterner who came with a sense of discovery, a fresh eye on the landscape. Helen had given the land back to Dan, and Sheila Frederick had chained him to it, coming back out of his youth like a lost bookend, with a phone call saying *I don't look the same, you know*, and because none of them did—it had been thirty years—it meant she was still pretty. She lived in a bright new river-shore condo in Chestertown. She was still pretty, but now when she relaxed, her mouth settled into a tight line of bitterness. Their last night, two years ago, after a year of fighting, she told Dan she worried about his aloneness, not his loneliness which was, she said, her problem and a female one at that, but his aloneness as he rattled around that huge house day after day, with no company but that harsh and unforgiving Lucille. From her, this talk and prediction of a solitary life was a threat; to Dan, at that moment, anyway, being alone was perfect freedom.

Dan finally waved Perlee out of his office without anything further said. These lugs, he could move them around like furniture and they'd never ask why. Dan looked out his office window onto the Queen Anne's County courthouse park, a crosshatching of herringbone brick pathways shaded under the broad leaves of the tulip trees. At the center gathering of the walks was a statue of Queen Anne that had been rededicated by Princess Anne herself. She was only a girl at the time but could have told that wildly enthusiastic crowd a thing or two about history, if they'd chosen to listen. Dan had done well by his children, if today was any indication. They were free not because they had to be, but because they wanted to be. Rachel won a job offer from three thousand miles away because she was that good. My God, how would he bear it when she was gone? And Nick was reaching adulthood with a passion, on the wings of some crazy notion about literary deconstruction that, who knew? could well be what they all needed to hear and understand. So, in many ways, his thoughts ended with this sad girl, this Patty Keith, who seemed the single part of his life that didn't have to be, yet it was she who had been tugging him into depression and ruminations on the bondages of family and place all afternoon.

On the way home he stopped at Mitchell Brothers Liquors, a large windowless block building with a sign on the side made of a giant *S* that formed the first letter of "Spirits, Subs, and Shells." The shells, of course, were the kind you put into shotguns and deer rifles. The Mitchells were clients of his and were very possibly the richest family in town. He bought a large bottle of Soave and at the last minute added a jug of Beefeaters, which was unusual enough for Doris Mitchell to ask if he was having a party. He answered that Nick was home with a girlfriend that looked like trouble, and he was planning to drink the gin himself.

The summer kitchen was empty when he stepped out, gin and tonic in hand. A shower and a first drink had helped. He might have hoped for the three of them, now fully relaxed, to be there trading stories, but instead they came out one by one, and everyone was carrying something to read. He supposed Patty was judging him for staring out at the trees and water, no obscure Eastern European novel in his hand. Nick was uncommunicative, sullen really, this sullenness in the place of the sparkling joy he used to bring into the house. Dinner passed quickly. Afterwards, Patty insisted that Nick take her to the dock and show her the stars and the lights of Kent Island the way, she said firmly, he *promised* he would. Rachel and Dan turned in before they got back, and Dan read *Newsweek* absently until the last of the doors had closed, and he slipped out of his room for one of his house checks, the changing of the guard from the mortals of evening and the ghosts of the midwatch. He was coming back to his room when he heard a cry from Nick's room. In shame and panic he realized that they were making love, but before he could flee he heard her say. "No. No." It wasn't that she was being forced, he could tell that immediately; instead, there was a harshness to it that, even as a father is repelled at the idea of listening to his son have sex, forced Dan to remain there. He had not taken a breath, had not shifted his weight off the ball of his left foot; if anyone had come to the door he would not have been able to move. There was more shuffling from inside, a creak as they repositioned in the old sleigh bed. "*That's* right," said Patty firmly finally. "Like *that*. Like that." Her voice, at least, was softer now, clouded by the dreaminess of approaching orgasm. "Like that," she breathed one last time, and came with a thrust. But from Nick, this whole time, there had not been a word, not a grunt or a sound, so silent he was that he might not have been there at all.

"I think she's a witch," said Rachel. They were on their post-breakfast walk again, this time both of them digging in their heels in purposeful strides.

Dan let out a disgusted and fearful sigh.

"No, I mean it. I think she's using witchcraft on him."

"If you'll forgive the statement, it's cuntcraft if it's anything."

"That's pretty, Dad," she said. They had already reached the water and were turning into the mowed field. "But I'm telling you, it's spooky."

All night Dan had pictured Patty coming, her legs tight around Nick's body, her thin lips clenched pale, and her white teeth dripping blood.

"She controls him. She tells him what to do," said Rachel. "If this were Salem she'd be hanging as we speak."

They had now walked along the hayfield fence line through the brown grass, and said nothing more as they turned for the house, its lime-brushed brick soft and golden in the early morning sun.

"It won't last. He'll get over her," he said.

"Yes, but the older you are the longer it takes to grow out of things, wouldn't you say?"

Dan nodded; Rachel, as usual, was quite right about that. It had taken him six months to figure out that Sheila Frederick was one of the worst mistakes of his life, and another seven years to do something about it. It would not have been so bad if it weren't for the kids. He could admit and confess almost everything in his life except for the fact that he had known, for years, how much they hated her. They hated her so much that when it was over, Nick didn't even bother to comment except to tell Dan he'd seen her twice slipping family teaspoons into her purse.

They skirted the graveyard and without further discussion bypassed the house for another tour. As they went by, Dan glanced over his shoulder, and there she was, Derrida in hand, a small voracious lump that had taken over a corner of the summer kitchen. He looked up at the open window where Nick was working.

"I think I'd better marry Henry," said Rachel.

"He's a very nice guy. You know how fond of him I am," said Dan.

"Nice, but not very interesting. Is that what you mean?"

"Not at all. But as long as you put it this way, I think this Patty Keith is interesting."

"So what are we going to do about Miss Patty?" asked Rachel.

"Well, nothing. What can we do? Nick's already mad at me; I'm not going to give him reason to hate me by butting into his relationships."

"But someday Nick's going to wake up, maybe not for a year, or ten years, and he'll realize he's just given over years of his life to that witch, and then isn't he going to wonder where his sister and father were all that time?"

"It doesn't work that way. Believe me. You don't blame your mistakes in love on others."

Rachel turned to look at him fully with just the slightest narrowing of focus. It was an expression any lawyer, from the first client meeting to the last summary to the jury, had to possess. "Are you talking about Mrs. Frederick?" she said finally.

"I suppose I am. I'm not saying others don't blame you for the mistakes you make in love." Without any trouble, without even a search of his memory, Dan could list several things Sheila had made him do that the kids should never, ever forgive. What leads us to live our lives with people like that?

"No one blames you for her. The cunt."

Dan was certain that Rachel had never before in her whole life used that word. He laughed, and so did Rachel, and he put his arm on her shoulder for a few steps.

She said faintly, with an air of summary, "I really think you're making a mistake. I believe she's programming him. I mean it. I think she's dangerous to him and to us. It happens to people a lot more resilient and less sensitive than Nick."

"We'll see." They walked for a few more minutes, in air that was so still the motion of their steps felt like relief. Again Rachel was right; he was a less sensitive man than his son but he had been equally powerless to resist the eight years he had spent with Sheila. Dan couldn't answer for his own life, much less Nick's, so they completed their dejected morning walk and climbed the brick steps to the back portico. As they reached the landing, he took his daughter in his arms again and said, "God, Rachel, I'm going to miss you."

When they came back Patty was in the kitchen talking to Lucille. From the sound of it she had been probing for details about Nick as a boy, which could have been a lovely scene if it hadn't been Patty, eyes sharp, brain calculating every monosyllabic response, as if, in the middle of it, she might take issue with Lucille and start correcting her memories. It's not the girl's fault, thought Dan; it's just a look, the way her face moves, something physical. There was no way for Patty to succeed with Lucille; no girl of Nick's could have done better. It's not Patty's fault, Dan said to himself; she's trying to be nice but she just doesn't have any manners; her parents haven't given her any grace. He said this to himself again later in the morning when she poked her head into his study and asked if his collection of miniature books was valuable. Mother obviously did not deal in miniatures although, Dan supposed, she would be eager to sell Audubons to IBM. Dan answered back truthfully that he didn't know, some of his books may be valuable, as a complete collection it could be of interest to someone. She took this information back with her to the summer kitchen. Dan watched her walk down the hall, a short sweatshirt that exposed the hollow of her back and a pair of those tight jersey pants that made her young body look solid as a brick.

Dan did not see Nick come down, did not hear whether he had finished his chapter and whether that was enough for Patty. At lunch Rachel noted that the Orioles were playing a day game, and Dan had to remind himself again that except for sailing, the athlete in the family was the girl, that she'd been not only older but much more physical than her brother. He remembered how he and Helen had despaired about Nick, a clinger, quick to burst into tears at the first furrowing of disapproval; how Dan had many times caught a tone from the voices in the school playground right across the street from his office, and how he had often stopped to figure out if it was Nick's wail he heard, or just the high-pitched squeals of the girls, or the screech of tires on some distant street. And how curious it was that with this softness also came irrepressible energy, the force of the family, as if he saved every idea and every flight of joy for Dan and Rachel. Yet it had been years now that Nick had turned it on for him.

For once, Patty seemed content to sit at the sidelines while Rachel and Nick continued with the Orioles. Name the four twenty-game winners in 1971, said Rachel, and Nick, of course, could manage only the obvious one, Jim Palmer. Rachel's manners—they were Lucille's doing as much as his, Dan reminded himself—compelled her to ask Patty if she could do any better; Patty made a disgusted look and went back to her crab salad. At that point Dan saw the chance he had been waiting for, and he turned to Nick and told him he had to go see a client's boat—a Hinckley—that was rammed by a drunk at Chestertown mooring. "Come on along and we'll catch up," he said offhandedly. He looked straight into Nick's eyes and would not allow him to glance toward Patty.

"Hey, great," said Nick after the slightest pause. "How about later in the afternoon?"

"Nope. Got to go at low tide. The boat sank." His tone was jocular, the right tone for cornering his son before Patty could move, before she started to break into the conversation with her "Wait a minute" and her "I don't understand." Rachel moved fast as well and quickly suggested, in a similar tone, that they, in the meantime, would go see the Wye Oak, the natural wonder of the Eastern Shore. "We can buy T-shirts," said Rachel.

"But . . ."

A few minutes later Dan and Nick were on the road in Dan's large Buick. There was considerable distance between them on the seat. "I hope Patty doesn't mind me stealing you like this," Dan said finally.

Nick could not hide his discomfort, but he waved it all off.

"Women," said Dan.

Nick let out a small laugh. He was sitting with his body turned slightly toward the door, gazing out at the familiar sights, the long chicken sheds of McCready's Perdue operation, the rustic buildings of the 4-H park under the cool shade of tall loblolly pines.

"So how's it going? The novel."

Good, he said. He'd finished his chapter.

"You know," said Dan, working to something he'd planned to say, "I'm interested to read it anytime you're ready to show it. I won't mention it again, just so long as you know. I can't wait to see what it's about."

"Oh," said Nick, "it's not really *about* anything, not a plot, anyway. I'm more interested in process. It's kind of part of a critical methodology."

Dan wanted to ask what in the world that meant, but could not. "Patty seems interested. I'm sure that's helpful."

"Patty's energy," Nick said, finally turning straight on the seat, "is behind every word."

"She certainly is a forceful girl." Dan realized his heart was pounding, and that it was breaking as he watched Nick come to life at the mention of her name.

"She tore the English department at Columbia *apart*." He laughed at some private memory that Dan really did not want to hear. "I know she's not for everyone, but I've never known anyone who takes less shit in her life."

And I love her, he was saying. I'm in love with her because she doesn't take shit from anyone. Not like you, Dan heard him think, who is living out his life a prisoner of family history. Not like you who let Mrs. Frederick lock me out the night I ran away from my finals in freshman year. Dan supposed the list was endless.

And at this impasse something could well have ended for him and Nick. It would not come as a break, a quarrel, but it would also not come unexpectedly or undeserved. In the end, thought Dan, being Nick's father didn't mean he and his son couldn't grow apart; didn't mean a biological accident gave him any power over the situation. It meant only that it would hurt more. He could not imagine grieving over friends he once loved with all his heart and now never saw. The Hellmans, how he had loved them, and where in the world were they now? But Nick, even if he never spoke to him again, even if this Patty Keith took him away to some isolation of spirit, Dan would know where he was and feel the pain.

"So why so glum, Dad?" said Nick, a voice very far away from the place where Dan was lost in thought.

"What?"

"I mean, we're going to see a wreck, a Hinckley, for Christ's sake, and you're acting like you owned it yourself."

They were crossing the long bridge over the Chester, lined, as always, with market fisherman sitting beside plastic pails of bait and tending three or four poles apiece. Twenty years ago they'd all been black, now mostly white, but there had not been too much other change in this seventeenth-century town; Dan had never known how to take this place, old families jostling to the last brick even as they washed and sloshed their way down Washington Street on rivers of gin. But it was a lovely town, rising off the river on the backsides of gracious houses, brick and slate with sleeping porches resting out over the tulip trees in a line of brilliant white slats. Dan looked ahead at this pleasant scene while Nick craned his neck out to the moorings.

"Oh yes," he said. "There's a mast at a rather peculiar angle."

The boat was a mess, lying on its side on a sandbar in a confused struggle of lines, a tremendous fibrous gash opening an almost indecent view of the forward berths. Nick rowed them out in a dinghy no one knew who owned; he was full of cheer, free, no matter what, on the water. The brown sandbar came up under them at the edge of the mooring like a slowly breaching whale. As they came alongside, Nick jumped out and waded over to the boat, peered his head through the jagged scar, and then started hooting with laughter.

"What is it?" said Dan.

Nick backed his head out of the hull. "Porn videos. God, there must be fifty of them scattered over the deck."

Dan quickly flashed a picture of his rather proper Philadelphia client, who could have no idea that his most secret compartment had been burst in the crash.

"Jesus," said Nick. "Here's one that is actually called *Nick My Dick*. It's all-male."

"Stop it. It's none of your business," said Dan, but he could not help beaming widely as he said this, and together they plowed the long way back through the moorings, making loud and obnoxious comments about most of the boats they passed. Dan doubted any of these tasteless, coarse stinkpots, all of the new ones featuring a dreadful palette of purples and plums, contained a secret library to compare with the elegant white Hinckley's. After they returned the boat they strolled up Washington Street to the court square and stopped for an ice cream at one of the several new "quality" establishments that had begun to spring up here. Dan hoped, prayed, only that Sheila Frederick, who lived here, would not choose this moment to walk by, but if she did she would simply ignore him anyway, which would not be a bad thing for Nick to see.

But it was all bound by the return, as if Nick were on furlough. And it was certain to be bad, Dan could sense it by now as they turned through the gates back to the farm. This time, when they re-entered the summer kitchen, the Derrida remained raised. As far as Dan could tell she had made little headway in this book, but she stuck to it through Nick's stray, probing comments about their trip. For the first time she struck Dan as funny, touchingly adolescent, with her tight little frown and this pout that she seemed helpless, like a twelve-year-old, to control. No, she had *not* gone to see the Wye Oak. No, she did not wish for any iced tea.

This is how it went for the rest of the day and into the evening. She's in quite a snit, said Rachel when they passed in the front hall, both of them pretending not to be tiptoeing out of range of the summer kitchen, which had seemed to grow large and overpowering around that hard nub of rage. Nick also circled, spending some of the time reading alongside the girl, some of the time upstairs writing a whole new chapter, perhaps a whole new volume, as penance. It was Lucille's day off, and normally eating at the kitchen table gave the family leave to loosen up, a kind of relief from the strictures of life. Patty sat but did not eat, just made sure that everyone understood, as Nick might have said, that she wouldn't take his shit. Dan could not imagine what she was telling herself, how she had reconstructed the events of the afternoon to give her sufficient reason for all this. In the silence, everything in the kitchen, the pots and pans, the appliances and spices, seemed to close in, all this unnecessary clutter. The pork chops tasted like sand; the back of the chair cut into his spine. He tried to picture how she might describe this to friends, if she had any. He could not guess which one of them had earned the highest place in this madness, but he knew which one of them would pay. He'd seen it in couples all his life, these cycles of offense and punishment, had lived the worst of it himself with Sheila Frederick. When she finally left the table, and Nick followed a few minutes later—he gave a kind of shrug but his face was blank—Rachel tried to make a slight joke of it. "We are displeased," she said.

"No. This is tragic," said Dan. "She's mad."

They cleaned the dishes, and after Rachel kissed him good night he went out into the darkness of the summer kitchen. The air, so motionless all week, was still calm but was beginning to come alive; he could hear the muffled clang of the bell buoy a mile into the river. A break in the heat was coming; the wildlife that never stopped encroaching on this Chesapeake life always knew about the weather in advance, and the voices became softened and sharp. The squirrels' movements through the trees or across the lawns became quick dashes from cover to cover; the beasts and beings were ready, even to a lone firefly, whose brief flashes gave only a staccato edginess to a darkening night. Dan felt old; he was tired. For a moment or two his unspoken words addressed the spirits of the house—they too never stopped encroaching—but he stopped abruptly because he knew, had known since a boy, that if he let them in he would never again be free of them. He wondered if Helen would be among them. He waited long enough, deep into this skittish night, for everyone to be asleep; he could not stand the thought of hearing a single sound from Nick's room. But when he finally did turn in he could not keep from hesitating for a moment at the door, much as he and Helen used to when the children were infants, and they needed only the sound of a moist breath to know all was well.

Under the door he saw that the light was on, and through it he heard the low mumble of a monotone. It was her, and it was just a steady drone, a break now and again, a slightly higher inflection once or twice. It was a sheet of words, sentences, if they were written, that would swallow whole paragraphs, and though Dan wanted to think this unemotional tone meant her anger was spent, he knew immediately that this girl was abusing his son. She was interrogating him without questions; she was damning him without accusations, just this litany, an endless rosary of rage. It could well have been going on for hours, words from her mad depths replacing Nick's, supplanting his thoughts. He could make out no phrase except, once, for a distinct "What we're discussing here . . ." that was simply a pause in the process as she forced him to accept not only her questions, but her answers as well. He did not know how long he stood there; he was waiting, he realized after a time, for the sound of Nick's voice, because as Dan swayed tired back and forth in the hall, he could imagine anything, even that she had killed him and was now incoherently continuing the battle over his body. When finally the voice of his son did appear, it was just two words. "Christ, Patty." There was only one way to read these two names: he was begging, pleading, praying for her to stop. And then the drone began again.

He closed his bedroom door carefully behind him, and sat by his bay window in an old wingback that had been Helen's sewing chair. Her dark mahogany sewing table was empty now, the orderly rows of needles and spooled threads scattered over the years. The wide windows beckoned him. He could feel no breezes on his sweating forehead and neck, but the air was flavored now with manure, milk, gasoline, and rotting silage, a single essence of the farm that was seeping in from the northwest on the feet of change. He stared out into the dark for a long time before he undressed, and was still half awake when the first blades of moving air began to slice through the humidity. He was nodding off when later, on his pillow, he heard the crustacean leaves of the magnolias and beeches begin to clatter in the wind.

The house was awakened by the steady blow, an extravagance of air and energy after these placid weeks of a hot August. Dan could hear excited yips from the kitchen, as if the children were teenagers once again; he thought, after what he had heard and the hallucinations that plagued him all night long, that he was dreaming an especially cruel vision of a family now lost. But he went down to the kitchen and they were all there: Rachel, as usual grumpy and slow moving in the morning and today looking matronly and heavy in her long unornamented nightgown; Patty, standing on the other side by the refrigerator with a curiously unsure look; Lucille at her most abrupt, wry best; and Nick, wearing nothing but his bathing suit, pacing back and forth, filled with the joy and energy only a few hours ago Dan had given up as lost forever.

"A real wind," he said. "A goddamn hurricane."

"Shut your mouth with that," said Lucille happily.

"We're going to sail all the way to the *bridge*," he continued, and poked Rachel in the side with a long wooden spoon until she snarled at him.

"I've got to wash my hair," said Rachel.

"Fuck your hair."

Lucille grabbed her own wooden spoon and began to move toward him, and he backed off toward Patty, who was maybe tired out from her efforts the night before, or maybe just so baffled by this unseen Nick that even she could not intrude. Nick picked her up by the waist and spun her around. She was in her short nightgown and when Nick grabbed her he hiked it over her underpants; even as Dan helplessly noticed how sexy her body was, he recoiled at the thought of Nick touching it. With mounting enthusiasm, Dan watched this nervy move and wondered whether it would work on her, but she struggled to get down and was clearly furious as she caught her footing.

"I agree with Rachel," she said. It was probably, Dan realized, the first time she'd ever used Rachel's name.

Nick persisted. "Wind like this happens once a year. It might blow out."

"It could be flat calm again by lunch," said Dan.

She turned quickly on Dan as if he hadn't the slightest right to give an opinion, to speak at all. "I *understand*," she whined. "I just think this is a good chance for him to get work done."

It was "him," Dan noticed. He waited for Nick's next move and almost shouted with triumph when it came.

"Fuck work." As he said this, a quite large honey locust branch cracked off the tree outside the window and fell to a thud through a rustle of leaves.

Patty screwed her face into a new kind of scowl—she had more frowns, thought Dan, and scowls and pouts than any person he ever met—and announced, "Well I'm not going. I'm going to get *something* done."

"Derrida?" said Dan. He was still giddy with relief.

She glared.

"Oh, come on, sweetie," Nick coaxed. "You won't believe what sailing in wind like this is like." He tried cajoling in other ways, promises of unbroken hours of work, a chance to see the place from the water; he even made public reference to the fight of the day before when he told her a sail would "clear the air after that awful night." He could be worn down by this. Dan knew; he could still lose. But earlier in the conversation Rachel had slipped out and now, with a crash of the door that was probably calculated and intentional, she came back into the kitchen in her bathing suit—she really should watch her weight, Dan couldn't avoid thinking—and that was all the encouragement Nick needed.

Dan walked down to the water with them and sat on the dock as they rigged the boat. The Dacron sails snapped in slicing folds; the boom clanked on the deck like a road sign flattened to the pavement in a gale. "Is it too much?" he called out. Of course it was; under normal circumstances he would be arguing strenuously that it was dangerous. They all knew it was too much. Nick called back something, but he was downwind and the sound was ripped away as soon as he opened his mouth. They cast off and in a second had been blown a hundred feet up the creek. They struggled quickly to haul in the sails; Rachel was on the tiller and Dan wished she wasn't because she was nowhere near the sailor Nick was; she would have been better on the sheets where her brute strength could count. But she let the boat fall off carefully and surely, and all of a sudden the wind caught the sails with a hollow, dense thud, and as they powered past the dock upwind toward the mouth of the creek, Dan heard Nick yell, full voice and full of joy, "Holy shit!"

When he got back to the house she was in her place in the summer kitchen. How tired he was of her presence, of feeling her out there. All the time—it was maybe nothing more than a family joke, but it was true—she had been sitting in his chair. Nick may have told her, or she may have even sensed it. He walked through the house and was met, as he expected, as he had hoped, with an angry, hostile stare.

"You don't approve of water sports, I gather?" he said, ending curiously on a slightly British high point.

She fixed him in her gimlet eyes; this was the master of the Columbia English department.

"Not interested?" he asked again.

"As a matter of fact, I don't approve of very much around here."

"I'm sorry for that," he said. He still held open the possibility that the conversation could be friendly, but he would not lead it in that direction. "It hasn't seemed to have gone well for you."

"There's nothing wrong with *me*."

"Ah-ha."

"I think you're all in a fantasy."

Dan made a show of looking around at the walls, the cane and wicker furniture, and ended by rapping his knuckles on the solid table. He shrugged. "People from the outside seem to make a lot more of this than we do," he said.

She leaned slightly forward; this was the master of his son. "It's not for me to say, but when you read Nick's novel you'll know where *he* stands."

The words exploded from him. "How dare you bring Nick's novel into this."

"Why do you think he wanted to come here, anyway?"

"Patty," said Dan, almost frightened by the rage that was now fevering his muscles, "when it comes to families, I really think you should let people speak for themselves. I think you should reconsider this conversation."

"You have attacked me. You have been sarcastic to me. I have nothing to apologize for." She made a slight show of returning to her book.

"Tell me something. What are your plans? What are your plans for Nick?"

"Nick makes his own plans."

It was not a statement of fact; it was a threat, a show of her larger power over him. "And you? What are your plans?"

"I'm going to live my own life and I'm not going to pretend that all this family shit comes to anything."

"Whose family? Yours or Nick's?"

"You mean do I plan to marry Nick? So I can get my hands on this?" She mimicked his earlier gesture. "I suppose that's why from the second, the very second I walked in, you have disapproved of me. Well, don't worry"—she said this with a patronizing tone, addressing a child, a pet—"the only thing I care about around here is Nick and . . ." She cut herself off.

"And what?"

"And his work. Not that it matters to you."

"Oh, cut the crap about his work. You want his soul, you little Nazi, you want any soul you can get your hands on."

She pounded the table with her small fist. "What we're talking about here . . ." she shouted, and Dan's body recoiled with this phrase, "is the shit you have handed out, and I'll cite chapter and verse, and—"

"Patty, Patty." He interrupted her with difficulty. "Stop this."

"I have some power, you know."

"Patty, I think it would be better for everyone if you left. Right now."

"What?"

"You heard me."

"You would throw me out?" She did, finally, seem quite stunned. "And just what do you think Nick's going to do when he gets back?"

"I don't know. But I will not tolerate you in my house for another minute."

She slammed her feet down on the brick floor and jumped up almost as if she planned to attack him, to take a swing at him. "O.K., I will. I'm not going to take this shit."

She marched through the kitchen, and a moment or two later he heard a door slam. He moved from his seat to his own chair; suddenly the view seemed right again, the pecan lined up with the blue spruce by the water, and the corner of the smokehouse opened onto a hay land that had, from this vantage, always reminded him of the fields of Flanders. A few minutes later he heard a heavy suitcase being dragged over the yellow pine staircase, the steel feet striking like golf spikes into the Georgian treads. He heard a mumble as she came to the kitchen to say something tactical to Lucille, perhaps to give her a note for Nick or to play the part of the tearful girl unfairly accused. He heard the trunk of her car open and he pictured her hefting her large bag, packed with dresses and shorty nightgowns and diaphragms and makeup, over the lip of her BMW, and then she was off, coming into view at the last minute in a flash of red.

Dan heard Lucille's light step, and then saw her face peer out onto the summer kitchen. As many times as Dan had tried to make her change, she never liked to come into a room to say something, but would stand in the doorway and make everyone crane their necks to see her.

"Mister Dan?"

"Lucille, *please* come out."

She took two steps. "You're in a mess of trouble now."

He held his arms up. "What could I do?"

"You just gotta make sure you're picking a fight with the right woman."

Dan looked away as she said this, and hung his head slightly, as if he expected her to say plenty more. But when he glanced back up she was smiling, such a rare and precious event.

"I got six of my own to worry about," she said. The wind was singing through the screens in a single, sustained high note. "But I do hope to the good Lord that those babies are O.K. out in this storm."

Dan stayed in the summer kitchen all morning. The winds weren't going to die down this time—he knew that the moment he woke up—it was a storm with some power to it and it would bring rain later in the day. He ate lunch in his study, and around two went down to the dock. The water was black and the wind was slicing the wave tops into fine spray. No one should be out in this, and not his two children. He pictured them, taking turns at the tiller as the boat pounded on the bottoms and broke through the peaks in a shattering of foam. He wasn't worried yet; he'd selected that big boat for days like this. It would swamp before it would capsize and they could run for a sandy shore any time they wanted. The winds would send them back to this side; he'd sailed more than one submerged hulk home as a boy, and he'd left a boat or two on the beach and hiked home through the fields. This was the soul of the Chesapeake country, never far from land on the water, the water always meeting the land, always in flux. You could always run from one to the other. The water was there, in the end, with Sheila, because he had triumphed over her, had fought battles for months in telephone calls that lasted for hours and evenings drowned in her liquors, until one morning he had awakened and listened to the songs from the water and realized that he was free.

He lowered his legs over the dock planking and sat looking out into the bay. From this spot, he had watched the loblolly pines on Carpenter's Island fall one by one across the low bank into the irresistible tides. When the last of the pines had gone the island itself was next, and it sank finally out of sight during the hurricanes of the fifties. Across the creek Mr. McHugh's house stood empty, blindfolded by shutters. What was to become of the place now that the old man's will had scattered it among nieces and nephews? What was to happen to his own family ground if Rachel went to Seattle for good and Nick . . . and Nick left this afternoon, never to come back?

Dan tried to think again of what he would say to Nick, what his expression should be as they closed up on the mooring, what his first words should cover. But the wind that had already brought change brushed him clean of all that and left him naked, a man. He could not help the rising tide of joy that was coming to him. He was astonished by what had happened to him. By his life. By the work he had done, the wills, the clients, all of them so distant that he couldn't remember ever knowing them at all. By the wife he had loved and lost on the main street of Easton, and by the women who had since then come in and out of life, leaving marks and changes he'd never even bothered to notice. By the children he fathered and raised, those children looking out from photographs over mounds of Christmas wrappings and up from the water's edge, smiles undarkened even by their mother's death. By his mistakes and triumphs, from the slap of a doctor's hand to the last bored spadeful of earth. It was all his, it all accumulated back toward him, toward his body, part of a journey back through the flesh to the seed where it started, and would end.

HELPING

Robert Stone

One gray November day, Elliot went to Boston for the afternoon. The wet streets seemed cold and lonely. He sensed a broken promise in the city's elegance and verve. Old hopes tormented him like phantom limbs, but he did not drink. He had joined Alcoholics Anonymous fifteen months before.

Christmas came, childless, a festival of regret. His wife went to mass and cooked a turkey. Sober, Elliot walked in the woods.

In January, blizzards swept down from the Arctic until the weather became too cold for snow. The Shawmut Valley grew quiet and crystalline. In the white silences, Elliot could hear the boards of his house contract and feel a shrinking in his bones. Each dusk, starveling deer came out of the wooded swamp behind the house to graze his orchard for whatever raccoons had uncovered and left behind. At night he lay beside his sleeping wife listening to the baying of dog packs running them down in the deep moon-shadowed snow.

Day in, day out, he was sober. At times it was almost stimulating. But he could not shake off the sensations he had felt in Boston. In his mind's eye he could see dead leaves rattling along brick gutters and savor that day's desperation. The brief outing had undermined him.

Sober, however, he remained, until the day a man named Blankenship came into his office at the state hospital for counseling. Blankenship had red hair, a brutal face, and a sneaking manner. He was a sponger and petty thief whom Elliot had seen a number of times before.

"I been having this dream," Blankenship announced loudly. His voice was not pleasant. His skin was unwholesome. Every time he got arrested the court sent him to the psychiatrists and the psychiatrists, who spoke little English, sent him to Elliot.

Blankenship had joined the Army after his first burglary but had never served east of the Rhine. After a few months in Wiesbaden, he had been discharged for reasons of unsuitability, but he told everyone he was a veteran of the Vietnam War. He went about in a tiger suit. Elliot had had enough of him.

"Dreams are boring," Elliot told him.

Blankenship was outraged. "Whaddaya mean?" he demanded.

During counseling sessions Elliot usually moved his chair into the middle of the room in order to seem accessible to his clients. Now he stayed securely behind his desk. He did not care to seem accessible to Blankenship. "What I said, Mr. Blankenship. Other people's dreams are boring. Didn't you ever hear that?"

"Boring?" Blankenship frowned. He seemed unable to imagine a meaning for the word.

Elliot picked up a pencil and set its point quivering on his desk-top blotter. He gazed into his client's slack-jawed face. The Blankenship family made their way through life as strolling litigants, and young Blankenship's specialty was slipping on ice cubes. Hauled off the pavement, he would hassle the doctors in Emergency for pain pills and hurry to a law clinic. The Blankenships had threatened suit against half the property owners in the southern part of the state. What they could not extort at law they stole. But even the Blankenship family had abandoned Blankenship. His last visit to the hospital had been subsequent to an arrest for lifting a case of hot-dog rolls from Woolworth's. He lived in a Goodwill depository bin in Wyndham.

"Now I suppose you want to tell me your dream? Is that right, Mr. Blankenship?"

Blankenship looked left and right like a dog surrendering eye contact. "Don't you want to hear it?" he asked humbly.

Elliot was unmoved. "Tell me something, Blankenship. Was your dream about Vietnam?"

At the mention of the word "Vietnam," Blankenship customarily broke into a broad smile. Now he looked guilty and guarded. He shrugged. "Ya."

"How come you have dreams about that place, Blankenship? You were never there."

"Whaddaya mean?" Blankenship began to say, but Elliot cut him off.

"You were never there, my man. You never saw the goddamn place. You have no business dreaming about it! You better cut it out!"

He had raised his voice to the extent that the secretary outside his open door paused at her word processor.

"Lemme alone," Blankenship said fearfully. "Some doctor you are."

"It's all right," Elliot assured him. "I'm not a doctor."

"Everybody's on my case," Blankenship said. His moods were volatile. He began to weep.

Elliot watched the tears roll down Blankenship's chapped, pitted cheeks. He cleared his throat. "Look, fella . . ." he began. He felt at a loss. He felt like telling Blankenship that things were tough all over.

Blankenship sniffed and telescoped his neck and after a moment looked at Elliot. His look was disconcertingly trustful; he was used to being counseled.

"Really, you know, it's ridiculous for you to tell me your problems have to do with Nam. You were never over there. It was me over there, Blankenship. Not you."

Blankenship leaned forward and put his forehead on his knees.

"Your troubles have to do with here and now," Elliot told his client. "Fantasies aren't helpful."

His voice sounded overripe and hypocritical in his own ears. What a dreadful business, he thought. What an awful job this is. Anger was driving him crazy.

Blankenship straightened up and spoke through his tears. "This dream . . ." he said. "I'm scared."

Elliot felt ready to endure a great deal in order not to hear Blankenship's dream.

"I'm not the one you see about that," he said. In the end he knew his duty. He sighed. "O.K. All right. Tell me about it."

"Yeah?" Blankenship asked with leaden sarcasm. "Yeah? You think dreams are friggin' boring!"

"No, no," Elliot said. He offered Blankenship a tissue and Blankenship took one. "That was sort of off the top of my head. I didn't really mean it."

Blankenship fixed his eyes on dreaming distance. "There's a feeling that goes with it. With the dream." Then he shook his head in revulsion and looked at Elliot as though he had only just awakened. "So what do you think? You think it's boring?"

"Of course not," Elliot said. "A physical feeling?"

"Ya. It's like I'm floating in rubber."

He watched Elliot stealthily, aware of quickened attention. Elliot had caught dengue in Vietnam and during his weeks of delirium had felt vaguely as though he were floating in rubber.

"What are you seeing in this dream?"

Blankenship only shook his head. Elliot suffered a brief but intense attack of rage.

"Hey, Blankenship," he said equably, "here I am, man. You can see I'm listening."

"What I saw was black," Blankenship said. He spoke in an odd tremolo. His behavior was quite different from anything Elliot had come to expect from him.

"Black? What was it?"

"Smoke. The sky maybe."

"The sky?" Elliot asked.

"It was all black. I was scared."

In a waking dream of his own, Elliot felt the muscles on his neck distend. He was looking up at the sky that was black, filled with smoke-swollen clouds, lit with fires, damped with blood and rain.

"What were you sacred of?" he asked Blankenship.

"I don't know," Blankenship said.

Elliot could not drive the black sky from his inward eye. It was as though Blankenship's dream had infected his own mind.

"You don't know? You don't know what you were scared of?"

Blankenship's posture was rigid. Elliot, who knew the aspect of true fear, recognized it there in front of him.

"The Nam," Blankenship said.

"You're not even old enough," Elliot told him.

Blankenship sat trembling with joined palms between his thighs. His face was flushed and not in the least ennobled by pain. He had trouble with alcohol and drugs. He had trouble with everything.

"So wherever your black sky is, it isn't Vietnam."

Things were so unfair, Elliot thought. It was unfair of Blankenship to appropriate the condition of a Vietnam veteran. The trauma inducing his post-traumatic stress had been nothing more serious than his own birth, a routine procedure. Now, in addition to the poverty, anxiety, and confusion that would always be his life's lot, he had been visited with irony. It was all arbitrary and some people simply got elected. Everyone knew that who had been where Blankenship had not.

"Because, I assure you, Mr. Blankenship, you were never there."

"Whaddaya mean?" Blankenship asked.

When Blankenship was gone Elliot leafed through his file and saw that the psychiatrists had passed him upstairs without recording a diagnosis. Disproportionately angry, he went out to the secretary's desk.

"Nobody wrote up that last patient," he said. "I'm not supposed to see people without a diagnosis. The shrinks are just passing the buck."

The secretary was a tall, solemn redhead with prominent front teeth and a slight speech disorder. "Dr. Sayyid will have kittens if he hears you call him a shrink, Chas. He's already complained. He hates being called a shrink."

"Then he came to the wrong country," Elliot said. "He can go back to his own."

The woman giggled. "He *is* the doctor, Chas."

"Hates being called a shrink!" He threw the file on the secretary's table and stormed back toward his office. "That fucking little zip couldn't give you a decent haircut. He's a prescription clerk."

The secretary looked about her guiltily and shook her head. She was used to him.

Elliot succeeded in calming himself down after a while, but the image of the black sky remained with him. At first he thought he would be able to simply shrug the whole thing off. After a few minutes, he picked up his phone and dialed Blankenship's probation officer.

"The Vietnam thing is all he has," the probation officer explained. "I guess he picked it up around."

"His descriptions are vivid," Elliot said.

"You mean they sound authentic?"

"I mean he had me going today. He was ringing my bells."

"Good for Blanky. Think he believes it himself?"

"Yes," Elliot said. "He believes it himself now."

Elliot told the probation officer about Blankenship's current arrest, which was for showering illegally at midnight in the Wyndham Regional High School. He asked what probation knew about Blankenship's present relationship with his family.

"You kiddin'?" the P.O. asked. "They're all locked down. The whole family's inside. The old man's in Bridgewater. Little Donny's in San Quentin or somewhere. Their dog's in the pound."

Elliot had lunch alone in the hospital staff cafeteria. On the far side of the double-glazed windows, the day was darkening as an expected snowstorm gathered. Along Route 7, ancient elms stood frozen against the gray sky. When he had finished his sandwich and coffee, he sat staring out at the winter afternoon. His anger had given way to an insistent anxiety.

On the way back to his office, he stopped at the hospital gift shop for a copy of *Sports Illustrated* and a candy bar. When he was inside again, he closed the door and put his feet up. It was Friday and he had no appointments for the remainder of the day, nothing to do but write a few letters and read the office mail.

Elliot's cubicle in the social services department was windowless and lined with bookshelves. When he found himself unable to concentrate on the magazine and without any heart for his paperwork, he ran his eye over the row of books beside his chair. There were volumes of Heinrich Muller and Carlos Casteneda, Jones's life of Freud, and *The Golden Bough*. The books aroused a revulsion in Elliot. Their present uselessness repelled him.

Over and over again, detail by detail, he tried to recall his conversation with Blankenship.

"You were never there," he heard himself explaining. He was trying to get the whole incident straightened out after the fact. Something was wrong. Dread crept over him like a paralysis. He ate his candy bar without tasting it. He knew that the craving for sweets was itself a bad sign.

Blankenship had misappropriated someone else's dream and made it his own. It made no difference whether you had been there, after all. The dreams had crossed the ocean. They were in the air.

He took his glasses off and put them on his desk and sat with his arms folded, looking into the well of light from his desk lamp. There seemed to be nothing but whirl inside him. Unwelcome things came and went in his mind's eye. His heart beat faster. He could not control the headlong promiscuity of his thoughts.

It was possible to imagine larval dreams traveling in suspended animation undetectable in a host brain. They could be divided and regenerate like flatworms, hide in seams and bedding, in war stories, laughter, snapshots. They could rot your socks and turn your memory into a black-and-green blister. Green for the hills, black for the sky above. At daybreak they hung themselves up in rows like bats. At dusk they went out to look for dreamers.

Elliot put his jacket on and went into the outer office, where his secretary sat frowning into the measured sound and light of her machine. She must enjoy its sleekness and order, he thought. She was divorced. Four red-headed kids between ten and seventeen lived with her in an unpainted house across from Stop & Shop. Elliot liked her and had come to find her attractive. He managed a smile for her.

"Ethel, I think I'm going to pack it in," he declared. It seemed awkward to be leaving early without a reason.

"Jack wants to talk to you before you go, Chas."

Elliot looked at her blankly.

Then his colleague, Jack Sprague, having heard his voice, called from the adjoining cubicle. "Chas, what about Sunday's games? Shall I call you with the spread?"

"I don't know," Elliott said. "I'll phone you tomorrow."

"This is a big decision for him," Jack Sprague told the secretary. "He might lose twenty-five bucks."

At present, Elliot drew a slightly higher salary than Jack Sprague, although Jack had a Ph.D. and Elliot was simply an M.S.W. Different branches of the state government employed them.

"Twenty-five bucks," said the woman. "If you guys have no better use for twenty-five bucks, give it to me."

"Where are you off to, by the way?" Sprague asked.

Elliot began to answer, but for a moment no reply occurred to him. He shrugged. "I have to get back," he finally stammered. "I promised Grace."

"Was that Blankenship I saw leaving?"

Elliot nodded.

"It's February," Jack said. "How come he's not in Florida?"

"I don't know," Elliot said. He put on his coat and walked to the door. "I'll see you."

"Have a nice weekend," the secretary said. She and Sprague looked after him indulgently as he walked toward the main corridor.

"Are Chas and Grace going out on the town?" she said to Sprague. "What do you think?"

"That would be the day," Sprague said. "Tomorrow he'll come back over here and read all day. He spends every weekend holed up in this goddamn office while she does something or other at the church." He shook his head. "Every night he's at A.A. and she's home alone."

Ethel savored her overbite. "Jack," she said teasingly, "are you thinking what I think you're thinking? Shame on you."

"I'm thinking I'm glad I'm not him, that's what I'm thinking. That's as much as I'll say."

"Yeah, well, I don't care," Ethel said. "Two salaries and no kids, that's the way to go, boy."

Elliot went out through the automatic doors of the emergency bay and the cold closed over him. He walked across the hospital parking lot with his eyes on the pavement, his hands thrust deep in his overcoat pockets, skirting patches of shattered ice. There was no wind, but the motionless air stung; the metal frames of his glasses burned his skin. Curlicues of mud-brown ice coated the soiled snowbanks along the street. Although it was still afternoon, the street lights had come on.

The lock on his car door had frozen and he had to breathe on the keyhole to fit the key. When the engine turned over, Jussi Björling's recording of the Handel Largo filled the car interior. He snapped it off at once.

Halted at the first stoplight, he began to feel the want of a destination. The fear and impulse to flight that had got him out of the office faded, and he had no desire to go home. He was troubled by a peculiar impatience that might have been with time itself. It was as though he were waiting for something. The sensation made him feel anxious; it was unfamiliar but not altogether unpleasant. When the light changed he drove on, past the Gulf station and the firehouse and between the greens of Ilford Common. At the far end of the common he swung into the parking lot of the Packard Conway Library and stopped with the engine running. What he was experiencing, he thought, was the principle of possibility.

He turned off the engine and went out again into the cold. Behind the leaded library windows he could see the librarian pouring coffee in her tiny private office. The librarian was a Quaker of socialist principles named Candace Music, who was Elliot's cousin.

The Conway Library was all dark wood and etched mirrors, a Gothic saloon. Years before, out of work and booze-whipped, Elliot had gone to hide there. Because Candace was a classicist's widow and knew some Greek, she was one of the few people in the valley with whom Elliot had cared to speak in those days. Eventually, it had seemed to him that all their conversations tended toward Vietnam, so he had gone less and less often. Elliot was the only Vietnam veteran Candace knew well enough to chat with, and he had come to suspect that he was being probed for the edification of the East Ilford Friends Meeting. At that time he had still pretended to talk easily about his war and had prepared little discourses and picaresque anecdotes to recite on demand. Earnest seekers like Candace had caused him great secret distress.

Candace came out of her office to find him at the checkout desk. He watched her brow furrow with concern as she composed a smile. "Chas, what a surprise. You haven't been in for an age."

"Sure I have, Candace. I went to all the Wednesday films last fall. I work just across the road."

"I know, dear," Candace said. "I always seem to miss you."

A cozy fire burned in the hearth, an antique brass clock ticked along the marble mantel above it. On a couch near the fireplace an old man sat upright, his mouth open, asleep among half a dozen soiled plastic bags. Two teenage girls whispered over their homework at a table under the largest window.

"Now that I'm here," he said, laughing, "I can't remember what I came to get."

"Stay and get warm," Candace told him. "Got a minute? Have a cup of coffee."

Elliot had nothing but time, but he quickly realized that he did not want to stay and pass it with Candace. He had no clear idea of why he had come to the library. Standing at the checkout desk, he accepted coffee. She attended him with an air of benign supervision, as though he were a Chinese peasant and she a medical missionary, like her

father. Candace was tall and plain, more handsome in her middle sixties that she had ever been.

"Why don't we sit down?"

He allowed her to gentle him into a chair by the fire. They made
a threesome with the sleeping old man.

"Have you given up translating, Chas? I hope not."

"Not at all," he said. Together they had once rendered a few fragments of Sophocles into verse. She was good at clever rhymes.

"You come in so rarely, Chas. Ted's books go to waste."

After her husband's death, Candace had donated his books to the
Conway, where they reposed in a reading room inscribed to his memory, untouched among foreign-language volumes, local genealogies,
and books in large type for the elderly.

"I have a study in the barn," he told Candace. "I work there.
When I have time." The lie was absurd, but he felt the need of it.

"And you're working with Vietnam veterans," Candace declared.

"Supposedly," Elliot said. He was growing impatient with her
nodding solicitude.

"Actually," he said, "I came in for the new Oxford *Classical
World*. I thought you'd get it for the library and I could have a look
before I spent my hard-earned cash."

Candace beamed. "You've come to the right place, Chas, I'm
happy to say." He thought she looked disproportionately happy. "I
have it."

"Good," Elliot said, standing. "I'll just take it, then. I can't really
stay."

Candace took his cup and saucer and stood as he did. When the
library telephone rang, she ignored it, reluctant to let him go. "How's
Grace?" she asked.

"Fine," Elliot said. "Grace is well."

At the third ring she went to the desk. When her back was turned,
he hesitated for a moment and then went outside.

The gray afternoon had softened into night, and it was snowing.
The falling snow whirled like a furious mist in the headlight beams on
Route 7 and settled implacably on Elliot's cheeks and eyelids. His
heart, for no good reason, leaped up in childlike expectation. He had
run away from a dream and encountered possibility. He felt in possession of a promise. He began to walk toward the roadside lights.

Only gradually did he begin to understand what had brought him there and what the happy anticipation was that fluttered in his breast. Drinking, he had started his evening from the Conway Library. He would arrive hung over in the early afternoon to browse and read. When the old pain rolled in with dusk, he would walk down to the Midway Tavern for a remedy. Standing in the snow outside the library, he realized that he had contrived to promise himself a drink.

Ahead, through the storm, he could see the beer signs in the Midway's window warm and welcoming. Snowflakes spun around his head like an excitement.

Outside the Midway's package store, he paused with his hand on the doorknob. There was an old man behind the counter whom Elliot remembered from his drinking days. When he was inside, he realized that the old man neither knew nor cared who he was. The package store was thick with dust; it was on the counter, the shelves, the bottles themselves. The old counterman looked dusty. Elliot bought a bottle of King William Scotch and put it in the inside pocket of his overcoat.

Passing the windows of the Midway Tavern, Elliot could see the ranks of bottles aglow behind the bar. The place was crowded with men leaving the afternoon shifts at the shoe and felt factories. No one turned to note him when he passed inside. There was a single stool vacant at the bar and he took it. His heart beat faster. Bruce Springsteen was on the jukebox.

The bartender was a club fighter from Pittsfield called Jackie G., with whom Elliot had often gossiped. Jackie G. greeted him as though he had been in the previous evening. "Say, babe?"

"How do," Elliot said.

A couple of men at the bar eyed his shirt and tie. Confronted with the bartender, he felt impelled to explain his presence. "Just thought I'd stop by," he told Jackie G. "Just thought I'd have one. Saw the light. The snow . . ." He chuckled expansively.

"Good move," the bartender said. "Scotch?"

"Double," Elliot said.

When he shoved two dollars forward along the bar, Jackie G. pushed one of the bills back to him. "Happy hour, babe."

"Ah," Elliot said. He watched Jackie pour the double. "Not a moment too soon."

For five minutes or so, Elliot sat in his car in the barn with the engine running and his Handel tape on full volume. He had driven over from East Ilford in a baroque ecstasy, swinging and swaying and singing along. When the tape ended, he turned off the engine and poured some Scotch into an apple juice container to store providentially beneath the car seat. Then he took the tape and the Scotch into the house with him. He was lying on the sofa in the dark living room, listening to the Largo, when he heard his wife's car in the driveway. By the time Grace had made her way up the icy back-porch steps, he was able to hide the Scotch and rinse his glass clean in the kitchen sink. The drinking life, he thought, was lived moment by moment.

Soon she was in the tiny cloakroom struggling off with her overcoat. In the process she knocked over a cross-country ski, which stood propped against the cloakroom wall. It had been more than a year since Elliot had used the skis.

She came into the kitchen and sat down at the table to take off her boots. Her lean, freckled face was flushed with the cold, but her eyes looked weary. "I wish you'd put those skis down in the barn," she told him. "You never use them."

"I always like to think," Elliott said, "that I'll start the morning off skiing."

"Well, you never do," she said. "How long have you been home?"

"Practically just walked in," he said. Her pointing out that he no longer skied in the morning enraged him. "I stopped at the Conway Library to get the new Oxford *Classical World*. Candace ordered it."

Her look grew troubled. She had caught something in his voice. With dread and bitter satisfaction, Elliot watched his wife detect the smell of whiskey.

"Oh God," she said. "I don't believe it."

Let's get it over with, he thought. Let's have the song and dance.

She sat up straight in her chair and looked at him in fear.

"Oh, Chas," she said, "how could you?"

For a moment he was tempted to try to explain it all.

"The fact is," Elliot told his wife, "I hate people who start the day cross-country skiing."

She shook her head in denial and leaned her forehead on her palm and cried.

He looked into the kitchen window and saw his own distorted image. "The fact is I think I'll start tomorrow morning by stringing head-high razor wire across Anderson's trail."

The Andersons were the Elliots' nearest neighbors. Loyall Anderson was a full professor of government at the state university, thirty miles away. Anderson and his wife were blond and both of them were over six feet tall. They had two blond children, who qualified for the gifted class in the local school but attended regular classes in token of the Andersons' opposition to elitism.

"Sure," Elliot said. "Stringing wire's good exercise. It's life affirming in its own way."

The Andersons started each and every day with a brisk morning glide along a trail that they partly maintained. They skied well and presented a pleasing, wholesome sight. If, in the course of their adventure, they encountered a snowmobile, Darlene Anderson would affect to choke and cough, indicating her displeasure. If the snowmobile approached them from behind and the trail was narrow, the Andersons would decline to let it pass, asserting their statutory right-of-way.

"I don't want to hear your violent fantasies," Grace said.

Elliot was picturing razor wire, the Army kind. He was picturing the decapitated Andersons, their blood and jaunty ski caps bright on the white trail. He was picturing their severed heads, their earnest blue eyes and large white teeth reflecting the virginal morning snow. Although Elliot hated snowmobiles, he hated the Andersons far more.

He looked at his wife and saw that she had stopped crying. Her long, elegant face was rigid and lipless.

"Know what I mean? One string at Mommy and Daddy level for Loyall and Darlene. And a bitty wee string at kiddie level for Skippy and Samantha, those cunning little whizzes."

"Stop it," she said to him.

"Sorry," Elliot told her.

Stiff with shame, he went and took his bottle out of the cabinet into which he had thrust it and poured a drink. He was aware of her eyes on him. As he drank, a fragment from old Music's translation of *Medea* came into his mind. "Old friend, I have to weep. The gods and I went mad together and made things as they are." It was such a waste; eighteen months of struggle thrown away. But there was no way to get the stuff back in the bottle.

"I'm very sorry," he said. "You know I'm very sorry, don't you, Grace?"

The delectable Handel arias spun on in the next room.

"You must stop," she said. "You must make yourself stop before it takes over."

"It's out of my hands," Elliot said. He showed her his empty hands. "It's beyond me."

"You'll lose your job, Chas." She stood up at the table and leaned on it, staring wide-eyed at him. Drunk as he was, the panic in her voice frightened him. "You'll end up in jail again."

"One engages," Elliot said, "and then one sees."

"How can you have done it?" she demanded. "You promised me."

"First the promises," Elliot said, "and then the rest."

"Last time was supposed to be the last time," she said.

"Yes," he said, "I remember."

"I can't stand it," she said. "You reduce me to hysterics." She wrung her hands for him to see. "See? Here I am, I'm in hysterics."

"What can I say?" Elliot asked. He went to the bottle and refilled his glass. "Maybe you shouldn't watch."

"You want me to be forbearing, Chas? I'm not going to be."

"The last thing I want," Elliot said, "is an argument."

"I'll give you a fucking argument. You didn't have to drink. All you had to do was come home."

"That must have been the problem," he said.

Then he ducked, alert at the last possible second to the missile that came for him at hairline level. Covering up, he heard the shattering of glass, and a fine rain of crystals enveloped him. She had sailed the sugar bowl at him; it had smashed against the wall above his head and there was sugar and glass in his hair.

"You bastard!" she screamed. "You are undermining me!"

"You ought not to throw things at me," Elliot said. "I don't throw things at you."

He left her frozen in her follow-through and went into the living room to turn the music off. When he returned she was leaning back against the wall, rubbing her right elbow with her left hand. Her eyes were bright. She had picked up one of her boots from the middle of the kitchen floor and stood holding it.

"What the hell do you mean, that must have been the problem?"

He set his glass on the edge of the sink with an unsteady hand and turned to her. "What do I mean? I mean that most of the time I'm putting one foot in front of the other like a good soldier and I'm out of it from the neck up. But there are times when I don't think I will ever be dead enough—or dead long enough—to get the taste of this life off my teeth. That's what I mean!"

She looked at him dry-eyed. "Poor fella," she said.

"What you have to understand, Grace, is that this drink I'm having"—he raised the glass toward her in a gesture of salute—"is the only worthwhile thing I've done in the last year and a half. It's the only thing in my life that means jack shit, the closest thing to satisfaction I've had. Now how can you begrudge me that? It's the best I'm capable of."

"You'll go too far," she said to him. "You'll see."

"What's that, Grace? A threat to walk?" He was grinding his teeth. "Don't make me laugh. You, walk? You, the friend of the unfortunate?"

"Don't you hit me," she said when she looked at his face. "Don't you dare."

"You, the Christian Queen of Calvary, walk? Why, I don't believe that for a minute."

She ran a hand through her hair and bit her lip. "No, we stay," she said. Anger and distraction made her look young. Her cheeks blazed rosy against the general pallor of her skin. "In my family we stay until the fella dies. That's the tradition. We stay and pour it for them and they die."

He put his drink down and shook his head.

"I thought we'd come through," Grace said. "I was sure."

"No," Elliot said. "Not altogether."

They stood in silence for a minute. Elliot sat down at the oilcloth-covered table. Grace walked around it and poured herself a whiskey.

"You are undermining me, Chas. You are making things impossible for me and I just don't know." She drank and winced. "I'm not going to stay through another drunk. I'm telling you right now. I haven't got it in me. I'll die."

He did not want to look at her. He watched the flakes settle against the glass of the kitchen door. "Do what you feel the need of," he said.

"I just can't take it," she said. Her voice was not scolding but measured and reasonable. "It's February. And I went to court this morning and lost Vopotik."

Once again, he thought, my troubles are going to be obviated by those of the deserving poor. He said, "Which one was that?"

"Don't you remember them? The three-year-old with the broken fingers?"

He shrugged. Grace sipped her whiskey.

"I told you. I said I had a three-year-old with broken fingers, and you said, 'Maybe he owed somebody money.'"

"Yes," he said, "I remember now."

"You ought to see the Vopotiks, Chas. The woman is young and obese. She's so young that for a while I thought I could get to her as a juvenile. The guy is a biker. They believe the kid came from another planet to control their lives. They believe this literally, both of them."

"You shouldn't get involved that way," Elliot said. "You should leave it to the caseworkers."

"They scared their first caseworker all the way to California. They were following me to work."

"You didn't tell me."

"Are you kidding?" she asked. "Of course I didn't." To Elliot's surprise, his wife poured herself a second whiskey. "You know how they address the child? As 'dude.' She says to it, 'Hey, dude.'" Grace shuddered with loathing. "You can't imagine! The woman munching Twinkies. The kid smelling of shit. They're high morning, noon, and night, but you can't get anybody for that these days."

"People must really hate it," Elliot said, "when somebody tells them they're not treating their kids right."

"They definitely don't want to hear it," Grace said. "You're right." She sat stirring her drink, frowning into the glass. "The Vopotik child will die, I think."

"Surely not," Elliot said.

"This one I think will die," Grace said. She took a deep breath and puffed out her cheeks and looked at him forlornly. "The situation's extreme. Of course, sometimes you wonder whether it makes any difference. That's the big question, isn't it?"

"I would think," Elliot said, "that would be the one question you didn't ask."

"But you do," she said. "You wonder: Ought they to live at all? To continue the cycle?" She put a hand to her hair and shook her head as if in confusion. "Some of these folks, my God, the poor things cannot put Wednesday on top of Tuesday to save their lives."

"It's a trick," Elliot agreed, "a lot of them can't manage."

"And kids are small, they're handy and underfoot. They make noise. They can't hurt you back."

"I suppose child abuse is something people can do together," Elliot said.

"Some kids are obnoxious. No question about it."

"I wouldn't know," Elliot said.

"Maybe you should stop complaining. Maybe you're better off. Maybe your kids are better off unborn."

"Better off or not," Elliot said, "it looks like they'll stay that way."

"I mean our kids, of course," Grace said. "I'm not blaming you, understand? It's just that here we are with you drunk again and me losing Vopotik, so I thought why not get into the big unaskable questions." She got up and folded her arms and began to pace up and down the kitchen. "Oh," she said when her eye fell upon the bottle, "that's good stuff, Chas. You won't mind if I have another? I'll leave you enough to get loaded on."

Elliot watched her pour. So much pain, he thought; such anger and confusion. He was tired of pain, anger, and confusion; they were what had got him in trouble that very morning.

The liquor seemed to be giving him a perverse lucidity when all he now required was oblivion. His rage, especially, was intact in its salting of alcohol. Its contours were palpable and bleeding at the borders. Booze was good for rage. Booze could keep it burning through the darkest night.

"What happened in court?" he asked his wife.

She was leaning on one arm against the wall, her long, strong body flexed at the hip. Holding her glass, she stared angrily toward the invisible fields outside. "I lost the child," she said.

Elliot thought that a peculiar way of putting it. He said nothing.

"The court convened in an atmosphere of high hilarity. It may be Hate Month around here but it was buddy-buddy over at Ilford Courthouse. The room was full of bikers and bikers' lawyers. A colorful crowd. There was a lot of bonding." She drank and shivered.

"They didn't think too well of me. They don't think too well of broads as lawyers. Neither does the judge. The judge has the common touch. He's one of the boys."

"Which judge?" Elliot asked.

"Buckley. A man of about sixty. Know him? Lots of veins on his nose?"

Elliot shrugged.

"I thought I had done my homework," Grace told him. "But suddenly I had nothing but paper. No witnesses. It was Margolis at Valley Hospital who spotted the radiator burns. He called us in the first place. Suddenly he's got to keep his reservation for a campsite in St. John. So Buckley threw his deposition out." She began to chew on a fingernail. "The caseworkers have vanished—one's in L.A., the other's in Nepal. I went in there and got run over. I lost the child."

"It happens all the time," Elliot said. "Doesn't it?"

"This one shouldn't have been lost, Chas. These people aren't simply confused. They're weird. They stink."

"You go messing into anybody's life," Elliot said, "that's what you'll find."

"If the child stays in that house," she said, "he's going to die."

"You did your best," he told his wife. "Forget it."

She pushed the bottle away. She was holding a water glass that was almost a third full of whiskey.

"That's what the commissioner said."

Elliot was thinking of how she must have looked in court to the cherry-faced judge and the bikers and their lawyers. Like the schoolteachers who had tormented their childhoods, earnest and tight-assed, humorless and self-righteous. It was not surprising that things had gone against her.

He walked over to the window and faced his reflection again. "Your optimism always surprises me."

"My optimism? Where I grew up our principal cultural expression was the funeral. Whatever keeps me going, it isn't optimism."

"No?" he asked. "What is it?"

"I forget," she said.

"Maybe it's your religious perspective. Your sense of the divine plan."

She signed in exasperation. "Look, I don't think I want to fight anymore. I'm sorry I threw the sugar at you. I'm not your keeper. Pick on someone your own size."

"Sometimes," Elliot said, "I try to imagine what it's like to believe that the sky is full of care and concern."

"You want to take everything from me, do you?" She stood leaning against the back of her chair. "That you can't take. It's the only part of my life you can't mess up."

He was thinking that if it had not been for her he might not have survived. There could be no forgiveness for that. "Your life? You've got all this piety strung out between Monadnock and Central America. And look at yourself. Look at your life."

"Yes," she said, "look at it."

"You should have been a nun. You don't know how to live."

"I know that," she said. "That's why I stopped doing counseling. Because I'd rather talk the law than life." She turned to him. "You got everything I had, Chas. What's left I absolutely require."

"I swear I would rather be a drunk," Elliot said, "than force myself to believe such trivial horseshit."

"Well, you're going to have to do it without a straight man," she said, "because this time I'm not going to be here for you. Believe it or not."

"I don't believe it," Elliot said. "Not my Grace."

"You're really good at this," she told him. "You make me feel ashamed of my own name."

"I love your name," he said.

The telephone rang. They let it ring three times, and then Elliot went over and answered it.

"Hey, who's that?" a good-humored voice on the phone demanded.

Elliot recited their phone number.

"Hey, I want to talk to your woman, man. Put her on."

"I'll give her a message," Elliot said.

"You put your woman on, man. Run and get her."

Elliot looked at the receiver. He shook his head. "Mr. Vopotik?"

"Never you fuckin' mind, man. I don't want to talk to you. I want to talk to the skinny bitch."

Elliot hung up.

"Is it him?" she asked.

"I guess so."

They waited for the phone to ring again and it shortly did.

"I'll talk to him," Grace said. But Elliot already had the phone.

"Who are you asshole?" the voice inquired. "What's your fuckin' name, man?"

"Elliot," Elliot said.

"Hey, don't hang up on me, Elliot. I won't put up with that. I told you go get that skinny bitch, man. You go do it."

There were sounds of festivity in the background on the other end of the line— a stereo and drunken voices.

"Hey," the voice declared. "Hey, don't keep me waiting, man."

"What do you want to say to her?" Elliot asked.

"That's none of your fucking business, fool. Do what I told you."

"My wife is resting," Elliot said. "I'm taking her calls."

He was answered by a shout of rage. He put the phone aside for a moment and finished his glass of whiskey. When he picked it up again the man on the line was screaming at him. "That bitch tried to break up my family, man! She almost got away with it. You know what kind of pain my wife went through?"

"What kind?" Elliot asked.

For a few seconds he heard only the noise of the party. "Hey, you're not drunk, are you fella?"

"Certainly not," Elliot insisted.

"You tell that skinny bitch she's gonna pay for what she did to my family, man. You tell her she can run but she can't hide. I don't care where you go—California, anywhere—I'll get to you."

"Now that I have you on the phone," Elliot said, "I'd like to ask you a couple of questions. Promise you won't get mad?"

"Stop it!" Grace said to him. She tried to wrench the phone from his grasp, but he clutched it to his chest.

"Do you keep a journal?" Elliot asked the man on the phone. "What's your hat size?"

"Maybe you think I can't get to you," the man said, "but I can get to you, man. I don't care who you are, I'll get to you. The brothers will get to you."

"Well, there's no need to go to California. You know where we live."

"For God's sake," Grace said.

"Fuckin' right," the man on the telephone said. "Fuckin' right I know."

"Come on over," Elliot said.

"How's that?" the man on the phone asked.

"I said come on over. We'll talk about space travel. Comets and stuff. We'll talk astral projection. The moons of Jupiter."

"You're making a mistake, fucker."

"Come on over," Elliot insisted. "Bring your fat wife and your beat-up kid. Don't be embarrassed if your head's a little small."

The telephone was full of music and shouting. Elliot held it away from his ear.

"Good work," Grace said to him when he had replaced the receiver.

"I hope he comes," Elliot said. "I'll pop him."

He went carefully down the cellar stairs, switched on the overhead light, and began searching among the spiderwebbed shadows and fouled fishing line for his shotgun. It took him fifteen minutes to find it and his cleaning case. While he was still downstairs, he heard the telephone ring again and his wife answer it. He came upstairs and spread his shooting gear across the kitchen table. "Was that him?"

She nodded wearily. "He called back to play us the chain saw."

"I've heard that melody before," Elliot said.

He assembled his cleaning rod and swabbed out the shotgun barrel. Grace watched him, a hand to her forehead. "God," she said. "What have I done? I'm so drunk."

"Most of the time," Elliot said, sighting down the barrel, "I'm helpless in the face of human misery. Tonight I'm ready to reach out."

"I'm finished," Grace said. "I'm through, Chas. I mean it."

Elliot rammed three red shells into the shotgun and pumped one forward into the breech with a satisfying report. "Me, I'm ready for some radical problem solving. I'm going to spray that no-neck Slovak all over the yard."

"He isn't a Slovak," Grace said. She stood in the middle of the kitchen with her eyes closed. Her face was chalk white.

"What do you mean?" Elliot demanded. "Certainly he's a Slovak."

"No he's not," Grace said.

"Fuck him anyway. I don't care what he is. I'll grease his ass."

He took a handful of deer shells from the box and stuffed them in his jacket pockets.

"I'm not going to stay with you. Chas. Do you understand me?"

Elliot walked to the window and peered out at his driveway. "He won't be alone. They travel in packs."

"For God's sake!" Grace cried, and in the next instant bolted for the downstairs bathroom. Elliot went out, turned off the porch light and switched on a spotlight over the barn door. Back inside, he could hear Grace in the toilet being sick. He turned off the light in the kitchen.

He was still standing by the window when she came up behind him. It seemed strange and fateful to be standing in the dark near her, holding the shotgun. He felt ready for anything.

"I can't leave you alone down here drunk with a loaded shotgun," she said. "How can I?"

"Go upstairs," he said.

"If I went upstairs it would mean I didn't care what happened. Do you understand? If I go it means I don't care anymore. Understand?"

"Stop asking me if I understand," Elliot said. "I understand fine."

"I can't think," she said in a sick voice. "Maybe I don't care. I don't know. I'm going upstairs."

"Good," Elliot said.

When she was upstairs, Elliot took his shotgun and the whiskey into the dark living room and sat down in an armchair beside one of the lace-curtained windows. The powerful barn light illuminated the length of his driveway and the whole of the back yard. From the window at which he sat, he commanded a view of several miles in the direction of East Ilford. The two-lane blacktop road that ran there was the only one along which an enemy could pass.

He drank and watched the snow, toying with the safety of his 12-gauge Remington. He felt neither anxious nor angry now but only impatient to be done with whatever the night would bring. Drunkenness and the silent rhythm of the falling snow combined to make him feel outside of time and syntax.

Sitting in the dark room, he found himself confronting Blankenship's dream. He saw the bunkers and wire of some long-lost perimeter.

The rank smell of night came back to him, the dread evening and quick dusk, the mysteries of outer darkness: fear, combat, and death. Enervated by liquor, he began to cry. Elliot was sympathetic with other people's tears but ashamed of his own. He thought of his own tears as childish and excremental. He stifled whatever it was that had started them.

Now his whiskey tasted thin as water. Beyond the lightly frosted glass, illuminated snowflakes spun and settled sleepily on weighted pine boughs. He had found a life beyond the war after all, but in it he was still sitting in darkness, armed, enraged, waiting.

His eyes grew heavy as the snow came down. He felt as though he could be drawn up into the storm and he began to imagine that. He imagined his life with all its artifacts and appetites easing up the spout into white oblivion, everything obviated and foreclosed. He thought maybe he could go for that.

When he awakened, his left hand had gone numb against the trigger guard of his shotgun. The living room was full of pale, delicate light. He looked outside and saw that the storm was done with and the sky radiant and cloudless. The sun was still below the horizon.

Slowly Elliot got to his feet. The throbbing poison in his limbs served to remind him of the state of things. He finished the glass of whiskey on the windowsill beside his easy chair. Then he went to the hall closet to get a ski jacket, shouldered his shotgun, and went outside.

There were two cleared acres behind his house; beyond them a trail descended into a hollow of pine forest and frozen swamp. Across the hollow, white pastures stretched to the ridge line, lambent under the lightening sky. A line of skeletal elms weighted with snow marked the course of frozen Shawmut Brook.

He found a pair of ski goggles in a jacket pocket and put them on and set out toward the tree line, gripping the shotgun, step by careful step in the knee-deep snow. Two raucous crows wheeled high overhead, their cries exploding the morning's silence. When the sun came over the ridge, he stood where he was and took in a deep breath. The risen sun warmed his face and he closed his eyes. It was windless and very cold.

Only after he had stood there for a while did he realize how tired he had become. The weight of the gun taxed him. It seemed infinitely

wearying to contemplate another single step in the snow. He opened
his eyes and closed them again. With sunup the world had gone blazing blue and white, and even with his tinted goggles its whiteness
dazzled him and made his head ache. Behind his eyes, the hypnagogic
patterns formed a monsoon-heavy tropical sky. He yawned. More than
anything, he wanted to lie down in the soft, pure snow. If he could do
that, he was certain that he could go to sleep at once.

He stood in the middle of the field and listened to the crows. Fear,
anger, and sleep were the three primary conditions of life. He had
learned that over there. Once he had thought fear the worst, but he had
learned that the worst was anger. Nothing could fix it; neither alcohol
nor medicine. It was a worm. It left him no peace. Sleep was the best.

He opened his eyes and pushed on until he came to the brow that
overlooked the swamp. Just below, gliding along among the frozen
cattails and bare scrub maple, was a man on skis. Elliot stopped to
watch the man approach.

The skier's face was concealed by a red-and-blue ski mask. He
wore snow goggles, a blue jumpsuit, and a red woolen Norwegian hat.
As he came, he leaned into the turns of the trail, moving silently and
gracefully along. At the foot of the slope on which Elliot stood, the
man looked up, saw him, and slid to a halt. The man stood staring at
him for a moment and then began to herringbone up the slope. In no
time at all the skier stood no more than ten feet away, removing his
goggles, and inside the woolen mask Elliot recognized the clear blue
eyes of his neighbor, Professor Loyall Anderson. The shotgun Elliot
was carrying seemed to grow heavier. He yawned and shook his head,
trying unsuccessfully to clear it. The sight of Anderson's eyes gave him
a little thrill of revulsion.

"What are you after?" the young professor asked him, nodding
toward the shotgun Elliot was cradling.

"Whatever there is," Elliot said.

Anderson took a quick look at the distant pasture behind him and
then turned back to Elliot. The mouth hole of the professor's mask
filled with teeth. Elliot thought that Anderson's teeth were quite as he
had imagined them earlier. "Well, Polonski's cows are locked up," the
professor said. "So they at least are safe."

Elliot realized that the professor had made a joke and was smiling.
"Yes," he agreed.

Professor Anderson and his wife had been the moving force behind an initiative to outlaw the discharge of firearms within the boundaries of East Ilford Township. The initiative had been defeated, because East Ilford was not that kind of town.

"I think I'll go over by the river," Elliot said. He said it only to have something to say, to fill the silence before Anderson spoke again. He was afraid of what Anderson might say to him and of what might happen.

"You know," Anderson said, "that's all bird sanctuary over there now."

"Sure," Elliot agreed.

Outfitted as he was, the professor attracted Elliot's anger in an elemental manner. The mask made him appear a kind of doll, a kachina figure or a marionette. His eyes and mouth, all on their own, were disagreeable.

Elliot began to wonder if Anderson could smell the whiskey on his breath. He pushed the little red bull's-eye safety button on his gun to Off.

"Seriously," Anderson said, "I'm always having to run hunters out of there. Some people don't understand the word 'posted.'"

"I would never do that," Elliot said, "I would be afraid."

Anderson nodded his head. He seemed to be laughing. "Would you?" he asked Elliot merrily.

In imagination, Elliot rested the tip of his shotgun barrel against Anderson's smiling teeth. If he fired a load of deer shot into them, he thought, they might make a noise like broken china. "Yes," Elliot said. "I wouldn't know who they were or where they'd been. They might resent my being alive. Telling them where they could shoot and where not."

Anderson's teeth remained in place. "That's pretty strange," he said. "I mean, to talk about resenting someone for being alive."

"It's all relative," Elliot said. "They might think, 'Why should he be alive when some brother of mine isn't?' Or they might think, 'Why should he be alive when I'm not?'"

"Oh," Anderson said.

"You see?" Elliot said. Facing Anderson, he took a long step backward. "All relative."

"Yes," Anderson said.

"That's so often true, isn't it?" Elliot asked. "Values are often relative."

"Yes," Anderson said. Elliot was relieved to see that he had stopped smiling.

"I've hardly slept, you know," Elliot told Professor Anderson. "Hardly at all. All night. I've been drinking."

"Oh," Anderson said. He licked his lips in the mouth of the mask. "You should get some rest."

"You're right," Elliot said.

"Well," Anderson said, "got to go now."

Elliot thought he sounded a little thick in the tongue. A little slow in the jaw.

"It's a nice day," Elliot said, wanting now to be agreeable.

"It's great," Anderson said, shuffling on his skis.

"Have a nice day," Elliot said.

"Yes," Anderson said, and pushed off.

Elliot rested the shotgun across his shoulders and watched Anderson withdraw through the frozen swamp. It was in fact a nice day, but Elliot took no comfort in the weather. He missed night and the falling snow.

As he walked back toward his house, he realized that now there would be whole days to get through, running before the antic energy of whiskey. The whiskey would drive him until he dropped. He shook his head in regret. "It's a revolution," he said aloud. He imagined himself talking to his wife.

Getting drunk was an insurrection, a revolution—a bad one. There would be outsize bogus emotions. There would be petty moral blackmail and cheap remorse. He had said dreadful things to his wife. He had bullied Anderson with his violence and unhappiness, and Anderson would not forgive him. There would be damn little justice and no mercy.

Nearly to the house, he was startled by the desperate feathered drumming of a pheasant's rush. He froze, and out of instinct brought the gun up in the direction of the sound. When he saw the bird break from its cover and take wing, he tracked it, took a breath, and fired once. The bird was a little flash of opulent color against the bright-blue sky. Elliot felt himself flying for a moment. The shot missed.

Lowering the gun, he remembered the deer shells he had loaded.

A hit with the concentrated shot would have pulverized the bird, and he was glad he had missed. He wished no harm to any creature. Then he thought of himself wishing no harm to any creature and began to feel fond and sorry for himself. As soon as he grew aware of the emotion he was indulging, he suppressed it. Pissing and moaning, mourning and weeping, that was the nature of the drug.

The shot echoed from the distant hills. Smoke hung in the air. He turned and looked behind him and saw, far away across the pasture, the tiny blue-and-red figure of Professor Anderson motionless against the snow. Then Elliot turned again toward his house and took a few labored steps and looked up to see his wife at the bedroom window. She stood perfectly still, and the morning sun lit her nakedness. He stopped where he was. She had heard the shot and run to the window. What had she thought to see? Burnt rags and blood on the snow. How relieved was she now? How disappointed?

Elliot thought he could feel his wife trembling at the window. She was hugging herself. Her hands clasped her shoulders. Elliot took his snow goggles off and shaded his eyes with his hand. He stood in the field staring

The length of the gun was between them, he thought. Somehow she had got out in front of it, to the wrong side of the wire. If he looked long enough he would find everything out there. He would find himself down the sight.

How beautiful she is, he thought. The effect was striking. The window was so clear because he had washed it himself, with vinegar. At the best of times he was a difficult, fussy man.

Elliot began to hope for forgiveness. He leaned the shotgun on his forearm and raised his left hand and waved to her. Show a hand, he thought. Please just show a hand.

He was cold, but it had got light. He wanted no more than the gesture. It seemed to him that he could build another day on it. Another day was all you needed. He raised his hand higher and waited.

CLOTHING

John L'Heureux

Conor had been a Jesuit for sixteen years now, and an ordained priest for three of those years. He was a member of the long black line; he had faded into the woodwork; he was a minor cog in a vast machine. This is how he thought of himself, in images not his own but drawn from the rules of the Society of Jesus, from conversations in the rec room, from admonitions of Superiors. Life was bland, uneventful, with few successes and no dangers to speak of. The habit does finally make the man, he told himself.

There were sources of anxiety, to be sure, but not really dangers, not terrible temptations. A drink too many, perhaps, or imprudence in speech (telling sophomores in a high school English class that "Cardinal Spellman, quite simply, is a fascist"), or undue intimacy with the mother of one of his students (Mrs. Butler and that funny business at the pool). But nothing serious, nothing to worry about. Still, habit or no habit, there was something very wrong. Something—he searched for the word—hopeless.

And then, in the spring of his fourth year as a priest, he was officially transferred from the prep school where he taught in Connecticut to the retreat house in downtown Boston, the transfer to be effective in summer. Suddenly it all seemed impossible to him: the vow of obedience, the awful loneliness, the waste of his talent as a poet. He had published two books, and they had been well received by reviewers, but what was he doing—as a priest—writing poems at all? And why?

He went into a prolonged depression. He prayed. He drank too much. He flirted, deep in his subconscious, with the idea of suicide. Finally, while there was still a week to go before his transfer to Boston, it came to him that he did not have to die to get out, he just had to get out.

Conor went to his major superior, the Provincial, and said he wanted some time to consider his vocation, he had come to a point where he had to do this one thing, for himself. It was the 1960s and in the aftermath of Vatican II half his priest friends had already left, but Conor did not want to just leave. He wanted to make a decision at least as rational and prayerful as the decision he had made sixteen years earlier when he entered. Conor paused in his declamation and appraised the Provincial, who looked bored, and so he took a deep breath and said that while he was thinking through this problem, he did not want to work in, did not even want to live in, the retreat house.

"I see," the Provincial said. "How's your drinking?"

Conor thought about that for a while, rejected the idea of a smart aleck response, and said, "Well, the drinking will always be a problem . . . for any of us, I suppose, but I think I've got it under control. What I'm talking about, Father, isn't a crisis of booze, or even a crisis of faith. It's a crisis of hope. I don't hope anymore."

"Hope, schmope," the Provincial said. "Look. You're just one of over a thousand men we have to deal with, Conor. Things are changing. In the old days I'd have simply told you to go to the retreat house or get the hell out, but we can't do that anymore. Superiors have to *confer* with a subject now, we have to consult his *needs*, we have to *adapt*. So look, I'm short on time; I've conferred and I've consulted and I've adapted. What do you want?"

"Well, I thought . . ."

"Where are you going to live, first of all?"

"Well, I thought I'd stay right where I am."

"And do what?"

"Well, I thought I'd continue to write my poetry, and reviews. And give readings. I thought I'd . . . pray."

"And who's supporting you, please, while you're writing this poetry?"

"Well, I thought, the Jesuits. I've given sixteen years of my life, after all, and . . . well, I thought . . ."

"Well, you thought. Well, you thought. Think again, my friend, and when you do, be very clear on one thing." He leaned across the desk to make his point. "The Society of Jesus owes you . . . *nothing*. Got it? Nothing."

Conor felt hot, and dizzy. The Provincial seemed to come in very close to him, their faces almost touching, and then he pulled away, and his desk with him. Conor was isolated suddenly, lost, a small ridiculous figure in a world that in seconds had become distant from him. He saw himself as he was: self-absorbed, pretentious, absurd. As if, in this huge organization of brilliant and holy men, he could possibly matter: ridiculous. He had deceived himself with this self-important talk about hope. The room tipped away from him and he wanted to hide.

Then all at once, something inside him said no, and at that instant the room righted itself. Words came to him and Conor leaned forward to say, But I want my life. I have a right to my life. It's my only hope.

But instead, he heard himself saying in a strange voice, almost a child's voice, "Of course you're right, Father. I'll go to the retreat house. I'll try harder."

And in the long silence that followed, he said, "Hope isn't that important anyway."

A year later—after seventeen weekend retreats to laymen and laywomen, after thirty talks to high school students on sex and marriage, after five Cana conferences and many baptisms and innumerable confessions, after a brief love affair with a divorcée (Mrs. Butler, who left her husband and family and came to Boston to find herself; she found herself, eventually, in AA) and a long love affair with a former nun (Alix, whom he intended to marry as soon as he got his walking papers from the Jesuits)—a year later, Conor made formal application to leave the Jesuits and to be reduced to the lay state. He was assigned an interrogator, Fr. Casey, a man in his seventies with a perpetual cough and a bad cigarette habit.

"*Interrogator?*" Conor asked. "*Reduced* to the lay state?"

"Just technical terms, boy," Fr. Casey said. "Don't get jumpy now; they told me you're the jumpy type. Poetry."

Conor said nothing. He was doing this not for himself but for Alix, who had her own code of morality. She would have sex with him, she would even live with him, but she would not marry him except in the Catholic Church. Love is fine, she said, and so is sex, so long as there is love, but marriage outside the Church was unthinkable; it did violence to her integrity. And so he was doing this for her, submitting himself to a final humiliation so that they could be married as Catholics.

For over an hour Conor sat with his right hand on the little blue book that enshrined the Rules of the Society of Jesus, the blue book itself resting on a Douay version of the Holy Bible, while he answered questions about whether his parents had married from love or obligation, whether he was a wanted or unwanted baby, whether they had proposed the priesthood to him or he had come upon the idea himself. Conor answered and contradicted himself and then answered again. Fr. Casey dutifully wrote down everything he said.

Telling himself he had only to hang on and eventually this nightmare would be over, Conor concentrated on the priest's handwriting: perfect little letters of the same height and slant, perfectly controlled, perfectly legible. Perfection in the smallest of things. Would this never end? Finally Conor's patience gave out.

"Why are you writing down every word I say? This is going to take forever!"

Fr. Casey looked up, amused. He had all eternity ahead of him. "I have to," he said. "This is a legal document. It will be sent to Rome. You've been in the Jesuits for seventeen years; it doesn't seem to me very unreasonable to ask you to spend a few hours getting out."

"But who could answer these questions?" Conor said, exasperated. "This whole process is designed to prove that I never really had a vocation, that somehow I was forced into this. But you're not going to make me say that. I was *not* forced into the priesthood. I did *not* enter the Jesuits under any misconceptions. I *did* understand fully what I was doing."

There was a long silence in the room. Conor was about to apologize, but said instead: "I entered the priesthood of my own free will, and now it's because of my own free will that I want out. I want to be my own man. I want to make my own mistakes. I want to be free."

"Free," Fr. Casey said, the word loaded with meaning.

"To make my own mistakes," Conor said.

Another long silence. "We'll try again." Fr. Casey lit a new cigarette and said, "This is going to take hours, son, so I'd suggest you cool down. Now, as to the question of your vocation: to what do you

attribute it; to what exact person or event or moment? It's very important, so I want you to think. Are you thinking?"

Conor thought, and said nothing. It was as if the priest had not
heard a word he'd said.

An hour later Fr. Casey had moved on to other topics. How often
did Conor masturbate? Never. Very good, but when did you stop? I
never began. Never? Never at all? No, never. Why? What was the matter? A long pause, and then another cigarette, and more irritation on
Conor's part, but no explosion this time.

"And has there been any sexual congress with *others* during the
past years?"

"Yes," Conor said; a non-equivocal answer.

"Frequently?"

"Sometimes."

"Women? More than one?"

"Two."

"Men?"

"No men."

"Ah." Fr. Casey took out his handkerchief and mopped his brow.
Conor laughed, thinking the priest meant to be funny.

"Yes?" Fr. Casey was puzzled.

"No. I mean, we're nervous. Or at least I am."

"Now, about these women." He paused, significantly.

"The first was an affair. It was just sex. I broke it off after two
weeks. Confessed it, of course. The other is love; a love affair, if you
want; but it's permanent. We're going to marry as soon as my papers
come through."

"*If* they come through."

"*When* they come through."

"Be careful." Fr. Casey held his pen suspended for a moment in
the air.

"Father, I've been careful and I'm all done. I've given sixteen
years of honest service to God, and one year of very muddled service
that was meant to be for God but that ended up being for me, I guess,
because it's getting me out. And I don't particularly care what *you*
think of me or what *Rome* thinks of me, because it's myself I've got to
live with. And all I want from you is *out*. I'm done. Like it or not, I'm
free."

"You go too far." Fr. Casey's voice was suddenly the voice of God. "You go too far."

I'll do it for Alix, Conor told himself, and bowed his head as if he were sorry for his outburst.

"You are dealing with Mother Church, and she is a very indulgent Mother indeed. But even mothers can be pushed too far. Do you understand me?"

Later, hours later, when Conor was leaving Fr. Casey's room, he turned and said with a kind of innocent surprise: "I suddenly remembered. Your question about my vocation, about when exactly I knew I had one? It's just come back to me: I was a child, about five or six, and I had a terrible quarrel with my mother about something or other. It was shortly after that quarrel that I began thinking I'd be a priest; not because I wanted to, but because it just seemed inevitable."

"It doesn't matter now," Fr. Casey said. "I've finished taking notes."

Months went by and Conor moved from the retreat house into a studio apartment. At last a letter arrived asking that he come to the Provincial's office to sign and receive his decree of laicization. He signed and, with that signature, he was reduced to the lay state.

But when he moved from his studio into Alix's apartment just before the wedding, Conor discovered that—for some reason he could not explain—he still had in his possession his Jesuit habit: the cassock, the cincture, the Roman collar.

What was he to do with them? Obviously he couldn't keep them. Nor could he just throw them out.

The awful session with Fr. Casey came back to him, and then the scene in the Provincial's office where he had signed away his Jesuit allegiance, surrendered the practice of his priesthood. No, he did not want to see those men again. Anger, resentment, shame; none of these described what he felt, but he knew he could not face them again for a long long time.

"Betrayal," he said aloud, and though there was no connection in his mind between the word he said and the idea that came to him, he realized at once what he would do.

He folded the habit carefully and lay it on the bed. He folded the cincture in halves, and then in halves again, and then once more. He lay the white plastic collar on top of the habit and cincture.

He stared at the clothes for a moment and then, with purpose, he picked them up and draped them over his left arm.

He walked the five blocks to the retreat house and went in the door to the public chapel. Though it was early afternoon, the chapel was very dark, and it was a moment or two before Conor was certain that no one was there.

He knelt and said an Act of Contrition. Then he stood and placed the cassock carefully in the pew in front of him. He lay the cincture on the cassock, crossways, with the white plastic collar on top.

He turned to go, hesitated, and then quite deliberately turned back. He picked up the collar and, with no thought that it was sentimental or melodramatic to do so, he lifted it to his lips for the ritual kiss that custom and devotion had required of him for so many years.

He genuflected and walked out of the chapel, hopeful, free.

Conor sat in the rocking chair reading *Swiss Family Robinson* while his mother peeled carrots for the stew. They often spent Saturday mornings like this, Conor reading in the big rocker while his mother watered her plants or prepared meals or did the baking.

Conor was eight years old and there was nobody his age in this new neighborhood; his mother, trapped here by marriage and the Depression, missed her old chums in Springfield; and so they were friends, really; more like companions than mother and son.

But she was cross this morning, Conor could see, and she was not going to keep her promise.

"You should be outside, playing," she said.

"But what about the shoes?" Conor said, not looking up from his book. "We've got to go buy the shoes."

"I'm busy," she said, and tossed the last of the carrots into the pot.

Conor had been invited to Marianne Clair's birthday party that afternoon, and he had a present for her (one of his Thornton Burgess books; you couldn't tell it wasn't new), and so he was all set to go. Except for one thing. He had to have a new pair of shoes. He had only a single pair that he wore for school and for best, and somehow he must have scuffed the top of the toe on his right shoe because the leather had worn away and when he stood in front of the class to read, everybody could see his sock showing through.

Conor had not been able to tell his mother this, or tell her what happened yesterday in school when Miss Moriarty made him stop reading and insisted that Marianne share with the whole class whatever it was that she found so funny. He could never tell her this; he could never tell anyone. But last night he had prayed over and over that he would get the new shoes soon.

Two weeks ago his mother had said that maybe next Saturday they would take a bus downtown and buy him a new pair of shoes. A week later she had said the same thing again. But this morning she had already mentioned several times how busy she was, how many things she had to do. It would be only a while longer—he could tell—before she said he would just have to wait another week for the shoes.

She finished preparing the stew and in no time spread the kitchen table with newspaper, got out her bag of soil and her pots, and was busy transferring the first of the window plants from a small pot to a larger one.

Conor looked over at her without raising his head; this way he could watch without her knowing it. She rapped the plant out of its pot and held it upside down in her left hand while she scooped soil into the new pot with her right. Conor liked to watch her do this; she was quick and certain, juggling the plant and the pot, pressing down the new soil with her knuckles, making it all come out right. Everything she touched grew.

She looked up at him suddenly. "You should be outside, in the nice sun," she said. "It's too nice a day not to be outside."

"But when are we going to buy the shoes?" he asked, even though he had begun to suspect it was hopeless.

She said nothing.

"Mother? What about the shoes?"

"They'll have to wait," she said, her hands busier than ever with her potting.

"But you promised. You said."

She started on another plant, ignoring him.

"You promised. You never keep your promises."

"That's enough. Now stop, or you won't go to the party at all."

"What a cheater you are!"

"Conor!" she said, the last warning.

"You lied to me. You never intended to buy the shoes."

"That's it. That does it," she said. "You're spoiled and you're fresh and you're selfish, and you are not going to that party. Period."

"You just don't want to take me, that's all. You just don't want to buy me shoes."

"Go to your room! Now!"

"I hate you," Conor said, and headed—fast—for the door. "Besides, you're as homely as Mrs. Dressel."

It had popped into his head from nowhere. He had heard Mrs. Waters from next door say she thought Emily Dressel was the homeliest woman in town, and he had heard his mother repeat the comment to his father. He had heard them laugh and agree that it was probably true. His mother had said, "That poor woman; if I looked like that, I'd wear a hat with a veil."

So now he sat in his bedroom wondering why his mother had said nothing back to him. He had wanted to make her angry, to hurt her, badly, because she had ruined everything. Even if he said he was sorry and they were friends again, it wouldn't be the same. Even if she took him to get the shoes now, it wouldn't be the same. It was too late.

He would ignore her. He would be nice to her from now on, but never again the way he used to be. Well, that was what she deserved. She had earned her punishment.

He tried to go back to *Swiss Family Robinson* which, despite the speed of his escape from the kitchen, he had had the sense to take with him, but he couldn't concentrate on the words.

He wondered if she knew. Did she know that he was punishing her? And did she suspect that, in a way, he was relieved not to have to go to the party with all new kids?

She probably did. She probably knew, as he himself knew, that in a day or so, after he'd been punished for being fresh and after they'd gone without talking for a while, it would all be the same, and that next Saturday he would read some new book and she would bake cookies and all of this counted for nothing. He wanted to hurt her back, for good.

Instantly he realized how to do it.

He marched firmly out to the kitchen and stood beside her at the kitchen sink. She was holding one of the repotted plants near the faucet, getting it wet, but not too wet. She said nothing and so he waited. He would give her one more chance. But when she still remained silent, he said, "Do you want to know something? You really *are* as homely as Mrs. Dressel. And tomorrow or the next day when we're not mad at each other anymore, I'll tell you I didn't really mean it. I'll tell you I just said it to pay you back. But I do mean it, and—you know what—I'll mean it *then,* too, even when I say I don't. Because it's the truth."

His mother said nothing, but her face got hard-looking, and she shook. Suddenly the plant fell from her hands. The fresh soil spilled into the sink and the water from the faucet drilled hard on the plant until even the old soil fell away and the roots were exposed, but still she did nothing to save it. She only stared straight ahead.

Conor turned smartly and walked down the hall to his room. He shut the door behind him.

His face was hot and he felt dizzy, but not sick-dizzy. He was dizzy with a kind of power, a strange sense of who he was and what he could do. He looked around the room and everything seemed different. His bed was so small, and the chair too, and his bureau. Not exactly small, but distant; as if he had moved away from them, as if he had nothing to do with them anymore. Even his books looked different; they looked old, ancient; he knew everything that was in them. With one finger, with a single word from his mouth, he could dismiss them from existence. He was capable of anything now.

And at once he knew he must hide. But where? He went to his closet and climbed in among the slippers and boots and old toys, but that was not enough.

He took his bathrobe down from its hook and put it over his head. No. He was still not hidden.

He pulled down his shirts from the shelves, his pajamas, his underwear; in a frenzy he tore everything from the hangers, heaped the clothes in a mound on the closet floor. Still it was not enough.

He stripped himself then, adding his shirt and trousers to the pile on the floor, and, pulling the door tight behind him, crawled beneath the heavy pile of clothing and lay, for a time, hidden.

Hours later his mother found him there, still shaking with power and terror.

Alix was dying of metastatic liver cancer.

Hers was the typical case. While shaving beneath her arms one evening, she had noticed an odd little lump near the nipple of her left breast. The next morning she phoned her gynecologist, and almost before she had time to realize what was happening, she was recuperating from a radical mastectomy. At her third month checkup she seemed fine, but three months later a tumor appeared in her right breast and she had to undergo another mastectomy.

Two years passed, filled for Alix and Conor with a kind of desperate hope, and then the hoping was over. Alix developed a nagging cough, she began to lose weight, her fine white skin began to turn sallow. Even before the doctor examined her, he pronounced it cancer of the liver—final and fatal. Alix had been in the hospital for over a month now, with the promise of days to live, or hours. And still she had not complained.

Whenever he had a cold, Conor always said—by way of apology to her and acknowledgment to himself—that on his tombstone he wanted carved this simple inscription:

HE SUFFERED NO PAIN WITHOUT COMPLAINT.

What he could never understand, therefore, was how Alix could suffer so much and complain so little. Or rather, not at all.

He had sat by her bed each day, telling her about his classes (he taught English at Sacred Heart College), about her friends from school who had phoned to inquire how she was doing (she taught English at Sacred Heart Prep), about their German shepherd, Heidi. She had smiled, her hand resting lightly on his, and in her new voice—husky, strained, exhausted—she had done her best to cheer him up.

But now she slept all the time, or perhaps she was unconscious. Conor sat beside her bed, forcing himself to look at her emaciated hand or at the small mound her feet made beneath the covers, or at the reproduction of the Madonna della Strada on the wall opposite. Anywhere, but at her face.

Because the last time he had looked at her sleeping face, he had thought, Go. Please Go. I have never known you anyway. And he could not bear to think that again.

Conor had known her since that last terrible year in the priesthood, when he had prayed and drunk and made love to her and then gone to confession, promising he would end this affair, and he meant it, and then he would start all over again. How had she endured it? Endured him?

He shot a quick glance at her face. Her skin was smooth, taut to her skull, and with the advance of the disease the color had darkened from its natural white to a pale yellow and then to a deep tan; now it was a reddish brown, thin and hard to the touch. Her face was a deathmask made of copper.

This was not Alix.

He tried to summon some image of her, some proof that he had known her after all. He saw them walking on the beach with the dog; he saw them fighting, spitting out the angry words they would take back later; he saw them making love. But that was not it; that was not what he was looking for. He thought of her as she had been for the past two years, broken with cancer, and he remembered kissing the pink flesh where her breast used to be and looking up to see the single tear on her cheek. He thought of her in bed with him, her head twisting on the pillow, the sounds of her pleasure in his ear. But that was not the right image either. It was hopeless.

Then, just when he had given up, it came to him: the photo of Alix on the swing. She was five years old and she was wearing a birthday dress. She sat on the swing with both feet planted on the ground; her hands gripped the ropes solidly, easily; she looked straight into the camera. There was a smile on her face, a look of confidence, a sureness about everything in her world. Her eyes saw, and liked what they saw, and she was perfectly content. Hope was not even a question.

Conor fixed the picture firmly in his mind, smiled at the freshness, the inviolability of that child, and then he turned to look at Alix.

"The relentless compassion of God," he said aloud, and as if she had been waiting for him to say that, Alix opened her eyes and looked at him.

"Never," she said, and then something else which Conor could not make out.

He leaned over her to catch the words, and at once her eyes tipped upward in her head and she began to push away the sheets. "Help me," she said. "Oh help me with these." She sat up somehow and managed to kick the sheets free of her body. She clawed at the johnny tied loosely at her back; the string broke and she flung the thing on the floor. She was sitting up in the bed now, naked, staring, her eyes empty in her copper face. "Help me," she said once more. "I never loved."

"No," Conor said, taking her by the shoulders, turning her to look into his face. "No, that's not true," he said again, desperate this time. "You loved me. You always loved me."

She focused on Conor then and something came into her empty eyes, a kind of promise.

"And I loved you," he said, but already her eyes had begun to close. He lay her back on the bed, slowly, gently, and she seemed finally to be without life altogether. "No," Conor sobbed. "Oh, God, no. No." And then he thought he heard her echo him, "No. No."

He did not cover her dead body, but left it as it was, naked, decent. He stood by her bed and prayed, hoping against hope.

THE SKATER

Joy Williams

Annie and Tom and Molly are looking at boarding schools. Molly is the applicant, fourteen years old. Annie and Tom are the mom and dad. This is how they are referred to by the admissions directors. "Now if Mom and Dad would just make themselves comfortable while we steal Molly away for a moment . . ." Molly is stolen away and Tom and Annie drink coffee. There are brown donuts on a plate. Colored slides are slapped upon a screen showing children earnestly learning and growing and caring through the seasons. These things have been captured. Rather, it's clear that's what they're getting at. The children's faces blur in Tom's mind. And all those autumn leaves. All those laboratories and playing fields and bell towers.

It is winter and there is snow on the ground. They have flown in from California and rented a car. Their plan is to see seven New England boarding schools in five days. Icicles hang from the admissions building. Tom gazes at them. They are lovely and refractive. They are formed, and then they vanish. Tom looks away.

Annie is sitting on the other side of the room, puzzling over a mathematics problem. There are sheets of problems all over the waiting room. The sheets are to keep parents and kids on their toes as they wait. Annie's foot is bent fiercely beneath her as though broken. The cold, algebraic problems are presented in little stories. Five times as many girls as boys are taking music lessons or trees are growing at different rates or ladies in a bridge club are lying about their age. The characters and situations are invented only to be exiled to measurement. Watching Annie search for solutions makes Tom's heart ache. He remembered a class he took once himself, almost twenty years ago, a class in myth. In mythical stories, it seems, there are two ways to disaster. One of the ways was to answer an unanswerable question. The other was to fail to answer an answerable question.

Down a corridor there are several shut doors and behind one is Molly. Molly is their living child. Tom and Annie's other child, Martha, has been dead a year. Martha was one year older than Molly. Now Molly is her age. Martha choked to death in her room on a piece of bread. It was early in the morning and she was getting ready for school. The radio was playing and two disc jockeys called the Breakfast Flakes chattered away between songs.

The weather is bad, the roads are slippery. From the back seat, Molly says, "He asked what my favorite ice cream was and I said, 'Quarterback Crunch.' Then he asked who was President of the United States when the school was founded and I said, 'No one.' Wasn't that good?"

"I hate trick questions," Annie says.

"Did you like the school?" Tom asks.

"Yeah," Molly says.

"What did you like best about it?"

"I liked the way our guide, you know, Peter, just walked right across the street that goes through the campus and the cars just stopped. You and Mom were kind of hanging back, looking both ways and all, but Peter and I just trucked right across."

Molly was chewing gum that smelled like oranges.

"Peter was cute," Molly says.

Tom and Annie and Molly are at the Motel Lenore. Snow accumulates beyond the room's walls. There is a small round table in the room and they sit around it. Molly drinks cranberry juice from a box and Tom and Annie drink Scotch. They are nowhere. The brochure that the school sent them states that the school is located thirty-five miles from Boston. Nowhere! They are all exhausted and merely sit there, regarding their beverages. The television set is chained to the wall. This is indicative, Tom thinks, of considerable suspicion on the part of the management. There was also a four-dollar deposit on the room key. The management, when Tom checked in, was in the person of a child about Molly's age, a boy eating from a bag of potato chips and doing his homework.

"There's a kind of light that glows in the bottom of the water in an atomic reactor that exists nowhere else, do you know that?" the boy said to Tom.

"Is that right?" Tom said.

"Yeah," the boy said, and marked the book he was reading with his pencil. "I think that's right."

The motel room is darkly paneled and there is a picture of a moose between the two beds. The moose is knee-deep in a lake and he has raised his head to some sound, the sound of a hunter approaching, one would imagine. Water drips from his muzzle. The woods he gazes at are dark. Annie looks at the picture. The moose is preposterous and doomed. After a few moments, after she has finished her Scotch, Annie realizes she is waiting to hear the sound. She goes into the bathroom and washes her hands and face. The towel is thin. It smells as if it's been line-dried. It was her idea that Molly go away to school. She wants Molly to be free. She doesn't want her to be afraid. She fears that she is making her afraid, and she is afraid. Annie hears Molly and Tom talking in the other room and then she hears Molly laugh. She raises her fingers to the window frame and feels the cold air seeping in. She adjusts the lid to the toilet tank. It shifts slightly. She washes her hands again. She goes into the room and sits on one of the beds.

"What are you laughing about?" she says. She means to be offhand, but her words come out heavily.

"Did you see the size of that girl's radio in the dorm room we visited?" Molly says, laughing. "It was the biggest radio I'd ever seen. I told Daddy there was a real person lying in it, singing." Molly giggles. She pulls her turtleneck sweater up to just below her eyes.

Annie laughs, then she thinks she has laughed at something terrible, the idea of someone lying trapped and singing. She raises her hands to her mouth. She had not seen a radio large enough to hold anyone. She saw children in classes, in laboratories in some brightly painted basement. The children were dissecting sheep's eyes. "Every winter term in Biology you've got to dissect sheep's eyes," their guide said wearily. "The colors are really nice though." She saw sacks of laundry tumbled down a stairwell with names stenciled on them. Now she tries not to see a radio large enough to hold anyone singing.

At night, Tom drives in his dreams. He dreams of ice, of slick treachery. All night he fiercely holds the wheel and turns in the direction of the skid.

In the morning when he returns the key, the boy has been replaced by an old man with liver spots the size of quarters on his hands. Tom thinks of asking where the boy is, but then realizes he must be in school learning about eerie, deathly light. The bills the old man returns to Tom are soft as cloth.

In California, they live in a canyon. Martha's room is there, facing the canyon. It is not situated with a glimpse of the ocean like some of the other rooms. It faces a rocky ledge where owls nest. The canyon is full of small birds and bitter-smelling shrubs. There are larger animals too who come down in the night and drink from the pans of water the family puts out. Each evening they put out large white pans of clear water and in the morning the pans are muddy and empty. The canyon is cold. The sun moves quickly through it. When the rocks are touched by the sun, they steam. All of Martha's things remain in her room— the radio, the posters and mirrors and books. It is a "guest" room now, although no one ever refers to it in that way. They refer to it as "Martha's room." But it has become a guest room, even though there are never any guests.

The rental car is blue and without distinction. It is a four-door sedan with automatic transmission and a poor turning circle. Martha would have been mortified by it. Martha had a boyfriend who, with his brothers, owned a monster truck. The Super Swamper tires were as tall as Martha, and all the driver of an ordinary car would see when it passed by was its colorful undercarriage with its huge shock and suspension coils, its long orange stabilizers. For hours on a Saturday they would wallow in sloughs and rumble and pitch across stony creek beds, and then they would wash and wax the truck or, as Dwight, the boyfriend, would say, dazzle the hog. The truck's name was Bear. Tom and Annie didn't care for Dwight, and they hated and feared Bear. Martha loved Bear. She wore a red and white peaked cap with MONSTER TRUCK stenciled on it. After Martha died, Molly put the cap on once or twice. She thought it would help her feel closer to Martha but it didn't. The sweatband smelled slightly of shampoo, but it was just a cap.

Tom pulls into the frozen field that is the parking lot for the North-wall School. The admissions office is very cold. The receptionist is wearing an old worn Chesterfield coat and a scarf. Someone is playing a hesitant and plaintive melody on a piano in one of the nearby rooms. They are shown the woodlot, the cafeteria, and the arts department, where people are hammering out their own silver bracelets. They are shown the language department, where a class is doing tarot card readings in French. They pass a room and hear a man's voice say, "Matter is a sort of blindness."

While Molly is being interviewed, Tom and Annie walk to the barn. The girls are beautiful in this school. The boys look a little dull. Two boys run past them, both wearing jeans and denim jackets. Their hair is short and their ears are red. They appear to be pretending that they are in a drama, that they are being filmed. They dart and feint. One stumbles into a building while the other crouches outside, tossing his head and scowling, throwing an imaginary knife from hand to hand.

Annie tries a door to the barn but it is latched from the inside. She walks around the barn in her high heels. The hem of her coat dangles. She wears gloves on her pale hands. Tom walks beside her, his own hands in his pockets. A flock of starlings fly overhead in an oddly tight formation. A hawk flies above them. The hawk will not fall upon them, clenched like this. If one would separate from the flock, then the hawk could fall.

"I don't know about this 'matter is a sort of blindness' place," Tom says. "It's not what I had in mind."

Annie laughs but she's not paying attention. She wants to get into the huge barn. She tugs at another door. Dirt and flakes of rust smear the palms of her gloves. Then suddenly, the wanting leaves her face.

"Martha would like this school, wouldn't she," she says.

"We don't know, Annie," Tom says. "Please don't, Annie."

"I feel that I've lived my whole life in one corner of a room," Annie says. "That's the problem. It's just having always been in this one corner. And now I can't see anything. I don't even know the room, do you see what I'm saying?"

Tom nods but he doesn't see the room. The sadness in him has become his blood, his life flowing in him. There's no room for him.

In the admissions building, Molly sits in a wooden chair facing her interviewer, Miss Plum. Miss Plum teaches composition and cross-country skiing.

"You asked if I believe in *aluminum?*" Molly asks.

"Yes, dear. Uh-huh, I did," Miss Plum says.

"Well, I suppose I'd have to *believe* in it," Molly says.

Annie has a large cardboard file that holds compartmentalized information on the schools they're visiting. The rules and regulations for one school are put together in what is meant to look like an American passport. In the car's back seat, Molly flips through the book annoyed.

"You can't do anything in this place!" she says. "The things on your walls have to be framed and you can only cover sixty percent of the wall space. You can't wear jeans." Molly gasps. "And you have to eat breakfast!" Molly tosses the small book onto the floor, on top of the ice scraper. She gazes glumly out the window at an orchard. She is sick of the cold. She is sick of discussing her "interests." White fields curve by. Her life is out there somewhere, fleeing from her while she is in the back seat of this stupid car. Her life is never going to be hers. She thinks of it raining, back home in the canyon, the rain falling upon the rain. Her legs itch and her scalp itches. She has never been so bored. She thinks that the worst thing she has done so far in her life was to lie in a hot bath one night, smoking a cigarette and saying *I hate God.* That was the very worst thing. It's pathetic. She bangs her knees irritably against the front seat.

"You want to send me far enough away," she says to her parents. "I mean, it's the other side of the dumb continent. Maybe I don't even want to do this," she says.

She looks at the thick sky holding back snow. She doesn't hate God anymore. She doesn't even think about God. Anybody who would let a kid choke on a piece of bread . . .

The next school has chapel four times a week and an indoor hockey rink. In the chapel, two fir trees are held in wooden boxes. Wires attached to the ceiling hold them upright. It is several weeks before Christmas.

"When are you going to decorate them?" Molly asks Shirley, her guide. Shirley is handsome and rather horrible. The soles of her rubber boots are bright, horrible orange. She looks at Molly.

"We don't decorate the trees in the chapel," she says.

Molly looks at the tree stumps bolted into the wooden boxes. Beads of sap pearls golden on the bark.

"This is a very old chapel," Shirley says. "See those pillars? They look like marble, but they're just pine, painted to look like marble." She isn't being friendly, she's just saying what she knows. They walk out of the chapel, Shirley soundlessly, on her horrible orange soles.

"Do you play hockey?" she asks.

"No," Molly says.

"Why not?"

"I like my teeth," Molly says.

"You *do,*" Shirley says in mock amazement. "Just kidding," she says. "I'm going to show you the hockey rink anyway. It's new. It's a big deal."

Molly sees Tom and Annie standing some distance away beneath a large tree draped with many strings of extinguished lights. Her mother's back is to her, but Tom sees her and waves.

Molly follows Shirley into the cold, odd air of the hockey rink. No one is on the ice. The air seems distant, used up. On one wall is a big painting of a boy in a hockey uniform. He is in a graceful easy posture, skating alone on bluish ice, skating toward the viewer, smiling. He isn't wearing a helmet. He has brown hair and wide golden eyes. Molly reads the plaque beneath the painting. His name is Jimmy Watkins and he had died six years before at the age of seventeen. His parents had built the rink and dedicated it to him.

Molly takes a deep breath, "My sister, Martha, knew him," she says.

"Oh yeah?" Shirley says with interest. "Did your sister go here?"

"Yes," Molly says. She frowns a little as she lies. Martha and Jimmy Watkins of course know each other. They know everything but they have secrets too.

The air is not like real air in here. Neither does the cold seem real. She looks at Jimmy Watkins, bigger than life, skating toward them on his black skates. It is not a very good painting. Molly thinks that those who love Jimmy Watkins must be disappointed in it.

"They were very good friends," Molly says.

"How come you didn't tell me before your sister went here?"

Molly shrugs. She feels happy, happier than she has in a long time.

She has brought Martha back from the dead and put her in school. She has given her a room, friends, things she must do. It can go on and on. She has given her a kind of life, a place in death. She has freed her.

"Did she date him or what?" Shirley asks.

"It wasn't like that," Molly says. "It was better than that."

She doesn't want to go much further, not with this girl whom she dislikes, but she goes a little further.

"Martha knew Jimmy better than anybody," Molly says.

She thinks of Martha and Jimmy Watkins being together, telling each other secrets. They will like each other. They are seventeen and fourteen, living in the single moment that they have been gone.

Molly is with her parents in the car again on a winding road, going through the mountains. Tonight they will stay in an inn that Annie has read about and tomorrow they will visit the last school. Several large rocks, crusted with dirty ice, have slid upon the road. They are ringed with red cones and traffic moves slowly around them. The late low sun hotly strikes the windshield.

"Bear could handle those rocks," Molly says. "Bear would go right over them."

"Oh, that truck," Annie says.

"That truck is an ecological criminal," Tom says.

"Big Bad Bear," Molly says.

Annie shakes her head and sighs. Bear is innocent. Bear is only a machine, gleaming in a dark garage.

Molly can't see her parents' faces. She can't remember the way they looked when she was a baby. She can't remember what she and Martha last argued about. She wants to ask them about Martha. She wants to ask them if they are sending her so far away so that they can imagine Martha is just far away too. But she knows she will never ask such questions. There are secrets now. The dead have their secrets and the living have their secrets with the dead. This is the way it must be.

Molly has her things. And she sets them up each night in the room she's in. She lays a little scarf upon the bureau first, and then her things upon it. Painted combs for her hair, a little dish for her rings. They are the only guests at the inn. It is an old rambling structure on a lake. In a few days, the owner will be closing it down for the winter.

It's too cold for such an old place in the winter, the owner says. He had planned to keep it open for skating on the lake when he first bought it and had even remodeled part of the cellar as a skate room. There is a bar down there, a wooden floor, and shelves of old skates in all sizes. Window glass runs the length of one wall just above ground level and there are spotlights that illuminate a portion of the lake. But winter isn't the season here. The pipes are too old and there are not enough guests.

"Is this the deepest lake in the state?" Annie asks. "I read that somewhere, didn't I?" She has her guidebooks which she examines each night. Everywhere she goes, she buys books.

"No," the inn's owner says. "It's not the deepest, but it's deep. You should take a look at that ice. It's beautiful ice."

He is a young man, balding, hopelessly proud of his ice. He lingers with them, having given them thick towels and new bars of soap. He offers them venison for supper, fresh bread and pie. He offers them his smooth, frozen lake.

"Do you want to skate?" Tom asks his wife and daughter. Molly shakes her head.

"No," Annie says. She takes a bottle of Scotch from her suitcase. "Are there any glasses?" she asks the man.

"I'm sorry," the man says, startled. He seems to blush. "They're all down in the skate room, on the bar." He gives a slight nod and walks away.

Tom goes down into the cellar for the glasses. The skates, their runners bright, are jumbled upon the shelves. The frozen lake glitters in the window. He pushes open the door and steps out onto the ice. Annie, in their room, waits without taking off her coat, without looking at the bottle. Tom takes a few quick steps and then slides. He is wearing a suit and tie, his good shoes. It is a windy night and the trees clatter with the wind and the old inn's sign creaks on its chains. Tom slides across the ice, his hands pushed out, then he holds his hands behind his back, going back and forth in the space where the light is cast. There is no skill without the skates, he knows, and probably no grace without them either, but it is enough to be here under the black sky, cold and light and moving. He wants to be out here. He wants to be out here with Annie.

From a window, Molly sees her father on the ice. After a moment, she sees her mother moving toward him, not skating, but slipping forward, making her way. She sees their heavy awkward shapes embrace.

Molly sees them, already remembering it.

GRADUATION

Roxana Robinson

I drove up on Friday to Jeffrey's graduation. I went alone: Alex, Jeffrey's stepfather, was away on business and couldn't come till Saturday. St. George's is in Rhode Island, just past Newport. It's a four-hour trip from Manhattan, but I didn't mind the drive. The afternoon I left, I stood in the garage on Eighty-third Street, waiting for the attendant to bring my car. I started breathing deeply, big, long breaths, and I closed my eyes, as though I were standing in a windy meadow and not on the oil-stained concrete floor of the garage. I couldn't help it: I couldn't wait to start. I couldn't wait to be in the car, I couldn't wait to begin the racing surge along the smooth highways, every second drawing me closer to Jeffrey. If you have only one child, that child is at the heart of your life.

I reached St. George's around six. The school is on a wide hillside overlooking the ocean, and everything glitters with the light off the water, and the air is fresh with salt. The school buildings are red-brick Georgian with white trim, set with big old sugar maples. It was a clear day, early summer, with no wind. By the time I got there, shadows were stretching across the sloping lawns, turning the landscape majestic. Driving up the long driveway, I felt peaceful to be at this place, so calm and handsome.

I found Jeff in his room. It smelled rank, as always—a rich mixture of healthy young men, dirty socks, and industrial cleanser. And everything they owned—clothes, shoes, athletic equipment, electronic parts—was all in a great swirl, across the floor, on the beds and desks, in and out of the closets, like debris after a flood. It looked wonderful. My own room I want immaculate, each chair set in its own footprints on the carpet, but I love Jeff's room like this. It makes me laugh, all that energy.

Jeffrey was sitting on the bottom bunk bed, fiddling with his Walkman. He is tall now, and lanky, and his joints make odd angles. His limbs seemed to fill up the whole rectangle of the bed. He looked up and smiled when I came in. Each time I see him it is a tiny shock: he has come to look more and more like his father. In between, I forget this, but when I see him next it hits me again. Jeffrey has Bill's wide square face, short straight nose, his odd low eyebrows and muddy blond hair. In fact he looks exactly like his father when I first met him in college. It is a face that I once loved, and one which now makes my heart shrink.

I leaned over and put my arms around those smooth, strong young shoulders, closed my eyes, and willed the face to change into my son's again.

"Hi, Mom," he said.

I sat down next to him on the bed. "Well, I'm glad to see everyone's all packed," I said cheerfully, looking at the voluptuous heaps littering the room.

Jeffrey grunted, he had gone back to the Walkman. His roommate, Owen Schaefer, appeared. Owen is impossibly tall and thin, with no-color short hair that stands straight up from his forehead. He has been Jeff's best friend since freshman year, and I am a great fan of his.

"Hi, Mrs. Winslow."

"Hi, sweetie, how are you? Come over here and let me give you a kiss." Owen permitted this. "Are your parents coming up, I hope?"

"No, Mom, they're busy. They can't make graduation, they have a party this weekend," said Jeff, not looking up from the Walkman. I rolled my eyes and shook my head at Owen.

"Thank you, Jeff," I said, and Owen laughed. "What's the matter with the Walkman?" I asked Jeff. "The batteries?"

"No," said Jeffrey, his voice making it clear that the problem was too complicated for a maternal sensibility.

"He probably needs a new one," offered Owen solemnly.

"Right," said Jeff, pleased.

"Thank you, Owen," I said, and we all three laughed.

Jeffrey may be at the heart of my life, but I am not at the heart of his. I was, of course, when he was little. At first, you are your child's whole, whole world, and though you love him, though he is at the center of it, he is not your whole, whole world. For years the child is like a beloved anchor, dragging on you, slowing you down. He pleads with you constantly: to play with him, read to him, help him out. You do it, of course: you are all he has, and you love him. But infinitesimally and inexorably, things shift. When he is fifteen, you realize suddenly that the burden, the debt, has slid heavily and forever onto the other side, like the ball of mercury in a thermostat. Now you have become the supplicant: for the rest of your life you will be asking him to spend time with you, and feeling grateful when he does.

Jeff is eighteen, and my affection makes him uneasy. I don't care: I love him and he has to put up with it. When we first heard that he had gotten into St. George's, I said, "That's wonderful, sweetie! And I'll get a little apartment in Newport! I love Newport."

Jeffrey shook his head. "Very funny, Mom," he said. I could see him wondering if I was going to be one of those mothers who turn up too often, wearing the wrong clothes and saying mortifying things about rock music to his friends. I haven't done that. But this is how I feel: his presence in my life is huge, crucial, heartrending, in a way that mine will never again be in his.

Now Jeffrey keeps me at a distance, but he's supposed to: he's an adolescent boy. It means he's establishing himself as a separate person, not that he hates me for divorcing his father and marrying Alex Winslow.

I'm waiting for things to get better, and they're not so bad right now. There are times, like then, sitting next to Jeffrey on his unmade bed, in the wonderful chaos of his room, and being conscious of his smooth skin, the tender young bristles on his upper lip, the easy, supple strength of his limbs, breathing in the fresh, strange smell of him, and laughing with him and his roommate, when I feel so grateful I want to close my eyes. I wanted more children, but I am so glad at least that I have this one, so thankful to have been able to start a life like this: a miracle.

Jeff and I went out to an early dinner. I took him back to my hotel, in case he wanted to talk or watch TV or something after dinner.

The hotel was one of the old Newport mansions, and the rooms were handsome, oversize, and gloomy. We were alone in the dining room, and we took a table next to the ocean wall. We sat on either side of a cold, black window. We could feel the draft coming from it, and beyond it we could hear the invisible sea on the rocks. I looked around—at the long, ponderous curtains, the dim reaches of the ceiling, the solemn classical archways dividing the vast room.

"Can you imagine living here?" I said. "It's not what I'd call cozy. I hope they didn't have to have breakfast here every morning."

I was trying to stir Jeff up, but he just looked around and smiled. He didn't say anything. He drank some of his water.

"When you get back, we'll find a camp outfitter and take a day to get all your things for Alaska," I said. He is going kayaking this summer in Prince William Sound.

"Okay," said Jeff.

"Your trip will be so great," I said. "I want you to know that we never did things like that when I was your age. You went to Camp Wikkee-o-kee, in Maine, every summer until you were seventeen. After that you still went every summer, only then you were a counselor. No one ever asked us if we wanted to go kayaking in Alaska or trekking in Nepal or helicopter skiing in Cortina. In fact, *still* no one asks me," I finished up. I was sure Jeff would challenge me on this, as my childhood was not deprived, but he didn't. He laughed, but didn't answer. He was pretty quiet: I knew what was on his mind.

"Well, Alex is flying in early tomorrow. And your father and Susan, they're coming up tomorrow morning too?" I asked carefully. He never mentions his father to me, not ever.

"Yup," Jeff said.

"And you're having dinner with them tomorrow night," I said.

"Yup," said Jeff. This made him visibly uneasy, so I didn't ask where they were going.

"And then Alex and I will take you out to lunch on Sunday."

Jeff was eating carefully, watching his plate. His foot jiggled steadily under the table, a tiny, febrile throb. How could he not be uneasy? The next day we would all be there together, Bill and Susan, his new wife, and Alex and me and Jeffrey, which has never happened before. I was dreading it myself.

Bill and I have been divorced for four years, and he is still full of rage. He hasn't spoken to me in two and a half years; all communication is through lawyers, accountants, or his secretary. His secretary includes brief notes about plans when she forwards my school mail (there is some continuing mixup, and periodically the school sends my mail to Bill's office).

Last spring vacation Bill took Jeff skiing in Austria. By the terms of our agreement we are supposed to share Jeff's holidays. Bill was going to take him for the first week, and Alex and I would take him to Nassau with us for the second. The day Jeff left for Austria, after we had said good-bye, he stopped in the doorway of our apartment and turned. He was wearing his big red parka. His bag and boots were already on the elevator, and the car was waiting downstairs to take him to the airport. He put on one of his mittens, and jabbed at the door frame with his blunt mittened hand as he talked. He looked at the mitten instead of me.

"Mom," he said.

"What is it?" I asked. "Do you need money?" He seemed so troubled.

"No," he said, not looking up. "I'm not coming to Nassau."

"What do you mean?" I asked.

"Dad said he'd only take me skiing if I'd come for the whole vacation, both weeks. And he said I had to be the one to tell you. He said he wouldn't. He got really mad." Jeff spoke without raising his eyes to me, banging away at the door frame with his mitten. For a second I just stood there—I couldn't believe what I was hearing.

"But why didn't you tell me?" I asked. "Why did you wait until now to tell me?" My voice was angry.

Jeff's mitten stabbed at the brass door socket. "I don't know," he said resentfully.

But I went on. "What do you mean, you don't know? You knew I'd find out, Jeffrey, why didn't you tell me?" Unexpectedly, I began to cry, which I think I have never done in front of Jeff. I swept the tears off my cheeks with the backs of my hands.

"I didn't *want* to tell you!" Jeff said finally, looking up at me. He saw my face, and his own face crumpled. "Because I knew this would happen when I did," he said, and then, horribly, his voice broke, and darling Jeff, my large, sweet-smelling, kind Jeffrey, began to cry, too.

The car was waiting downstairs to take him to the airport. There was nothing for me to do but let him go. I put my arms around him and told him that it was all right. I told him to have a great time skiing, and that I loved him. What else could I do? Bill is good at getting what he wants. I knew how he had acted to Jeff: threatening and jeering, alternately. He's a bully, it's one reason I left him.

When they came back from skiing, of course I tried to reach Bill, but he would never take my calls. Finally my lawyer wrote a letter of complaint, but Bill never responded. My lawyer reminded me that the law is expensive and cumbersome to set in motion, and he asked me what, in the end, it was that I wanted to achieve? What I want to achieve is never to have Jeff put in that position again, and so now I let Bill do mostly what he wants. I suppose I hope that being placating will finally earn me absolution. In any case it will protect Jeff.

Bill's secretary sent the graduation information to me with a note saying that Bill wanted to have dinner with Jeff on the Saturday night after graduation. I suppose that night is the climax of the weekend, but I didn't argue. Anything is better than putting Jeff in the middle.

When Jeff and I left the hotel dining room he said he didn't feel like coming upstairs. He said he had to pack, which was visibly true, so I drove him back to school. When I stopped the car outside his dorm he didn't move or look at me. I knew what he was thinking, and I wished I could make things easier for him.

"Don't worry," I said, "it won't be so bad."

I hugged him. When he was small, things seemed so easy: I could make things whole and right, simply through the fact of my presence, my body. Things are different now, I am forty-two, and can no longer count on my body to do the things it used to.

Over his shoulder I could see the lights of the dorm, brilliant in the dark landscape. There was all that life in there, music thudding and doors slamming: that was where Jeff's world was now, not in my arms. He was too polite to pull away, but I could feel him aching to, to disconnect from me, so I pulled away first.

"Good night, sweetie," I said, "I'll see you tomorrow."

He opened the car door. "Good night, Mom," he said, "thanks for dinner." I nodded, and as he shut the door I waved to him as I started the car, and I drove off at once, so it wouldn't look as though I were yearning, wistful, abandoned.

When I got back to the hotel Alex called, from wherever he was.

"How's Jeff?" he asked. They are great friends, thank goodness.

"He's worried about tomorrow. Surprise."

"How about you?"

"I'm all right," I said, "Hurry up and get here."

"Don't worry," he said.

I read for a while and went to sleep. I felt fine that night. It was the next morning when I began to worry.

I woke up alone in that big bed, and anxiety closed down over me like a poisonous fog. I ordered breakfast, and got up and dressed, but it got worse. I stood in front of the mirror and my heart sank: how could I have bought this suit? Jeff would be embarrassed; Bill and Susan would laugh. It looked awful, but there was nothing else to wear. I turned from the mirror and went to stand in front of the window.

Why wasn't Alex here by now? Wasn't he late? Was he all right? I wondered if something had happened to him. No one would know where to find me, if it had. I wouldn't know until I got back home on Sunday. These things were skittering about on the top of my consciousness: I was trying to avoid the big things.

I was afraid that Bill would do something terrible, something public and humiliating, something that would discredit me as a mother. I couldn't think what it was he might do, but it was in my mind, like the nightmare when you have no clothes on in public: shame and degradation. I was worried that Jeff would be caught in the middle again, that he would be trapped, bullied, blackmailed into taking his father's side against me. I was afraid that his own graduation, instead of being a day full of pride and exultation for him, would be one of anguish and misery.

And then there was another thing, unconnected to what Bill did to Jeff or to me: why was it that Susan had had a baby, easily, at once, getting pregnant after one month of marriage, at the age of forty-one? I had tried to have more children, first with Bill, after Jeff was born, for the next eight years of our marriage. Then I had tried with Alex, for the four years of ours. I tried everything, everything. I started with pills and injections and unnatural couplings, and worked my way up to anesthesia, operations, terrible glittering steel and glass, bloody changes to the center of me. I let them do things that hurt, that went too deep. I didn't mind anything, though, I was greedy for it all. Each time I rode along on a high, blissful wave of conviction, until I was told once again that I had failed, my body had betrayed me again.

In the mirror I could see that my neck was thin, my skin was becoming parched. I was forty-two, and on the wane. The flow in me was subsiding. I would never have another baby. This whole part of me, this delicious current, this heavenly voluptuous flow of passion, this blissful, legitimate, uncomplicated tide of love would have only one object, ever. I would never have a whole enchanted circle of faces that were mine, that looked for me, that gave themselves up to me entirely, that needed my face for the completion of their world. I would never hold a baby on one hip, another small body leaning easily against my legs, a third rocking unsteadily toward me. It was what I had wanted; it wouldn't happen. That part of my life was gone, was over.

I try not to think about this—it does no good—but there are times when it hits me and the air seems to turn dark around me, as though I am in mourning. Then panic rises up in me: I am afraid that I will give way, that I will let this dark wave break over me.

I sat down now on the bed and folded my arms against my chest. "No," I said out loud, firmly. I held my arms tightly, pressing in hard. "No."

There was a discreet knock on the door: "Room service."

It was Alex. He stepped inside and gave me a big, slow, enveloping hug. All of him wrapped around me and squeezed. It felt wonderful. Alex kissed me and then stepped away.

"Don't you look terrific," he said.

"Really?" I asked, starting to laugh. One of the wonderful things about Alex, besides, of course, his generosity of spirit, is his sideways approach. He knew perfectly well that it wasn't the way I looked that was on my mind.

"Yes," he said, studying me carefully and nodding. "Susan will turn green when she sees you."

The graduation was in the gymnasium, and Bill and Susan sat on the other side of the room. Alex and I sat with Owen's parents, Jim and Libba Schaefer. The four of us clapped dutifully, and laughed at the jokes, and kicked each other when the hated French teacher was introduced. I yawned suddenly and horribly during the visiting dignitary's speech, and Libba poked me, and we both turned weepy when our sons stepped forward for their diplomas.

After the class marched out again we all began to follow them outside. Everyone was milling around on the lawn, and we inched our way through the crowd trying to find Jeff, and watching for Bill and Susan out of the corners of our eyes.

"There he is," I said to Alex, and we ploughed toward him. He was talking to the parents of a friend. His face was cautious, his hands busy rolling and unrolling his diploma. He seemed so nervous, I felt sorry for him. I threw my arms around him and kissed him.

"Congratulations, sweetie," I said. Alex hugged him, too, and Jeff's smile broke through. I introduced myself to the other parents, and we stood talking for a few minutes. I stood on tiptoe the whole time, trying not to let my heels sink into the soft lawn. My peripheral vision was in high gear. Bill and Susan were behind me, to my left, talking to someone I didn't know. They were edging their way toward us, and I could feel the back of my neck turn prickly. I wanted to be calm, I wanted to overwhelm them with poise, with amiability. But as I could feel them coming nearer I could feel my body beginning to subvert me. My pulse had speeded up, and I was having trouble breathing. Nothing seemed to work normally, and my face was turning stiff, I wouldn't be able to smile. Even moving my mouth to talk felt peculiar. I could feel them coming nearer.

I turned to Jeff and said, "We've told the Schaefers we'd all eat lunch together, I hope that's all right with you?"

"Uh," said Jeff, nervously.

"With your father and Susan, of course. I'm going to go find the Schaefers and get a table. You collect your father and come find us."

"Okay," said Jeff, without a flicker, and just as Bill and Susan arrived I fled. I nodded at Susan, but just barely, it might have been part of my turning away from Jeff. We made our way back to Jim and Libba. My ankles were shaking, from standing on tiptoe I thought, but my hand, holding the program, was shaking, too. My heart was pounding, and my whole peculiar body, without my permission, was in a state of wild alarm, as though I had had a near miss with an axe murderer.

But, miraculously, it turned out all right. At lunch we all sat at a round table. Jeff was between me and Bill. Alex sat next to me and Susan next to Bill. Jim Schaefer sat dutifully next to Susan and Libba next to Alex. Between the Schaefers was Owen. I subdued my nervous system. It was very civilized, and I was very proud of everyone. The two sides never had to speak to each other, and Bill and I let Jeff turn back and forth from one to the other in spurts. We were all animated—manic, really—and I could see Susan being charming, irresistible to Jim Schaefer. Alex is always charming, and he made Libba giggle. In an odd way, it wasn't too bad. It was excruciating, but it wasn't too bad: there we all were, sitting together, and nothing terrible had happened. Bill had done nothing after all. I thought, if this is the worst, it isn't so bad.

That night Alex took me to the most expensive restaurant in Newport, where we had too much to eat and too much to drink, and a lovely time. In the morning we made love, and so we were late to the chapel service, and had to stand in the doorway.

The chapel is small, graceful, and Gothic, and it was packed. I never even saw Bill and Susan. Jeff was next to Owen in the choir stalls. I thought how simple young faces they are. The boys looked so clean, so handsome and tidy; they had somehow managed to spring, immaculate, from that chaos they lived in, as they had emerged from the long, rumpled, complicated, chaotic process of childhood. Here they were at last, beautiful, loved, capable, ready to live their lives. It was a miracle.

Standing there, listening to the lovely, high, soaring voices asking "And did those feet, in ancient times," I felt exhilarated. It was partly relief: it was such a vast blessing to feel that it was over. Nothing had happened, we had all been polite, and maybe things would go on getting better. Maybe at last I had been forgiven. It was so lovely there, all of it, the rows of smooth, young faces in the choir, the high ceiling soaring over our heads, the pure white plaster walls, the hymns: it seemed enchanted. I thought, this is our reward, this is all we hope for, starting these children off, and it's more than enough.

Afterward Jeff hurried past us in a group of boys, his head down. He didn't see us, I guess, so I reached out to grab him.

"Wait a minute, Mister," I said. "Not so fast. Good morning," I leaned forward for a kiss but he ducked. It was too public for him, so I patted him on the shoulder instead.

"Oh, hi," he said, nervous. "Listen, I have to go. These are

Owen's pants. He needs to have them back, they're leaving right away."

I looked down: Jeff's white pants were rolled up over his ankles. "Oh," I said. "Why do you have Owen's pants, or is that a silly question?"

Jeff sighed elaborately. "Mine got red paint on them, remember? Now I've got to go. I'm keeping the Schaefers waiting."

I pushed him easily away. "Go," I said. "We'll come find you in your room."

We made our way there slowly, stopping to talk to people we had come to know in four years of Parents' Weekends. It was a triumphal procession. There were the favorite teachers, whose faces lit up when they saw us, who loved Jeff themselves, who honored our love of Jeff. There were the other parents, whose children had shared this school with Jeff, these four awkward, long years. We were happy to see one another, like survivors after a war. It was over, we had all succeeded. We all felt congratulatory, proud of one another and of ourselves.

Near the dormitory I saw Libba. I waved to her and called, "We're keeping the pants. They're much nicer than Jeff's."

She laughed, and as we came up she put her hand on my wrist. "Listen, I never saw where you were sitting last night," she said, "but I wanted to tell you how fabulous Jeff's speech was."

I stared at her. "Last night?" I said.

"At the dinner," said Libba.

"At the dinner," I repeated. "What dinner?" My heart started up again, pounding away like a fool. I didn't know what she was going to say, but I knew I didn't want to hear it. I didn't want this to go any further.

"What do you mean 'what dinner'? Here at the school, dummy," said Libba, "The senior class dinner. Jeff's speech was *wonderful*. Had you heard it before? Of course you must have. You must be so *proud* of him."

I stared at her, and I couldn't do it. I couldn't cover for myself, I couldn't think of any way to fill that terrible black space she was creating. I couldn't think of a sentence that would show that things were all right, that I had known this, that her words weren't scraping at the core of my heart. I couldn't do it. I just stood there and stared at her, and finally she realized what had happened.

"Oh, no," she said, and put her hand on my shoulder. It was too much, and I pulled back.

"Listen, we've got to arrange with Jeff about the car," I said loudly, "we'll see you later." I pushed ahead again, as though everything in the world depended on my getting through this crowd. Alex was next to me. I didn't know whether he had heard or not, but I couldn't tell him. It seemed as though they were words I could never say out loud, sounds that would kill my heart if I ever heard them again.

When we reached the dormitory we started down the hall, but there was a group milling around Jeff's room. As we got closer we could see what it was: Susan was standing in the doorway, right in the middle of it, so no one could pass by her. In her arms was a baby, Bill's second son. Susan held him with one arm; she had him propped easily on her hip, and her other hand was outstretched. She was smiling at Jeff's friends and introducing herself. "Hello, I'm Mrs. Carpenter," she was saying—my old name. As I came up she was shaking someone's hand and smiling.

"Good morning, Owen. Congratulations! Now, there's someone I want you to meet. You haven't met Graham, Jeff's little brother. Say hello, Graham," she said comically.

She turned to the baby, and jiggled him up and down, easily, as though she were used to having a baby on her hip. Then she picked up his small pink hand and made it look as though the baby were waving, saying hello to Owen Schaefer, my friend Owen, who stood there smiling back, who had shaken Susan's hand; Owen, who had betrayed me.

JUNGLE VIDEO

Ralph Lombreglia

Last night, the neighborhood skunks invaded my dreams. They emerged from the dumpster at the restaurant where I used to work and followed me to my old apartment building—a black-and-white throng nipping at my heels. Their pointy faces snuffled my shoes as my ex-girlfriend said that she wasn't alone and I couldn't come in. Then the skunks wiggled with me down endless lonely streets to a sound track of electric guitars, garbage cans tumbling over, and a peculiar popping noise that turned out to be people trading small-weapons fire from the rooftops. And just now, when crashing sounds from upstairs woke me, it all made more sense than you want your dreams to make: in the full light of morning my bedroom reeks of skunk. The little beasts must have been rooting outside the house all night.

I wrap a pillow around my head but it only amplifies the commotion above me. A man of average stature and need for rest, I live below the workplace of insomniac giants. Anita is six feet three, Dwight several inches taller. Their footfalls boom in the ceiling. Now they're knocking things over and screaming at each other.

I shuffle out to the kitchen in my robe. Someone has been down to make coffee. I pour myself a mug of it and head upstairs. All the second-floor offices are empty, so I push open the door to the big editing suite. The only light comes from the shimmering television screens and the tall racks of video decks and special-effects generators blinking against the wall: the hidden engines of Paradise Productions humming away in an old house on a working-class street in Boston. Nobody's here, either. The sounds are coming from the large attic-floor office overhead. I punch that intercom number on the telephone. The pandemonium stops and someone scrambles to answer. It's Dwight. "Why, Walter," he says. "How nice to hear your voice. Where are you?" Then I hear a loud grunt and the sound of the phone clattering to the floor.

After a minute Dwight gets on again. "Anita just tackled me," he says. "It's not a good time to talk. We're wrestling."

"It sounded like you were here in the editing room, right on top of my bed."

"We started down there."

"You wrestled up the stairs?"

"Yeah. Can I call you back? I'm in a half nelson right now." He hangs up, and the crashing and screaming begin again.

I look at the pictures flickering on the three color TVs above the editing table—faces and scenery we've been staring at all week, trying to get the first cut of a marketing tape ready for a big software outfit out on Route 128. A bowl of popcorn is on the video controller console, and stray kernels lead to the hot-air popper sitting on a stack of tape cassettes. As soon as I see it, I remember the racket it makes—a sound very much like small-weapon fire. At the other end of the table, our script is glowing on Anita's computer screen. I scroll through, up and down, and I find long passages of voice-over narration I've never seen. Sound bites we'd rejected long ago are back, whole sequences are moved to places we'd agreed were wrong, and most of the stuff I wrote is simply gone. All this since midnight, when I stumbled downstairs like a zombie.

They're playing music above me now and throwing each other against the walls. I head back down to take a shower and shave. Even the bathroom—its one window sealed shut behind the shower curtain—smells of skunk.

Nobody knows why the skunk population exploded this year, but they've taken over this neighborhood. I was walking down to the corner store one night in early spring when I saw my first gang of them, four bad customers staking out a nearby yard. Coming home with my six-pack, I found three more at the curb, heads poked through holes in a garbage bag. They looked up when they heard me coming, lettuce shreds dangling from their lips, and stared me down until I crossed the street. Then they went back to eating. Since then, I've seen skunks every night, scores of them traipsing through yards and working the gutters. We have our own family of four or five residing in tunnels beneath the unpruned shrubs; at twilight you can lean over the porch railing and watch them surface into our scrap of front lawn. We tell ourselves there's something wonderful about it—the natural world reasserting itself in the urban landscape.

I get dressed and go back upstairs. When I reach the attic office, Anita and Dwight are lying beneath an afghan on the pulled-out sofa bed, their clothes in a heap on the floor. They wave to me. "You really have to meet my friend Rebecca," Anita says.

I pretend not to know what she's talking about. She's been saying this for months, and so far she has failed to produce any such woman. She turns to Dwight. "I want Walter to meet Rebecca."

"Just say yes," Dwight says to me.

"Don't you people ever sleep?" I say. "Didn't you go home at all? I heard popcorn popping in the dead of night."

"We might catch a few winks right now," Dwight says.

"Now? Dwight, the client is coming here at three o'clock."

"Oh, we're in good shape with that," Anita says.

"We are?"

When I left last night she called it a terrible crisis.

"Sure, we're fine. After you went to bed, the Doctor showed up, and we all got this huge burst of energy and just started ripping it apart. You should have been there. We put on music and made pop-corn and got some really neat ideas. We changed everything all around. Wait till you see it."

Dwight yawns. "Actually," he says, "we still don't have that elusive thing they call the vision."

"That's true," Anita says. "But this is just the rough cut."

"Anita," I say. "We've been agreeing all week that it was working. We agreed it was fine."

She smiles, sticks her foot out from under the afghan, and pats me on the knee with her toes. "I did agree to those things," she says. "It makes you so sad when I don't."

Anita and Dwight and the Doctor went into business for themselves because they couldn't work for other people anymore. True, a number of people couldn't work with them anymore either, but that was just as well. They always had more offers than they could possibly take. They're practically famous. You've seen documentaries they've produced, news programs they've directed, public-affairs specials they've researched and written. But they always had to work when other people wanted them to work, and do what other people told them to do. After a number of years they wearied of it. And then, overnight, everybody needed a video to announce his or her essence to the world, and Anita and Dwight and the Doctor became a corporation.

Six months ago, on the darkest day of winter, I sublet the first floor from them, agreeing to share the kitchen and bath. For three years, I'd been living with Jeanette, across the river in Cambridge, waiting on tables and acting in any play I could find. Then Jeanette dug up a young law partner to take my place. She'd been unhappy from the beginning, she said, and that rocked me: next to her I couldn't act at all. After I moved here, I saw the video folks every day as they rambled through my apartment to get coffee or use the john. "Forget that woman, Walter," Anita would say whenever she drifted in or out. It became an incantation, and after a while it began to work. I did begin to forget. If I started to remember, I hung around with the busy, happy people upstairs. One night, while they screened some footage, Anita discovered that I could pick shots and write a script and do it for not much money. I've been in corporate video ever since.

When I left Anita and Dwight on the sofa bed, I went down to watch the new version of our tape. Anita is a visual person. With the help of her partners, she'd snipped all the logical threads we'd spent a week spinning out, and now we had twenty minutes of pictorial free association, cut to the music I heard in my dream. I made believe I was the client and asked myself what I thought. "Are you people out of your minds?" I replied.

Now we're in the editing room, and Anita is talking to the television. "Steady up, Doctor," she says, twisting a knob to make the tape go forward and back, looking for a decent place to cut into the shot. "Steady up, goddammit."

The Doctor himself shot the footage we're looking at right now. We call him the Doctor because he has a Harvard Ph.D.—anthropology: kinship patterns of cannibals or something. He's actually a decent amateur cameraman, but this is wobbling all over the place and going in and out of focus. It's a shot of many people sitting in an enormous room, busily using computers in a way that suggests roaring productivity and satisfaction. Happiness, even. We need a shot like this, Anita says, and she's right. We need it because our client's last software release contained enough horrific bugs to corrupt databases all across the country. Heads rolled, we gather, at their new building on 128. But now it's all fixed, they claim, and that's why we're making this tape. In a few weeks they're bringing their biggest customers to town for a gala product unveiling in a fancy hotel, where they'll feature the premiere of our video on a giant screen. So yes, of course, we need a shot like this. And we have plenty of them. Would Anita produce this assignment and not bring home a bucketful of such shots? But today she doesn't like them anymore. The light is wrong, or the angle is, or the people don't look excited enough. Something invisible to me bothers Anita about every one of the happy-user shots we already have.

Instead she wants to use this one the Doctor took last week in Harvard Square while he was wandering around with the hand-held camera. He ended up in a vast basement at his alma mater where students were testing a new system to make computers do their homework.

I tell Anita, "This footage has nothing to do with our client's business or products. Using it would be misleading and unethical. It would be pure video trickery. We cannot use this shot, Anita, and you know it."

"I like the way it looks," she tells me. And then she says, "Now if only we had that perfect testimonial from a satisfied purchasing agent."

I turn my head to the wall and pretend to be deaf. Earlier this week, she got the idea of shooting me as this hypothetical purchasing person. Working me in as an actor is one of Anita's themes, like fixing me up with her friend.

The intercom buzzes. It's Dwight. He wants me to come upstairs and talk to him. When I get up there he's sitting in his underpants at his computer, playing Phantom Flyer. "I'm at thirty thousand feet, and I just lost an engine," he says. "Not only that, my flaps are stuck. I'm going into a dive." On the computer screen the horizon line bobs up and down in the windshield of a jet cockpit. Finally it flies right up out of sight and the earth gets closer and closer. "This always happens," he sighs, leaning back and scratching his ribs until his plane hits the ground. We watch the colorful explosion together. "How about we go catch some breakfast?" he says.

"Dwight, are you crazy? I'm trying to help Anita fix this tape. I'm starting to think you have a self-destructive streak, Dwight."

He stands up and wanders over to the sofa bed. "I'm starting to think you're a worrywart," he replies, and begins to dress from the pile of garments on the floor. Dwight's taste in clothing is the stuff of legend. Today he's wearing the fruits of a recent sweep through Filene's Basement: pearl-gray over-the-calf hose, decorated with flying yellow geese, and maroon Italian loafers. He puts on the shoes before he puts on the pants—the shoes being delicate enough, and the electric-blue rayon trousers baggy enough, to allow for that—and finishes with a pink T-shirt that says OFFICIAL JAMAICAN BIKINI INSPECTOR. Then he puts his arm around my shoulders. "Fixing this tape is beside the point," he says.

"Oh, really," I say.

"Yes. Would you like me to tell you why?"

"Sure. Tell me."

"First you show me those home fries and eggs. And that ham."

Dwight's favorite diner is called the Pig 'n' Poke, over by the railway switching yards beneath the Mass Pike. From our booth, I can see a blue Conrail locomotive pulling boxcars through a tunnel.

Dwight piles fried egg onto a corner of toast and raises it in the air. "The tape you made with Anita was perfectly competent," he says, and he pushes the toast-egg assembly into his mouth.

I should be having something wholesome myself, not the French fries and root beer I've ordered. But taking real nourishment seems out of keeping with my present circumstances.

"The Doctor and I admired it when we watched it last night," Dwight goes on. "You could find work all over town with a demo reel of stuff like that. You could stop working for us and go make the same boring video everybody else is making. Yak about something, then show a picture of it. Yak some more, show another picture. Yak, picture, yak, picture, yak, picture, yak."

"That's what clients think a video is, Dwight. That's what they want."

He slices a piece of ham and folds it in half. "The first thing to remember about clients," he says, "Is that they don't know what they want. The second thing—this is the problem part—is that they think they do." He pops the ham in.

"What about the third thing?" I say.

"What third thing?"

"That a lot of money is getting spent, and it's their money."

"Wrong!" Dwight exclaims, pounding the table with the butt of his knife. The sugar shaker falls down and trickles a white mound next to the napkins like time running out. "Wrong, wrong, wrong. They signed a contract. That money belongs to us."

"Well, then the videotape is theirs."

"Nope, that's ours too. We're its creators." He picks up the fallen shaker and streams sugar into his cup. Then he stirs it and has a sip. "Wow, that's sweet," he says. "The third thing about clients—the real third thing—is that if you let them, they'll start doing your job for you. But they don't know how to do your job, see? And so in the end they're disappointed and it's your fault."

"They probably wouldn't have been disappointed, Dwight. They probably would have liked it, and we'd practically be done by now."

"That's even worse. Then we'd have to feel bad all alone, knowing we took the cheesy way out. A household of hacks with only themselves for comfort." He motions to the waitress for our check. "No," he says, "what we have to do is correctly identify our job and then do it. Now, what is our job?"

"To make a videotape."

He shakes his head. "Anybody could do that." He gets up with the check to pay it. "Our job is to be the brilliant media wizards."

Outside, I stop at the passenger door of Dwight's white '64 Bonneville—it's the only car he can find that's big enough for him to drive—but he strides right past it and out to the highway. "Where are you going?" I say, but he refuses to answer me. I have to run through traffic to catch him on the median strip.

"We have some research to do," he says.

Across the highway is a shopping center with an amusement arcade. I follow Dwight into a dim, cavernous space full of flashing machines and teenagers in T-shirts decorated with skulls and lightning bolts. The proprietor is behind the cash register in a dirty barber's smock. He waves greetings to Dwight, slaps a roll of quarters into one of Dwight's outstretched hands, plucks a ten-dollar bill from the other. Then Dwight leads me to a video game called Jungle Bungle. He taps the screen with his fingernail. On it is a list of the highest scores. Dwight's initials are two numbers from the top, next to yesterday's date.

"Yesterday? I thought you were out on a shoot yesterday."

"I was," he says. "But I must have had some free time." He puts two quarters in the machine. "OK, I'd like to hear a little meditation on computer software."

"I can't work this way, Dwight."

"We're falling on our faces with a big client today, bud, and you're the writer on this project."

He begins to play the game. The star of Jungle Bungle is an animated ape whose great joy in life is bananas. The player moves a joystick to make the ape run around and collect bananas and put them in a sack. At first it's easy—the yellow fruit is simply lying on the ground or hanging in bunches low in the trees. A few flicks of the joystick and Dwight has every banana there is. Then the machine plays a little tune and a new landscape slides into view.

"Insights?" Dwight asks. "Inspirations?"

"Dwight, this is totally irrelevant."

"How can you say that?" he says. "What about our client's sacred product? Isn't it the same thing? You travel around in a kind of environment and play with information—take a piece from here and move it over there. You know where they got that idea?"

"No."

Dwight's ape is now hunkering on the banks of a wide, fast-moving river.

"From ancient computer games," he says, "the ones the programmers played on the mainframes when they were college kids. You think it's gonna stop there? Five years from now, business software will look like Jungle Bungle. Trust me. The future always arrives as a game."

A riverboat appears with a magnificent freight of bananas. The ape clambers down to the water's edge to swim to the boat, but the black, humpy backs of many crocodiles surface in the river, and he scurries back up the bank. Then Dwight makes his move. He runs to the water and leaps right onto the nearest crocodile. When it turns around to bite him, Dwight bounds to the next and then the next, and in this way he makes it all the way to the boat, grabs the bananas, and, vaulting from monster to monster, comes all the way back. "First time I tried that I got eaten," he says happily.

Jungle environments come and go, with Dwight ingeniously racking up banana points. It's not until the eighth or ninth landscape that he finally makes a mistake, opening the wrong door in a temple full of fruit. Then it's my turn. Immediately, little monkeys in the trees drop coconuts on me and knock me out. Dwight's turn again, and he zips through the landscapes even faster than before. "The ape has to learn certain things," he says, "or he doesn't get to the next level of the game. But, of course, saying 'The ape has to learn' is like saying the computer 'knows' this or that."

"It's you who have to learn certain things."

"You bet. But in seeing it as the ape's situation you get this peculiar distance on yourself."

"It becomes something apart from you," I say.

"*You* become something apart from you."

"You become the ape."

"Yes!" Dwight says.

We return from the amusement arcade to find a metallic-khaki BMW sitting in the drive. Dwight runs the Bonneville up onto the curb, jumps out, and dashes onto the porch and into the house. Even from the outside I can hear him slamming upstairs in his usual way, three steps at a time.

"And here's Walter!" Anita says when I step into the editing suite. "Walter's our writer. He wrote this script."

"Oh," the clients say, "the writer," and they shake my hand—two men and a woman about my age. They're all wearing gray business suits, but it's easy to pick out the alpha male. He shakes my hand much harder than the beta male does, talks like a drill sergeant, and shoots laser eyebeams into my face. The beta male has an open, friendly nature—a classic beta trait.

The Doctor has been teaching me the theory of creatures in groups. He's a scholar of such things, and it seems to serve him well.

He winks at me from across the room. The Doctor himself is an alpha male, but a special breed whose alpha strategy is to pretend that he isn't.

Anita has polished up the golden Emmy statues and arranged them on a shelf above the editing table. I nudge her over there with my hip. "I didn't write one word of this and you know it," I whisper. She gives my ribs a little squeeze. "It's showtime!" she announces, handing out yellow legal pads.

We settle into the expensive office chairs, and she lets the video roll. A helicopter shoots the company's headquarters at dawn, we go inside for a vérité-like tour, programmers have lunch in the cafeteria and say mysterious things, the employee volleyball team plays a game to some tasty electric jazz. I hear furious scratching on the legal pads. Five minutes in, the alpha male wants Anita to stop the tape.

"No stopping," she says. "It breaks up the flow."

I should be thinking about damage control, but instead I'm thinking that Anita's talents are as wasted on corporate PR as they were on documentaries. She's more like the queen of video rock and roll. Her ending is a great scene of software people at their terminals arguing about the best place to get Chinese food. Then the screen goes blank.

"Are you people out of your minds?" the alpha male says. "This isn't what we talked about. This isn't what you said you were going to do. What about the story we agreed on?"

"There's tons of story in there," Anita says. "Don't you think?"

"What happened to all the shots of the president at his desk?"

This often happens at these screenings—the first problem is that their boss isn't in it enough. "They were dull," I say, sniffing for emphasis. You have to be looking for it, but even with the air-conditioner on and the windows closed, the slightest trace of skunk is still discernible. "What did you want, the same boring video everybody else is making?"

"But he's not in it at all!" the woman says. "He happens to be the founder of this company."

"When I was working in the bush," the Doctor says, "I often observed the wisest rulers not taking part in certain rituals. They enjoyed the spectacle of the ceremonial tribe."

"Other reactions?" Dwight says.

The beta male pipes up. "I thought it had some great energy," he says. "It made the company seem like fun."

The alpha male shoots him an unmistakable look of shut-your-face. "The product isn't even mentioned once!" he exclaims. "This was supposed to be about the bugs. You were supposed to talk about how this new version of the product eliminates all those bugs."

"People don't want to hear about bugs," Dwight says.

"That's right," I put in. "Haven't they heard enough?"

The alpha male gets out of his chair. "We tell you what we want and we leave you alone, and you get freaky on us. I'm giving you a week to fix this tape."

"Fixing this tape is beside the point," I say.

"Oh, really," he says.

"Anybody can puff a product," Dwight says. "We're vision people. We work with the big themes."

"Fine," the alpha male says. "You have a week to find one."

He snaps his briefcase shut and stomps off to the stairs with his colleagues in line behind him. Only the friendly male turns to wave goodbye. We peek down to the street through the venetian blinds and watch them drive away.

The Doctor puts his arm around Anita's shoulders. "Rough cuts are always—you know—rough," he says.

"Rough?" Anita says. "I think we just entered lawsuit territory."

"The other guy liked it," I say, but Anita just shakes her head. I've never seen her so discouraged.

"Is anybody hungry?" Dwight inquires.

"I could eat a little something," the Doctor says.

Chinese food always cheers Anita up. "Kung-pao chicken?" I say to her. "Scallops in spicy garlic sauce? Szechuan shrimp?"

"I don't want anything," she says.

"All the more Hunan octopus for me," Dwight says, leading us down the stairs.

It proves to be a pretty summer afternoon, with the heat letting up and blue sky and puffs of cloud above the mostly brown two- and three-family houses that line our street. I tap Dwight's shoulder. "Can we talk about something? Tenant to landlord?"

"Uh-oh," he says, following me down the drive.

I take him around back where we keep the garbage barrels.

They're on their sides, lids off, bags ripped open. Trash is strewn across the ground like the past rushing before our eyes—every piece of junk mail we've received this week mingled with the remains of all the food we've eaten. And hovering above the devastation is the abiding aura of skunk.

"I bought these really good garbage cans," Dwight says.

"I think the raccoons help them take off the lids," I say. "They have thumbs or something."

"I just want to point out that if we start killing them we're going up against the whole ecosystem. There must be thousands on the waiting list for the next available house."

"I don't want to kill them," I say.

"Good," Dwight says, heading back up the drive. "Let's clean it up later." And then, gazing out over the rooftops, he says, "Why do they have to mess with our minds?"

"The skunks?"

"No, these people," he sighs, flapping his hand at the sky.

It's still Happy Hour when we arrive at the Chinese place our video-taped programmers voted the best. A lovely young woman brings our drinks. Perhaps on account of her loveliness we order too much food, and only items printed in red.

"To Anita, our brilliant producer!" I say, raising my glass.

"To Anita!" Dwight and the Doctor chime in.

Anita drinks up and gives us a smile. She's coming out of it. "I wish Rebecca could have made it to dinner," she says to the table at large. And then, to me, she adds, "Rebecca loves hot food."

"Anita, I'm just wondering," I say. "Is there any reason to think that Rebecca might have made it to dinner? Tonight, I mean?"

"Oh, well, she was supposed to stop by this afternoon, that's all. But with Rebecca you never know."

"He knows that," Dwight says.

"I've told her all about you," Anita says.

"Just nod your head," Dwight says.

"Rebecca's very nice," the Doctor says. "Who have you got lined up for me?"

"I thought you were promised to a chieftain's daughter," Anita says.

"I am. But you can have many wives in that culture."

The food arrives and we lay into it, chopsticks and beer bottles flashing in the air. Our eyes water and our noses liquify, and we never let our glasses get empty.

"I'm a simple person," the Doctor says, once we've begun to slow down. He always says that when he's about to take charge. "I was in the bank the other day and they couldn't tell me how much money I had. You know why?"

"Let me guess," Dwight says. "We're getting too dependent on technology."

"Cars are OK," the Doctor says. "I like my toaster oven. But there's something creepy about computer stuff. I can't relate to it."

"Well, it's totally nonhuman," I say.

"Don't say that," Anita says. "We can't say nonhuman."

"But isn't it true?" I say. "If you think about it, the blind faith is almost unbelievable. People trust their whole lives—*their money*—to these incomprehensible creations beyond their control. When have human beings ever trusted anything like that?"

Dwight rises from his chair with a peculiar smile, squinting as though dazzled by brilliant lights. "I just had an idea," he says. "I have to go call somebody."

The fortune cookies come while he's on the phone. Anita and the Doctor receive identical predictions: great success awaits them around the corner. Dwight returns to find that he will meet an influential stranger. "Your friends are your greatest wealth," I read aloud from my own slip of paper, and we drain our glasses in a toast to that. Then I put the fortune in my wallet for safekeeping. It actually says, YOU WILL HAVE A LONG AND HAPPY FILE.

Outside, a thin orange line remains in the sky to the west. In the Bonneville, the stick-on digital dashboard clock says 2:17 without specifying morning or afternoon. It's wrong either way; we're driving home in a twilight the pearl gray of Dwight's new socks.

"Can I fix this tape in one week?" Anita asks.

"I was thinking you could, and then you said that," the Doctor says, sitting next to me in the back.

Dwight is taking a strange way home. In a neighborhood unknown to me he parks in front of a broken-down triple-decker. "I have to borrow a piece of equipment," he says, running into the house, and then he emerges with a big cardboard box, which he stows in the trunk. When we pull into our drive, he says, "I'd like to have a little partners' meeting upstairs right now. Walter, while we're doing that would you mind cleaning up the garbage out back?"

"Sure, Dwight," I say. "You guys have a meeting, I clean up the trash."

He gives me his famous smile and pinches my cheek. "You're playing a very important role," he says.

In the backyard I make sure I'm working alone—skunks have no fear and maybe no brains, and if you're not careful you can saunter right onto their heads—and then I scrape up the garbage with a shovel and broom. The little enforcers have been systematic, no coffee filter left unturned. I'm hosing down the blacktop and rinsing off my hands when the Doctor appears, humping two big cases of lighting gear down the driveway.

"Guess what?" he says, heading into the backyard. "We're having a little shoot."

"Now?" I say.

"Exciting, isn't it?" Anita says brightly, coming after him with her computer screen in her hands. Dwight brings up the rear with a folding table and the big orange extension cord. He sets those things down and crooks a finger to beckon me back up the driveway.

"Now, Dwight? We're having a shoot now?"

"Inspiration doesn't punch a clock, Walter. You know that. Plus, this idea has to be shot at night. It won't have the same spooky look in the daytime."

"Oh. Am I working on the script out here?"

"No, you're not." He opens his trunk, takes out the big box, and walks to the house. "Let's go to your place," he says on the porch. I open the door and follow him down the hall to my room. He drops the box on my bed. "How do you feel, Walter?" he asks.

"I feel great," I say.

"Good. Close your eyes," he says. "It's a surprise."

I close my eyes. Dwight holds something fuzzy up under my chin. I open my eyes again. A great expanse of black fur spreads from my neck to the floor. I peek into the opened cardboard box. It contains the head of a gorilla.

"What's this for, Dwight? Who's gonna wear this?"

He looks at me the way you look at a child; then he lays the furry body in my arms and rests the head on top. "Congratulations, Walter. You'll be directed by the lovely Anita."

I've had bad parts before, but always within my own species. I don't even know how you do this. "Do I keep my shoes on?" I ask.

"You don't keep anything on," Dwight says. "This is an action role in a heavy outfit. You'll be too hot if you're dressed in there. Plus, you'll feel more feral without your pants." He holds up an outstretched hand. "You're on in five," he says, and waves goodbye.

I get out of my clothes and into the suit. Powerful polyester fumes envelop me; I smell like new wall-to-wall carpet. I stand before the full-length closet mirror. Sticking out of the enormous black body, my little human face looks pathetic, so I put on the head, and when I consult the mirror again a change takes place in the chemistry of my brain. I bound out of the bedroom, huge shoulders squeezing through the doorway. The kitchen is flooded with white light, the window as bright as a television screen. My friends are in the backyard, arranging Anita's computer on the table at the edge of the lawn. I pad out to the enclosed back porch and watch them for a minute from there. Then I leap down into the lights and roar.

"Walter!" Anita cries. "I can't believe it! I can't believe how incredible you look! It is you, isn't it, Walter? *Walter?*"

I swipe at the air and run across the grass. The Doctor hoists the camera to his shoulder. "Kalimba, lord of the jungle!" he proclaims. "No creature dare trifle with mighty Kalimba!"

They have a small color monitor propped on the equipment cases so Anita can watch the framing of the shots. I lumber over there to see myself in it. I scratch my ribs and beat my chest. *"Hey,"* I say. *"I do look pretty scary, don't I?"* But inside the big, hollow head my voice is muffled and indistinct.

"Ruh, ruh, ruh," Dwight says, imitating the way I sound.

I hear an unfamiliar voice and spin around. A strange woman is standing in the shadows beside me. I jump back in surprise, lose my footing in the cumbersome suit, and fall down on the ground. Anita rushes over to help me up. "Kalimba," she says, managing to stop laughing for a moment, "this is Rebecca. Rebecca, Kalimba. Kalimba's the guy I've been telling you about," she says, and then she cracks up again.

Rebecca is wearing black jeans and a light-blue silky top and smiling very weakly. I put out my paw to shake her hand. She steps away and waves instead and puts her hands behind her back.

"My name is actually Walter," I say, waving in return. *"Can you hang around for a while? Until we finish this shoot? Maybe we could have a drink or something."*

"What's he saying?" Rebecca asks Anita.

"Beats me," Anita says. "We can't understand you, ape boy."

"Maybe if you took off your head," Rebecca suggests.

"Time to get to work, Kalimba," Dwight calls out. "No socializing with the females."

"Hide behind those bushes," Anita says. "I'll give you a cue."

A wall of scrappy hedges lines the property's rear edge, long stalks of jungly sumac trees sprouting up in the gaps. I crawl through and hide in the neighbor's backyard. Dwight trains the lights on my hiding place. The Doctor gets into position with the camera. And then Anita cries, "Kalimba, claw your way out through the trees!"

I burst through the vegetation and do my best King Kong in the lights, flailing and howling. Then I act amazed to see Anita's PC. I stalk it on all fours.

She improvises in a narrator's voice. *"Do you sometimes think computers weren't made for human beings?"* she says. *"Are you tired of searching for the right business software? Well, take a look at our products.* OK, Kalimba, look at the computer screen. Scratch your head. *They're certainly not primitive.* Now play with the computer. Tap on the keyboard and stuff. Great. Now jump up and down and act real happy. *But they're so easy to use, even a monkey can do it."*

I nod my head up and down and dance all around in apelike wonder. I point to the computer screen. I pound the ground with my feet. *"It's not an easy life for me here, Rebecca,"* I say. *"I slave over video scripts night and day, and then as soon as I finish one they change their minds and make me do it again. If things don't turn out right, I have to do this."*

"Ruh, ruh, ruh, ruh," Dwight says.

"We're rolling, Kalimba," Anita says. "Do more ape things."

I play with the computer again, acting out big monkey excitement over the shapes and colors on the screen. I lope across the lawn on my knuckles. I cling to the Empire State Building and swipe at the airplanes around my head. And then, while plucking nits out of my coat, I notice two big skunks sniffing around by the garbage cans. Dwight catches me looking and he looks too, and then he swings a movie light onto the racing-striped creatures. They sit up and blink their vacant little eyes.

"Get them!" Anita calls to the Doctor, and he moves in for the shot. *"We won't comment on our competition,"* she narrates. *"But we've seen them lurking around."*

"Hey, those are skunks!" Rebecca cries.

"Isn't it great?" Anita says. "They live here. They're ours."

But Rebecca panics and tries to run away across the grass. Dwight, always the heads-up producer, spins the Doctor around by his shirt so he can shoot her doing that. And me, I don't even need direction for this. Life is a video for me now. I step into Rebecca's path and sweep her up in my arms.

"Let us save you from our competitors!" Anita shouts.

Rebecca screams and kicks and demands that I let her go. But Dwight throws a handful of popcorn at my feet, the oblivious skunks mosey right over to get it, and Rebecca yields to my furry embrace. I glance down to watch the skunks having their snack. Seeing them up close like this is doing something odd to my mind. It's bringing back my dream—reminding me that skunks were my only companions when Jeanette turned me away from her door.

"Rebecca, you're doing great," I say. *"I think you have real star potential. Don't tell me you've never acted before."*

I look out across the yard at Anita and Dwight and the Doctor. I've never seen them so happy. I say to myself: Kalimba, these are the people who helped you when you were a miserable, lonely wreck. They gave you a new shot at life. They taught you their glamorous profession. These are your friends, Kalimba, your greatest wealth. And now what do they ask from you in return? Only that you stand in the bright movie lights with a woman in your arms and be everybody's charming hero.

"Relationships take faith and hope and cooperation," Anita narrates. *"We're a big software company, but we think of ourselves as a gentle giant. You can trust us with your precious data."*

Isn't it true?

RUE

Susan Dodd

Miss Rainey Roth of Wyoming, Rhode Island, did not believe in luck. Sixty-one years old, a self-sufficient woman with a business of her own, she had no time for hazy notions. People who believed in sudden strokes of good fortune, she thought, were simply seeking an excuse for idleness. Nothing was apt to help a person who wouldn't help herself.

This sensible attitude was not the least bit undermined or shaken when, on the fifteenth of September, Miss Rainey discovered she had won ten thousand dollars in the State Lottery. She became a winner (the word seemed remarkably foolish, applied to herself) not through luck, but through carelessness: someone had dropped the ticket on the path to her small herb and spice shop. Miss Rainey had never bought a lottery ticket in her life, and she wasn't sure whether her practical nature or her whimsical streak prompted her to save the numbered stub, to check it against the winning numbers announced in the paper a few days later. Either way, she was sure of one thing: she wasn't about to let the benefits of a rather silly accident alter her realistic outlook. Luck, instead. Luck was largely a matter of paying attention.

Miss Rainey was accustomed to making decisions. She rarely sought advice, made up her mind with an almost savage authority. On the day her winnings were confirmed, she remained in the potting shed behind her house, where she put up flavored vinegars and scented toilet waters, potpourris and pomander balls. The scents from the drying sheaves of lavender and comfrey and sweet basil cleared her head. By late afternoon, she knew precisely what she was going to do with the ten thousand dollars which had fallen so peculiarly into her lap:

She was going to keep her feet on the ground.

She was going to pay off the remainder of the business expansion loan she had taken out two years ago with the Wyoming branch of the Old Stone Bank of Providence (an outstanding balance of $3,764.25, according to her records).

And she was going to get herself a proper divorce. Legal. Official. Once and for all.

The following morning, Miss Rainey phoned the bank. Mr. Gencarella, the branch manager, sounded like a rejected suitor when she told him what she was about. He congratulated her, however, and agreed to make the necessary arrangements. Miss Rainey made one more call. Then, dressed in the gray tweed suit reserved for important business, she walked to the foot of her driveway. Her coarse, curly hair, still more black than gray, was tucked into a wool beret the color of wild chicory blossoms. A silk scarf of peacock feather print was loosely knotted at her throat. With a gray-gloved hand, she reversed a hand-painted wood sign. OPEN FOR BUSINESS . . . KINDLY CONSIDER THE WELL-BEING OF RESIDENT CATS AND VISITING CHILDREN. DRIVE WITH CAUTION was changed to CLOSED. No excuses. No promises.

The private investigator's office was in a nondescript six-story building in downtown Providence, within sight of the State Capitol. After checking the directory in the dim, narrow lobby, Miss Rainey took the stairs to the third floor. There was an elevator, but she was not of a mind to wait for it. She needed to stretch her legs after the long drive. At the top of the stairs, she followed a sign shaped like a pointing hand: FRANKLIN R. ALFINO, ROOM 302. It relieved her that the nature of Mr. Alfino's services was not specified on the sign or his door. She thought this boded well for his discretion. The floor of the short corridor, speckled marble, was wet, and ammonia fumes made her eyes water. She passed three unmarked doors with pebbled glass windows before reaching Room 302.

Its door ajar, Room 302 was just that—a room. Perhaps fifteen feet square, windowless, uncarpeted. It contained one desk (gray metal), three file cabinets (one oak, two green metal), a small black safe, and a man in shirtsleeves who looked nearly as old as she was. Miss Rainey was taken aback.

"I beg your pardon, I should have knocked," she said.

The man looked up slowly from the newspaper spread across his desk. "No problem. Mrs. Roth?"

"Miss."

The man smiled. "Miss Roth. Come on in." He waved casually toward a rickety folding chair she had not noticed beside his desk. "Have a seat." He did not rise or fold his newspaper. "What can I do for you?"

Miss Rainey occupied the chair gingerly and with the utmost reluctance. She could already see she had made a mistake. The office itself did not disturb her, though it was certainly shabby and less than clean. Still, it was utilitarian, like her own workroom in the former potting shed.

The man, however, was nothing like herself. More to the point, he was nothing like what she had imagined. A private investigator should, to her way of thinking, look alert, energetic . . . perhaps a bit sly. Mr. Franklin Alfino looked innocent and slothful. His narrow shoulders seemed pulled down by a center of gravity located in his soft, round belly. He had very little chin, no hair to speak of, and his brown eyes, too close together, looked sleepy. He reminded her of a Rhode Island Red laying hen. She was hardly surprised when he cackled.

"Don't like my looks, huh?" He leaned back in his swivel chair and stretched, exposing a rumpled shirttail. "That's the chance you take with the Yellow Pages."

"I beg your pardon?"

"Isn't that how you found me—the Yellow Pages?"

"In fact it is," Miss Rainey said.

"Figures." Alfino nodded. "Started with the A's, right?"

Miss Rainey felt herself flushing, as if she were caught in some ill-considered fib.

"Don't tell me Paulie Abrams is all booked-up?"

The fact of the matter was that Miss Rainey had ruled out Paul C. Abrams because she found his ad distasteful. She could muster little confidence in professional services commended to her attention by a large India-ink eye with spiky lashes. Franklin R. Alfino had been the second name in the phone book, limited to a simple line-listing. She had thought, or hoped, this might indicate reliability, seriousness of purpose. His appearance in the flesh, however, did much to counteract that favorable first impression.

"I think perhaps . . ."

"Looks aren't everything," Alfino said. "Mannix I ain't. But you could give me the benefit of the doubt."

"Mannix?" Miss Rainey fingered the soft leather strap of her handbag nervously.

"The T.V. glamour boys . . . weren't you expecting somebody like that?"

"I do *not* watch television, Mr. Alfino. Nor have I had occasion to require the services of a private investigator previously. I didn't know what to expect."

"Let me tell you something, then—free advice." Alfino was grinning, and the expression made him look a good deal less sleepy. "There's sixteen of us—private eyes—in Providence. Another five in Warwick. I know all these guys, and you can take my word for it—none of 'em look much better than I do. Fact is, you could do worse."

Miss Rainey said nothing for a moment, a doubtful and worried crease in her forehead. Finally, while Franklin Alfino continued to stare at her, she smiled. "Pretty is as pretty does," she said.

The detective cackled. "So what can I do for you, good lady?"

"I wish to locate my husband," Miss Rainey said.

"I thought you said it was 'miss.'"

"I prefer it. My husband and I have been . . . estranged for some time."

"Okay . . . miss. What happens then—when I find him, I mean?"

"I would like you to make whatever arrangements are necessary for him to divorce me."

"You want to get divorced?"

"I want," Miss Rainey said, calmly and distinctly, "for *him* to divorce *me.*"

"But—."

"I am willing to pay."

Alfino shrugged. "How much?"

"We'll cross that bridge when we come to it. In the meantime, he must be located."

"Whatever you say. Name?"

"Lorraine Elizabeth Roth."

"His, I mean."

"John Amos Dudley."

Franklin Alfino scribbled in the margin of his newspaper with a ballpoint pen. Without looking up, he asked in a monotone, "When and where, to the best of your knowledge, was Mr. Amos last seen?"

"*Dudley.*" Miss Rainey sighed. "Commander Dudley. Point Judith Pier. He sailed for Block Island. The bluefish were running. He never came back."

"So he may have drowned?"

"He did nothing of the kind."

"How do you know?"

"Because he wrote and told me so. A postcard. Of the Watch Hill carousel."

"Have you got this card?"

"Certainly not."

"Don't suppose it'd help much, anyway. He tell you where he was going?"

Miss Rainey sniffed. "'Where the spirit moved him,' he said." She saw Alfino trying to suppress a smile. "Even *I* had to be somewhat amused, Mr. Alfino."

Looking sheepish, the detective asked, "Why don't you call me Frank?"

"I'd rather not."

"I'm sorry?"

"Nothing to be sorry about," Miss Rainey said firmly. "I am simply not one for informality in business dealings."

Alfino studied her, and she saw she had been mistaken: his eyes were alert as a chicken hawk's.

"Back to business, then . . . Miss Roth. When did you receive this card?"

"I believe it was the first of July," Miss Rainey said.

"Postmarked—."

"The first of July, nineteen forty-three."

Franklin Alfino rubbed his eyes with his knuckles, as if he'd had cold water thrown in his face. "Ho, boy . . . ," he said.

"You can divorce *him*," her father's friend Judge Brimford had told her in nineteen forty-four, in his pleasant walnut-paneled study over-looking Narragansett Bay. "There is no earthly reason why you need ever set eyes on the scoundrel again, my dear." Rainey's father had recently died, and the Judge, retired, attempted to offer her *ad hoc* paternal advice and judicious affection.

Rainey had thanked the Judge and done nothing.

"*You* can divorce *him*," a Providence lawyer had pointed out in nineteen forty-six, when Rainey was buying the farm in Wyoming with the intention of beginning a new and independent life. "A legal notice is published. A brief wait. Then, if he doesn't appear—which we may assume he will not—the divorce is granted. *Pro forma.*"

"But *he* left *me*," Rainey said.

"Immaterial."

It was not immaterial to Rainey. She had thanked the lawyer and left.

"*You* can divorce *him*," Franklin Alfino told her now. "Much simpler."

"So I understand. That is not, however, what I want."

Alfino sighed. "Have it your way."

"I intend to," Miss Rainey replied. She did not leave until she had answered all the detective's questions and written him a check as a retainer.

Driving back to her farm, Miss Rainey Roth felt cautiously optimistic. Perhaps Franklin R. Alfino was unlikely to set the world on fire, but he knew how to take direction. And he was evidently not as befuddled as he looked. The hourly rate he proposed to charge for his services seemed reasonable. Besides, Miss Rainey didn't relish the prospect of another go at the Yellow Pages. The private investigators of greater Providence were probably not, as Alfino had suggested, a particularly congenial or impressive lot. Now that she had selected one, she might as well give him a chance, the benefit of the doubt.

Ten days later, Miss Rainey was arranging bittersweet and marsh grasses in lacquered Chinese baskets when she heard a car coming up the drive. Although her automotive knowledge was limited, she recognized the sound of a car in desperate need of a new muffler. She winced at the unwholesome racket upsetting the late morning calm, but kept on with her work. Footsteps scattered gravel on the path outside. She glanced through the small window and saw Franklin Alfino approaching the shop. She went out.

"You've found him?"

"Nothing yet. Sorry."

Miss Rainey tried to keep impatience from her tone. "What is it, then?"

"Had to come out this way, your neck of the woods. How about some lunch?"

"You want me to give you lunch?" she asked faintly.

Alfino tossed back his head and cackled, scaring off a squirrel from some nearby shrubbery. "I want to *take* you to lunch. There's a little tavern, not far . . . on the road to Exeter. How about it?"

Miss Rainey's usual lunch was a cup of sassafras or chamomile tea with saltines or a slice of buttered bread, and she frequently forgot to have that until three o'clock. She looked completely astonished at the detective's suggestion.

"Best cheeseburgers in Rhode Island. Chowder's homemade."

"I look a fright."

"Take off that smock thing and I wouldn't mind being seen with you." Alfino's eyes hooded sleepily. "Besides, I want to talk to you. Business," he said.

He drove more like a tourist than a detective—slow, aimless, his concentration adequate, but sporadic. Miss Rainey leaned back and looked out the window, waiting for him to speak. He did not. When he pulled up in front of the roadhouse—a place she had never visited, but assumed disreputable—she regretted the ride was over. The leaves were beginning to turn, and she realized that she always worked so hard at this time of the year that she scarcely had time to notice the colors of the season. "Bittersweet," she thought.

The Hilltop Tavern was as dilapidated inside as its exterior promised. The air was stale, smelling of beer, tobacco, cooking fat. Several men in work clothes sat at the bar, drinking and staring at a television screen high in a corner, suspended from the ceiling. Miss Rainey could see that they were watching on old horse opera. She thought she spotted John Wayne, huge, gravel-voiced, and very young. Alfino led her to a booth in the opposite corner of the room, and she chose the side of the table which placed her back to the television.

"Place doesn't look like much, does it?" Alfino said. The remark was offhand, but she got the feeling he was trying to gauge her reaction. She paused, pursing her lips.

"Pretty is as pretty does," she said at last.

The detective grinned. "Wait till the chowder—that's *beautiful*."

A stout middle-aged woman in a white nylon dress and an orange calico apron, who had been standing behind the bar watching television when they came in, approached the booth. "What can I get you?" No menu was on the table and none was offered.

"Chowder and a cheeseburger?" Alfino asked Miss Rainey.

"I believe just the chowder will do nicely, thank you."

He turned to the waitress, whose bored gaze was drifting back to John Wayne. "And bring the lady some johnnycakes, too. I'll have the chowder, onion rings, a burger medium-well, and a Narragansett draft. You want a beer?"

For a moment, Miss Rainey thought he was still addressing the waitress. "Oh . . . no, thank you."

"What'll you have to drink?"

"Tea?"

"Don't have it," the waitress said.

"Then a glass of water, please."

"You got any hard cider in yet?"

"Yup."

"Bring her one of those."

Miss Rainey opened her mouth to protest, but Franklin Alfino startled her speechless by reaching across the table and chucking her under the chin. "Trust me."

"That it?" the waitress asked.

"For now," Alfino said.

Miss Rainey waited until she felt sure the woman was out of hearing before she spoke. "Mr. Alfino—."

"I wish you wouldn't call me that." He sounded aggrieved.

"Please—."

"I know, I know . . . you don't believe in mixing business with pleasure." He hunched his shoulders and seemed to duck his rather large bald head. "But you did come out for lunch with me. How come?"

"I had nothing to offer you at home," Miss Rainey said.

Alfino raised his mournful eyes and smiled. "You're honest, I'll say that for you."

"I'm afraid I never learned not to be. I'm a very solitary person, Mr. Alfino. I've not had much need for tact and pleasantries."

"You went to college."

Miss Rainey felt accused by the flat statement. "That has nothing to do with it."

"Don't get your back up. I just meant you talk like a person with education."

"A young ladies' seminary. In Boston."

"A seminary . . . you mean like a priest? What, were you going to be a missionary or something?"

"A seminary was like a finishing school, Mr. Alfino."

"Yeah? Are you finished?"

She smiled.

"What'd they teach you there, on the level?"

"To speak like an educated person. Tact and pleasantries, too, I suppose . . . but I lacked the aptitude. Or have forgotten, perhaps."

"You're all right," the detective said. "Pleasant enough for me."

"Thank you." She felt flustered, like a schoolgirl.

"I'm going to college myself. Community college. Nights. Getting an associate's degree in accounting."

Miss Rainey blinked. "Why, that's very . . . commendable."

"Incredible, you mean." He laughed. "I'm sixty-four . . . don't ask."

"You look a good deal younger."

"Lady, you say you got no tact?"

Miss Rainey squirmed uncomfortably and the vinyl seat-padding under her squeaked. "You said we had business to discuss?"

Alfino's face resumed its somnolent expression. "I haven't been able to turn up a thing."

"So I gathered. I didn't expect this to be uncomplicated."

"Did you expect it to be expensive? Because I gotta tell you, the hours are mounting up."

Miss Rainey raised her chin. "I'll decide when I can no longer afford your services."

"Hey, don't get me wrong—I can use the work. But this could take months, and even then, it might be a blind alley. I'm just trying to be honest with you."

"Of course . . ."

"I hate wasting your money, when it'd be so easy to get you a divorce without finding your . . ."

250 / SUSAN DODD

"Husband," Miss Rainey said firmly. "I am still married to him."

"Sure. And you don't want to be—that I can understand. What I don't understand is—."

"You don't need to understand," she snapped.

The detective's nostrils and lips pinched, drawing together as if a swift and shocking blow had been dealt to him. The waitress returned, and Miss Rainey looked away. Plates, bowls, and glasses were set on the black formica table with unnecessary clatter.

Miss Rainey felt sorely distressed by her unintentional sharpness. "I'm sorry," she murmured.

"You're right, though, it's none of my business—that part of it."

The waitress sauntered off again.

"I suppose that I *do* want you to understand." The admission was clearly difficult for her.

"Never mind. Try the cider."

"He left me, so he should divorce me . . . people must take responsibility for what they do."

"You loved him?"

Miss Rainey looked severely at Franklin Alfino and did not speak for a full minute. He waited, watching her face with eyes that were alert under half-lowered lids.

"I did," she said finally. "But what's important is that I promised myself to him. And John Amos Dudley promised himself to me. Whether I loved him is beside the point, Mr. Alfino. I would have kept my promise regardless. I *have* kept it, for thirty-nine years."

Alfino shrugged. "No disrespect . . . but what's divorce gonna get you now?"

"Very little, I suppose you might say. But I've reached an age where I don't care to leave loose ends."

Franklin Alfino picked up a dented soup spoon and stirred thick white chowder in a gray plastic bowl. Behind wisps of steam, his face was troubled. Miss Rainey reached for the pepper. Neither of them started eating.

"May I ask you a question . . . a personal question, Mr. Alfino?"

"Shoot."

"What makes you go to college? Do you intend to become an accountant?"

His cheeks seemed to sag when he smiled, and the dark pockets under his eyes deepened. "I'm a little old to start over." He picked up a greasy salt shaker and held it, right-side-up, over his soup. "But I'm not . . . 'finished.' There are certain things that still interest me, things I'd like to understand . . . I never really had a chance to learn them until now."

"Precisely." Miss Rainey nodded. "I want John Amos Dudley to look me in the eye."

"You think if he does you'll understand something?"

"I rather doubt it."

"But you'd have a chance to try?"

"I believe we understand each other, Mr. Alfino."

The detective leaned across the table and gently tucked a paper napkin inside the high collar of Miss Rainey's blouse. The bristly back of his hand brushed her check. "Your johnnycakes are getting cold," he said. "Eat."

Several weeks passed with no word from Alfino. Miss Rainey was not surprised, but she was restless. She busied herself in the shop, preparing for the holiday trade. The second week in October, summer returned to New England. For four days, the sun beat down on the tin roof of the work shed, making it unbearably hot. Crickets chirped at night. The cats, Oleander and Hyssop, seemed stupefied.

Miss Rainey tried not to allow the extraordinary weather to disrupt her autumn routines. She packaged extra sage and thyme for Thanksgiving stuffing. She tied whole cloves and nutmeg, cinnamon stick and cardamom seed in tiny muslin sacks and designed a new label with instructions for "Wassail Bowl." When perspiration dripped into her eyes, she swiped impatiently at her brow with the back of her hand and thought how the heat would dry the herbs quickly, sealing in their flavors. She kept busy. She kept her feet on the ground. And she kept thinking of John Amos Dudley, who had courted her in a late Indian summer like this one, wed her the first week of Advent. Rainey had worn a silk shantung suit the color of champagne—it was wartime, Chantilly and satin were considered frivolous. Her bouquet of white tea roses was bordered with lavender and rosemary. Lavender for luck. And rosemary for remembrance.

John Amos Dudley was a local boy made good by war. A Lieutenant Commander in the Navy stationed at Quonset Point, he fought the enemy on paper. He was tight-lipped and clear-eyed when Rainey's father inquired about the specific nature of his duties.

Commander Dudley was a serious young man. Only Rainey Roth, with her high spirits and her quick tongue, could make him laugh in uniform. He was the son of a brakeman for the Providence and Worcester, and his family lived in a modest house near the railroad station in Westerly, Rhode Island. His mother had died of a stroke during the hurricane of '38, and his father's heart had failed the following year in a freightyard outside of Boston. John Amos was their only child.

Rainey met him at a tea dance at the Watch Hill Yacht Club on the last summer weekend of 1942. His dress whites were impeccably tailored and pressed and his eyes were the color of the hazy horizon over Montauk. They waltzed—something by Victor Herbert, she recalled—and the plum-colored sleeves of Rainey's afternoon gown had fluttered in three-quarter time against the uncompromising white of Commander Dudley's shoulders.

Now, the extraordinary warmth and fragrance of Indian summer revived her whirlwind romance, her scant months as a wife—continuing to live with her widowed father in the large, shingled house on the pond at Haversham, while John angled for weekend leave. She had still felt like a bride, when the bridegroom vanished, abandoning her and the war effort and the United States Navy, for bluefish and Block Island and the spirit that moved him.

"The spirit that moved him"—even now, nearly four decades later, Miss Rainey realized that she lacked the frailest notion what such a spirit might have been. On their wedding night, in a large cherry spool bed in the guest room at Haversham (her father had considerately gone fishing with Judge Brimford immediately following the ceremony), John had wept in her arms, confessing his longing to be a warrior of the sea. He had petitioned to be sent to the South Pacific, attached to a cruiser or battleship. The Navy's continued refusal to make him a hero perplexed and unmanned him. Rainey had stroked his wet cheeks, reassuring him of his manliness, secretly hoping to conceive a son as the proof her husband needed.

By late spring, John Amos Dudley had his assurances: he received orders to join a heavy cruiser in the Aleutian Islands and Rainey was carrying his child. In June, three days before he was to ship out, he sailed in a rented skiff toward Block Island, alone, with fishing gear borrowed from Rainey's father. Weeks later, when the Watch Hill post-card had come, Dr. Roth had quickly paid the owner of the skiff and purchased new fishing tackle. Rainey, at three and a half months, had miscarried the child she had been so certain was a son. She understood that the man to whom she had promised herself was a coward. Beyond that, however, "the spirit that moved him" eluded her.

It was this, the mysteriousness of John Amos Dudley's spirit, that most tormented Rainey. The yearning to see her husband's face once more was not prompted by passion or bitterness. Those, like the humiliation, had passed. But she could not abide knowing her life had been shaped and confined by something whose nature she failed so totally to grasp. And she supposed she wanted her husband to look her in the eye, to renounce her outright, because she still cherished a hope that she might yet make a man of him.

For a time, government men had come to the house at Haver-sham, full of probing questions about the Lieutenant Commander who disappeared. Rainey and her father were both shamed by the accusations implicit in their questions and their flat, official eyes. But there was nothing to hide. When she received the picture postcard of the Watch Hill carousel (a New York postmark), Rainey had relin-quished it to her government gladly. Her aging father, retired from medical practice, had been gentle, noncommittal, eager to avoid his daughter's gaze. He did not live to see the end of the war, and Rainey felt her disgrace shortened his life. In her innocence, she had consort-ed with the enemy.

Now, as the sun beat down on the tin roof, Miss Rainey Roth twisted stalks of marjoram into Advent wreaths, inhaled the heady smells of dill and basil and oregano, and looked back on the chapter of her life whose ending she would finally be able to write, thanks to a numbered chance carelessly dropped on her garden path. She fash-ioned nosegays of strawflowers to adorn the doorways of fussy women with cheerful, orderly families. She filled them out with sprigs of euca-lyptus for scent. Rosemary for remembrance. And she waited to hear from Franklin R. Alfino, Private Investigator.

The odd, misplaced hot spell passed and autumn returned. Now the air had teeth in it. Miss Rainey removed her woolen cardigans from the cedar chest in the attic and hung them outdoors to let the wind lessen the pungent odor of southernwood. On cold mornings, she plugged in a small electric heater in her workroom. She massaged her stiff fingers with warmed camphor oil at night.

It was a chilly overcast morning, and she was standing with her back to the heater, pasting hand-lettered labels on bottles of pale pink chive blossom vinegar, when Franklin Alfino returned. She did not hear him approach until he opened the door, setting her Japanese glass wind-chimes clashing.

"Good Heavens!" A handful of bright paper squares flew from her hands and floated to the floor.

The detective squatted awkwardly and began to gather up the scattered labels. "Scare you? Sorry."

"Startle a body out of her wits," Miss Rainey muttered.

Alfino straightened up and gave her a mildly reproving look.

"Don't mind me," she said.

"Get up on the wrong side of the bed?"

"It's getting up that matters." She tried to sound businesslike. "Have you something to report . . . or do you just happen to be 'in my neck of the woods' again?"

"Got anything around the house for lunch?"

"It's ten o'clock in the morning, Mr. Alfino."

The detective smiled good-naturedly. "I learned how to tell time at detective school, Miss Roth. Got any coffee?" He looked pointedly at an electric percolator on the corner of her workbench. It was plugged into an extension cord which reached, just barely, to an outlet halfway around the room.

"Herb tea. I do not approve of coffee."

"Don't know what you're missing. I'll settle for anything warm, though . . . even if it tastes like boiled socks."

Miss Rainey brewed tea in a tarnished copper kettle she took from the windowsill and placed it on the table along with two chipped earthenware mugs. Alfino cleared a space among the litter of vinegar bottles, labels, and glass cannisters of loose herbs. Without speaking, they sat side by side on the two rickety chairs which had once belonged to the austere dining room at Haversham. Miss Rainey took the mug without a handle and the chair with a loose hind leg.

"This isn't so bad," Alfino said.

"Lemon verbena, the herb of enchantment."

"You putting a spell on me?"

"I might try, if I thought for a moment it would get you down to business."

Alfino bowed deferentially. "All you gotta do is ask, good lady."

Miss Rainey's hands, trembling slightly, closed around her spotted brown mug. "I am asking," she said.

"I've found him."

"Where?"

"I don't know how to say this tactfully."

"Never mind that. Where is he?"

"In New Bedford. In a cemetery."

Miss Rainey Roth stared at Franklin Alfino. Her eyes, glistening with anger, were fiercely blue. "He's dead?"

"Almost fifteen years. I'm sorry . . ."

Her lips flattened out in a hard, straight line.

"Maybe it's just as well," Alfino said uncertainly.

Miss Rainey replied slowly, in a choked voice. "It simply is not . . . acceptable." She started to get up. Then, without warning, her mouth framing a small silent "o" of distress, she slumped to the floor in a dead faint.

She awoke on the horsehair sofa in her own front parlor. The air was musty, for the room was unused and unloved. Her father's fine furniture surrounded her, dusty and unforgiving. Franklin Alfino bent over her, covering her with his raincoat, a rumpled tan thing she had noticed when he first arrived: at last, something about him seemed to fall in with his occupation.

Miss Rainey came to like a person taking charge of a small emergency. "Don't fuss. I'm fine." When she sat up, too quickly, the color drained from her face. She dropped back against the sofa cushions. "I'm perfectly all right."

The detective wrapped the soiled sleeves of his coat around her shoulders. "Now, just take it easy for a few minutes."

"I never faint . . . must be coming down with something."

"A shock. Want some water?"

"What happened to him?"

"Your—."

"Husband," Miss Rainey said firmly.

"We'll talk about that later." Alfino looked uneasily around the cold, formal furniture. "Nice place you've got."

"We'll talk about it now, Mr. Alfino."

"You ought to—."

"Now," she repeated.

Alfino sighed. "Seems he drank himself to death. Put in a State institution in '65, died within a year. He was buried there. No living relatives, he told 'em."

Miss Rainey closed her eyes, nodding weakly.

"You sure you're all right?"

"He never even looked me in the eye." She turned her face to the rough, stern sofa-back, and the detective realized that she was weeping.

"It's finished," he said softly. "You're rid of him."

"No," she whispered. "I am not."

The following week, Miss Rainey sent a sizable check to Franklin R. Alfino, Private Investigator, for services rendered. She was free of debt, and nearly a thousand dollars were left from her lottery winnings. Her feet were on the ground, her business was unencumbered, her unfortunate past dead and buried. She tried to summon up satisfaction over the loose ends snipped from her life, and she kept about her work. In her herb garden, only the rue—that bitter shrub symbolizing repentance and said to restore second sight—remained green. She cut it back, pausing to bruise a handful of leaves and rub their oil on her forehead, for her head often ached. The Four Thieves . . . blind Adam . . . the Pharisees . . . it was a poor company she joined, anointing herself with rue.

The shop was doing a brisker business than in previous years. People seemed more interested in caring for themselves properly. Miss Rainey expanded her stock, devised more appealing labels and packaging, lectured at the town library and the Women's Club on the healing properties of common herbs. Exhausted at the end of each day, she took herself off to bed and courted sleep with hops tea and an inventory of her blessings. She was, after all, independent, content.

Something, however, had come over Miss Rainey Roth of Wyoming, Rhode Island. Mary Alice Potter, the town librarian, marked the change. So did Mr. Gencarella at the bank. Miss Rainey looked well enough, but her step seemed slightly less determined, her shoulders less straight. When she addressed the Friends of the Library, her ideas did not seem quite so "definite," Mary Alice said. The lines in her face were deeper, yet softer too, as if sorrow had won a victory over disapproval.

In short, Miss Rainey had been widowed.

The first Sunday of Advent was bitingly cold. A furious wind lashed the last leaves from the trees and brought small branches down with them. Wearing a severe black gabardine coat which had hung in the back of her closet for a dozen years, Miss Rainey went to the foot of her driveway, turned over her sign, and drove to New Bedford, Massachusetts, the port from which the stern Captain Ahab had pursued his great white nemesis.

She had called Franklin Alfino the day before for directions to the hospital. At first, he had refused to give them to her.

"What do you want to do that for?" he said. "Let the past stay buried."

"This is *my* concern," Miss Rainey told him.

"Mine, too."

"Why should you make it your business?"

"Like I told you, good lady, some things still interest me."

In the end, however, Alfino had given the directions and even offered to accompany her. Miss Rainey had turned him down with unaccustomed gentleness. "I must do this myself. It's between me and—."

"Your husband," he said. "I understand." The detective sounded sad and old.

"Franklin?"

"I thought you didn't want to call me that."

"Our business is finished now," Miss Rainey said.

The State hospital was located to the west of the city, several miles off a straight, little-used highway. The cemetery, Alfino had told her, was to the left of the main gate, behind a grove of pines.

Miss Rainey was stopped at the gate. She rolled down the car window and informed the elderly guard that she merely intended to visit the cemetery. He told her where to park and waved her on without curiosity, pulling a plaid muffler over his jaw.

There were no other visitors in the graveyard, a small square tract of land made monotonous with rows of plain markers. Miss Rainey had no trouble finding the plot she wanted. It was identified by a gray granite slab the size of a dress box: J. A. DUDLEY, 1917–1966.

Wind tore through the trees. There was a faint music from a nearby hospital building, but it could be heard only when the wind paused. The strains were brassy, but too sporadic for her to recognize. Miss Rainey stood beside the grave of her late husband, studying the two lines of letters and numbers meant to memorialize him, and trying to recall his face.

But even now, John Amos Dudley refused to look her in the eye. The face of the young Lieutenant Commander was darkly tarnished and dim, and the forty-nine-year-old drunkard buried here was unimaginable to her. Only a dazzling white sleeve and the color of the sky over Montauk came back to her. Miss Rainey waited. Behind the brutal wind, she thought she detected a waltz. But even as she listened, she knew she was making it up . . . as deftly as she had made up the contentment of her life.

When the breeze abated, the music made itself plain. A march— John Philip Sousa, if she wasn't mistaken. The false heartiness of parades and toy soldiers. Miss Rainey straightened her shoulders and gave a little shake of her head. Then she opened her handbag to remove a small pouch of unbleached muslin.

The dried herbs, mixed that morning, were comfortably rough and familiar to her fingers, something known and understood. She shook them from the sack, cupping them in the palm of her right hand. Then, when the wind picked up again, she tossed the handful of earth-toned bits and pieces into the swells of air. They flew from her hand and seemed to rise over her head before they dropped unevenly upon the final resting place of her estranged and long-gone husband:

> Rosemary for remembrance . . .
> Thyme for courage . . .
> And rue, the herb of grace.

THANKSGIVING DAY

Susan Minot

Gus and Rosie Vincent waited for their six children to crawl out of the station wagon and then slammed the doors. The Vincents were always the first to arrive.

They would pull up to the house in Motley, Massachusetts, where their father grew up, and crunch across the gravel, and in the doorway was Ma with her dark blue dress pleated from collar to waist and they would give her kisses, then file in to dump their coats in the coatroom and right away the first thing would be the smell of Pa's cigar. He waited in the other room. Every Thanksgiving they descended upon him and every year it was the same.

The three girls wore matching plaid skirts with plaid suspender straps. Caitlin and Sophie, who looked alike, had on hair bands of the same material. Delilah, the youngest daughter, was darker, with a short pixie. She said it wasn't fair she didn't get to have long hair too. The three boys came after, Gus and Sherman and Chickie, in grey flannels. Chickie's were shorts, since he was the baby.

For Sophie, the best thing was getting to see the cousins, especially the other Vincents. Bit, the only girl cousin, was Sophie's age, ten. And Churly was the oldest of everybody; he was fourteen. Churly and Bit arrived with Uncle Charles and Aunt Ginny. Sophie hesitated because sometimes you didn't give them a kiss. On Aunt Ginny's cardigan was the turkey pin she wore every year. The other cousins were the Smalls. Aunt Fran used to be a Vincent before she married Uncle Thomas. They had three boys. The oldest was Teever Small, who drooled.

Once everyone was there, the children had to put their coats back on for the annual picture. Bit had a white rabbit muff that Teever Small grabbed at, trying to flirt. "That's enough of that," said his father, but Bit had already snatched it back. Sophie felt how soft the fur was, thinking about the dead rabbit; the muff was in the shape of a rabbit too. The grown-ups shuffled everybody around, then stood beside Sophie's father, who had the camera. They crossed their arms against the cold, talking to one another and watching to make sure the kids didn't move.

"I'll be doggone," said Uncle Thomas. Sophie stared at his bow tie. "Will you look at that."

"A bunch of young ladies and young gentlemen," said Aunt Fran, smacking her orange lips. She had white hair like Ma's, except hers was short.

"Knock it off, Churly," Uncle Charles said.

Sophie turned around. Churly was smirking. He had a head shaped like a wooden golf club, with his long neck, and a crew cut like the other boys. Sophie looked back at the house and saw Ma inside, watching through the French doors.

After the picture was taken, Rosie Vincent told her children to say hello to Livia, and the cousins tagged along. The hall to the kitchen was dark, the floor with a sheen from the glow at the end. The kitchen was pale gray, with no lights on, and a white enamel table in the middle. Livia gave them pinched kisses, her eyes darting around the room, checking on food, on the children. She was huge and huffing in her white uniform. The kitchen smelled of Worcestershire sauce and turkey. "Are you behaving yourselves now?" She held up a shiny wooden spoon. When she was cooking, everything on Livia sweated, the steam rising behind her from the pots on the stove.

"Not me," Churly said. "I always try to be as naughty as possible."

Caitlin laughed while Sophie looked at Livia's face, which meant business. Livia sat down. "Now what are the seven blessed sacraments?" she asked, addressing Gus and Rosie's children—Catholic, thanks to their mother. Livia tipped one ear forward the way Sophie had seen the priest do in confession. Sophie fingered a tin Jell-O mold shaped like a fish, and Caitlin busied herself by tucking in Sherman's shirttails. No one answered. Livia rattled them off herself, slicing apples so the blade came right to her thumb without even looking. The cousin drifted off into the pantry as Livia thought up new questions—all having to do with catechism.

The dining-room table had already been set. The cranberry sauce had a spoon sticking out. Bit stole some mint wafers, reaching past the blue water goblets into the middle of the table, and gave one to Sophie. "It's okay," said Bit, noticing Sophie's expression.

"I saw that," Churly said from the doorway. Sophie blushed. He came in and whispered, "All right, you guys . . ." and she saw how his eyes were like those light-blue paperweights that had white lines of glass streaked from the middle. He leaned past them and plucked a candy out of the cut-glass boat. "Delish," he said. "Don't mind if I do."

In the living room, the grown-ups stood stirring drinks at the red-leather bar stand; then they sat down. Sophie's mother was the only one without a scotch or a Dubonnet. There was nothing to do while the grown-ups talked except to look around at each tiny thing. Three walls were covered with books, and over the mantelpiece was a portrait of Dr. Vincent, so dark and shiny that the lights reflected off it. One side of the room was all French windows, with dead vines at the edges. The windows overlooked the lawn. Beside the fireplace was a child's rocking chair with a red back, an antique. Gus had gotten to it first and was sitting there, holding onto his ankles, next to Ma's place on the sofa. They had the hard kind of sofas with wooden arms and wood in a curve along the back. You could tell it was Ma's place because of the brown smudge on the ceiling from her cigarette smoke.

The girls examined their grandmother. Her shoes, the pair her granddaughters liked the best, were pale lavender with pink trim and flat bows, her fancy shoes.

"Gussie," said Aunt Fran, the one person in the world who called Sophie's father that. She said it as if it tasted bad. "How'd you like the game?" The last time they had seen each other was at the Harvard halftime in October when they were stretching their legs under the bleachers. Gus, with his children, said, "Good day to you," as if he saw his sister every day, which he didn't, each walking in the opposite direction.

The grown-ups talked about the sports the boys were playing.

"Churly's on the debating team," said Uncle Charles. He was the oldest Vincent son.

"I certainly am," said Churly, the only one of the children taking up a seat. "Anyone want to argue?"

Under a lamp was a picture of Ma before she married. She was holding a plume of roses at her waist; her chin to the side, her dark eyes and dark hair swept up.

The grown-ups were talking about the woman next door who died after she cut her finger on a splinter from a Christmas-tree ornament. Ma said how appropriate it was that a pheasant appeared out of the woods at Mr. Granger's funeral.

"But *she* was the one who loved to shoot," said Aunt Fran with her Adam's apple thrust out.

"Terrible story about their son," said Sophie's mother. Her thumb rubbed her knuckle while the conversation continued.

They talked without looking at each other, their chairs all facing in. Aunt Fran addressed her remarks to the one spot in the room where no one sat or stood. She and Uncle Thomas were having a pond dug in the back of their house and by mistake the workers had struck a pipe. Aunt Fran and Uncle Thomas told the story at the same time, interrupting each other.

Uncle Charles said, "It's like a zoo at my house." When he made jokes, he barely cracked a smile. Bit was lucky, she got to have a pony and three dogs and sheep. "Our sheep just stand there in the rain," said Churly.

Uncle Charles said the chickens hated him. And now they had a turtle, with a chain attached to the loop on its shell so it wouldn't run away. "It chooses to sleep where I'm accustomed to park my car," he said.

"A what?" said Pa, angry at having to strain.

"Turtle," yelled Uncle Charles.

"Where's our turtle soup then?" Pa said and some of the family chuckled. Sophie didn't think he was kidding. He sat there still as a statue, his hands gripping the mahogany claws of his chair.

Caitlin was up at the bar with Churly, pouring a ginger ale. Sophie got Bit and Delilah to go to the owl room, and the boys followed. There were glass owls and a hollow brass owl with a hinge so its head lifted off, two china owls with flowers, owl engravings, and a needle-point of an owl that Caitlin had done from a kit. They had a game they played by closing their eyes and then going nose to nose with someone and saying, "One, two, three, Owl-lee, Owl-lee," and open-ing their eyes, imitating an owl. Delilah and Sherman were playing it.

Stretching down the corridor were group silhouettes of Vincent ancestors, black cutouts of children with ringlets, holding hoops, or men with bearded profiles. There were Pa's team pictures from Noble & Greenough and his class pictures from Harvard. All the faces in the photographs had straight noses and white eyeballs and hide-gray com-plexions. In one, Pa lay on his side, lengthwise, in front of everyone else. Sophie tried to match him with the Pa back in the living room. You never saw Pa smile, that was common knowledge, except in one picture the Vincents had at home, of Pa with the Senator. His job had been to write speeches, and, according to Sophie's mother, he got a dollar a year to do it. In the picture, his grin is closed, like a clown's. There was Pa in an army uniform—but Sophie knew the story of that. Pa missed the war, sailing to France on the exact day Armistice was declared. At the end of the hall, Sophie came to the picture of Pa's brother, the famous doctor who discovered the cure for a disease whose name she could never remember. He had died a long time ago.

When they drifted back into the living room, Uncle Charles was recalling when the lawn froze and they could skate over the sunken garden.

"Not true," said Pa, gurgling. "My lawn was never an ice rink."

"Sure," said Sophie's father. "Everything was frozen solid."

Pa said, "Never happened in my lifetime."

Uncle Charles clamped on his pipe with his back teeth. "Oh yes it did, Pa. You must be losing your memory." His voice was squeaky.

"Ma," demanded Pa.

With her perfectly calm face, Ma said, "I do remember it, yes." She looked at Pa and said gently, "It was when you were away."

"Nonsense," he said. "I never went anywhere."

The children's table was wobbly. This year Sophie got to sit at the big table, and Caitlin and Churly, too. Bit said she was glad to stay at the children's table where she wouldn't have to use good manners.

When the plates came, they had everything on them already, even creamed onions whether you liked them or not. Pa looked down at the food in front of him.

"Gravy, Grandpa?" shouted Aunt Fran. Half-frowning, he regarded her. She swung a silver ladle over his turkey, bringing it up with a flourish. "Yummy," she said in a booming voice.

Everyone at the table used loud voices—family behavior. When Sophie went out to go to the bathroom, she stood for a moment in the hall between the Chinese portraits and listened to the clatter behind her, the hollow echo from the high ceilings, Aunt Fran's hooting, the knives clicking on the china, her mother's voice saying something quietly to the little table. Sophie could tell Uncle Charles from his whine, and her grandmother was the slow voice enunciating each word the way old people do because they're tired of talking. Sophie went up close to study one Indian picture—you could see the tongue of the snake and the man's pink fingernails and even the horse's white eyelashes. Ma said they used one cat hair at a time to paint it. In the bathroom was the same brown soap shaped like an owl. The towels she used were so stiff it was like drying your hands with paper.

Sophie came back as Aunt Fran was saying, "He's a crook."

"Now stop that," said Ma, lifting her chin.

"Who is?" asked Churly, brightening.

"Never mind," said Ma to her knife and fork.

So Churly asked, "What'd he steal?"

Ma said. "They've started reshingling the house in North Eden." The Vincents went to Maine every summer. A drawer in one of the side tables was always kept pulled out—a red velvet slab with rows of arrowheads, ones that Pa had found on Boxed Island in Maine. You played Kick-the-Can on the sloping lawn after supper. When Churly was it, Sophie would let herself get caught. One time, playing spy, they saw Ma on her balcony with her hair all down, falling down her arms like a white shawl. Sometimes Ma and Pa were like ghosts. You'd see them pass behind a window in their house, or snapping out a light and vanishing. In the daytime, Ma's hair was twisted into a knot at the back.

Aunt Fran was wondering whether there didn't used to be a porch around the house out at Cassett Harbor, the old house. Uncle Thomas shouted, "That's right. Mrs. Lothrop said they'd have the Herreshoff teas on that porch."

"The correct term," said Ma, "is piazza."

"It must have been quite a view," said Sophie's mother.

"It's where you'd sit with your beaux," said Ma.

"We tore down the piazza," said Pa. Sophie was surprised he was listening.

Aunt Fran said, "I thought it burned down."

"Yes." Ma's nod was meant to end the discussion.

"How'd it burn down?" Churly asked. His long neck went up and his ears stuck out. Sophie felt herself flushing.

Pa said, "It–was–torn–down." His shoulders were round and low and his chin hovered inches above his plate.

Down at her end, Ma said, "The remainder was torn down, yes." Pa glared at her. His bottom lip drooped, as white as the rest of his face.

"How'd it burn down?" Churly asked eagerly.

Ma pulled some empty dishes over the tablecloth toward her. "You finish," she said. She stood up and carried some things to the sideboard, then glanced over the table to see what else to take. She piled small dishes on the turkey platter in front of Pa and went to lift it.

"Don't touch that," he said. He didn't look at her, or at the platter, but stared at the middle of the table.

"I think you're done," said his wife.

Sophie's mother pushed her chair back. "Let me. . . ." Her napkin bloomed like a white flower when she let go of it on the table.

"I'm not through," said Pa. "I want to pick." He didn't move.

"Now, Pa," said Aunt Fran. "We've got Livia's pies coming."

"Damn Livia's pies," he said. "Only occasionally you will disguise a voyage and cancel all that crap."

The little table fell quiet.

"I'm all ready for dessert," Uncle Thomas looked perky. "You ready for dessert there, Churly?"

Churly nodded, then looked to see what Pa would do next.

Caitlin and Sophie started to take their plates, but their mother gave them a stay-put look and made several quick trips through the swinging door.

Pa growled, "I've been eating goddamn custard all Monday."

Aunt Ginny asked, "What kind of pies do we have?" Each year they had the same: apple, mince and pumpkin. Everyone began saying which kind they wanted. Ma sat back down.

As they ate their pie and ice cream, Pa kept mumbling. "Bunch of idiots. . . . Going to knock it off like a bullhorn. . . . Newspaper, *then* cigar. . . ."

"No dessert for you, Pa?" Uncle Charles asked.

"I wouldn't set foot in there to piss," said Pa Vincent.

Ma went down and whispered into Pa's ear. No one could hear what she said, but Pa answered in a loud, slow voice, "Why don't you go shoot yourself?"

In the kitchen, Sophie and Caitlin watched Churly tell Livia. She fidgeted with pans and finally set them in the sink. "Your grandfather just needs his nap," said Livia. She studied the children's faces to see if they understood this. She was frowning. Her gaze drifted off and she turned her mammoth back to them, kept on sudsing things in the sink. She muttered, "He'll be wanting his . . ." but they couldn't hear what.

In the living room, the grown-ups were serving coffee. On the tray were miniature blue enamel cups, a silver bowl holding light-brown-sugar rocks, and chocolate mints in tissue paper envelopes.

Ma and Aunt Fran came down from upstairs where they had taken Pa.

"Everything all right?" bellowed Uncle Thomas. His wife scowled at him.

Ma took her place on the sofa. "Fine," she said. "Fine."

Rosie handed her a cup with a tiny gold spoon placed on the saucer. Delilah, her arm draped across her mother's knee, felt brave. "Was Pa mad at us?" she asked. Caitlin glared at her.

"Hah," shouted Uncle Charles, half-laughing, "he wasn't mad at me."

Sophie's father said, "He didn't know what he was saying, Delou." He was over by the window.

Ma sipped at the rim of her cup. Gus Vincent touched the curtain with one finger and gazed out. Rosie busily poured more coffee.

Looking at Delilah, Ma said, "He was not mad at you, dear."

Aunt Ginny looked up, surprised. "The turkey was delicious," she said.

"Oh shut up, Virginia," said Uncle Charles.

Sophie looked at Churly and noticed his ears sticking out and all his features flattened out, stiff, into a mask.

Uncle Thomas said, "Super meal, super." He jiggled the change in his pocket, waiting for something to happen.

"You can thank Livia for that." Ma set down her saucer. Sherman was in the rocking chair at her feet, lurching to and fro.

"Yes," said Rosie Vincent, "but you arranged it so beautifully."

Ma folded her hands. Her expression was matter-of-fact. "Actually, I don't think I've ever arranged anything beautifully in my whole life."

The grown-ups exchanged looks and for a moment there was no sound except for Sherman creaking in the rocking chair at Ma's feet. He got up, all at once aware of himself, and scurried to his mother. The chair went on rocking. Ma stared at it. Rocking empty, it meant something to her.

So she reached out one lavender shoe to still it, and did just that.

OFFERINGS

Joyce Kornblatt

On Sunday mornings, my mother tells me, my grandfather went to the Quincy Street pool and swam in the nude. My grandmother held this against him. It was not her sole complaint. Against her husband, she had two categories of grievances: bad habits and failures. Swimming in the nude was a bad habit, as were sleepwalking and cluttering. To the latter two, Pa took exception. He did not sleepwalk, he said; he needed solitude, and the middle of the night was the only time he could have it. He said the only walking he did was from the bedroom to the kitchen where he sat at the table, drank a cup of Postum, and studied the moon and the constellations. He told her that what she called clutter, he considered supplies: wood scraps, newspapers, string, jars, cracker boxes. Didn't he make his baby girls alphabet blocks from pieces of pine left over from the trestle table he built? Didn't he use the cracker boxes to start seedlings for the garden he grew each summer on the front porch of their second-floor flat in Boston, redwood planters brimming with marigolds and pansies, morning glories climbing the string trellis he strung between the porch posts? Didn't he wind up using all those newspapers to cover the broadloom when he painted the parlor's twelve-foot-high walls? No matter. Sleepwalking was sleepwalking. Clutter was clutter. My grandmother had recorded them under *bad habits,* and there were no erasures in *her* emotional ledger.

In the *failures* column, she entered "lack of ambition." My grandfather was the storekeeper, but his wife was the one in the family who kept the accounts.

His business was second-hand clothing. "Rags," my grandmother said. "Who can make a living from rags?"

"We do all right," Pa said. "We get along."

She wanted jewelry. She wanted to buy three yards of silk and take it to the dressmaker who would turn it into a tunic with stylish padded shoulders and bound bottonholes and a tasseled sash. She wanted to buy her shoes in Filene's Shoe Salon on the third floor instead of in the bargain basement where everything smelled musty and looked dull, even the patent leather, as if a fine rain of dust fell constantly on the discounted merchandise.

She wanted a piano, too. A baby grand. In Lithuania, she'd had a baby grand, and lessons once a week from Malke Weiss, who had trained at the conservatory at Minsk and claimed to have once met Stokowski.

"Did I come to America to lose everything I had?" my grandmother wailed.

"You came like we all did," her husband said. "To save your life."

Sundays, as soon as the weather warmed, my grandfather headed for the beach. He took his youngest daughter, my mother, with him. Nantasket, Wellfleet, Revere. Once they took the ferry to Martha's Vineyard, came home in the moonlight, and my grandfather "turned to silver," my mother says, "like a sculpture of a famous man."

In sleep, a bride in Pittsburgh, my mother returned to the ocean. Pa swung her over the waves. Their laughter rolled in again from that horizon line where memories bob like daring swimmers, like sailboats out too far for safety—rolled in to break beautifully and ferociously on the clean sand whose warmth she felt again in the landlocked rooms she lived in now, pieces of cardboard wedged against the cold in gaps between windows and frames. She would wake with the taste of salt in her mouth, her cheeks stiff with salt, her eyes red from its sting. "Nightmares," she lied to my father as he tried to console her. "Such terrible dreams."

They had lived in Pittsburgh for two years, but she was not used to it at all. My grandfather wrote her letters in his graceful hand: "Is it true you pay double for life insurance there? Are all the fish in the rivers dead?" The fish were not dead, and she hated the acrid smell from the mills, the furniture thick with soot, the mill whistles whining like wolves. Raised there, my father knew all the tricks for living in that sullied place, and he tried to teach them to her.

"It hurts to breathe," she would complain.

"Breathe like this, through your nose," he would tell her, a hand over his mouth as he demonstrated.

"The clothes get dirty as soon as I hang them on the line."

"Hang them in the bathtub," he would say, and one night came home with a drying rack for his wife to set in the claw-footed tub.

"In the middle of the day it's dark!" she would cry.

He would turn on all the lights in the apartment. "Now see? Who needs sunshine when you got Edison?"

"The ocean," she would weep. "I miss the beach."

And he would take her for walks around the municipal reservoir, the filtration plant's machinery churning in their ears.

It was 1943. My mother was three months pregnant with me, her ankles already swollen, her small breasts ballooning, the dark mother-line descending from her navel like a plunge of an anchor dropped into the sea. "I don't recognize myself," she said. "I don't know who I am."

"Don't talk foolish," my father said. "You're my wife."

In December, he was drafted. They had known he would be, but my parents were not people for whom the abstract future held much currency. She handed him the letter that had arrived that morning. He read in a quavering voice, as if the news were unexpected: "Greetings."

"I can't stay here alone," she said.

"You can stay with Lena," he said. His aunt and uncle lived two buildings down. "They have the extra room since Sammy joined."

"I'll go home," she said, reminding him of her heart's geography.

They packed up all their personal belongings. As each item disappeared into a container, it seemed to my mother that her young marriage itself was being dismantled, undone: a steamer trunk of clothing, towels, muslin sheets; a carton of chipped dishes, service for four—the "Silver Rose" pattern she'd found at the thrift shop where she'd also discovered the gilt-framed Rembrandt reproduction (for only a dollar) that she'd bought my father for his twenty-eighth birthday.

Years before, a high-school teacher had noticed my father's talent and provided him with the sketching pads his parents could not afford. For three years, my father had spent all his spare time filling the pages with drawings of bridges and birds and horse-drawn ice wagons plodding up slick cobblestoned hills. When he'd begun to love art more than anything else, knowing it would keep him poor forever (he had read that painters starved, turned to absinthe and cocaine, were always being evicted from their wretched quarters in the worst sections of Paris and New York), knowing his hobby could turn into an addiction, he threw his pencils away and hid the pads in the back of his closet. Years later I discovered them in a cardboard carton on which he'd printed "Art Work." I praised the fine detail, the subtle composition, the purity of line. "So what," he said. "Once upon a time, I had a knack. Now I'm just another working stiff."

Stiff was accurate: in the produce yards, he'd arrive at 4 A.M. to begin unloading the crates of fruits and vegetables the farmers brought in their pickup trucks, then reloading the goods into the vans of merchants who came to haggle with the farmers over the day's offerings. For my father, the pay was meager but dependable. In the beginning, he dreamed of a produce store someday, "being my own man," tried to see his years in the yards as "training in the business." To his new wife, who had come to Pittsburgh one summer to visit a cousin and been pursued by my father from bumper cars to ferris wheel to merry-go-round in a local amusement park, he brought gifts: bagfuls of bruised tomatoes, scarred peppers, lettuce going brown, dented apples, overripe bananas—bounty salvaged from the trash bin.

My mother made stews and soups, applesauce, banana bread. She grew proud of her domestic resourcefulness, resentful that it was required. What she wanted from him was one perfect melon, exotically sweet. If only once he had splurged, she might have forgiven him his common sense.

A year after my mother's wedding and departure from Boston, my grandfather sent her a present: a lace collar, brand new, from the upper levels of Filene's. Never mind that he had never given his own wife such a fine offering. He had no rival for his wife, no need for a canny courtship that struck the precisely right note between lament and aplomb. What he arrived at was a rather irresistible dignity that was, in fact, his actual nature.

Sometimes during those first two years of her marriage, my mother would catch my father staring at Rembrandt's portrait of the aristocrat in the plumed helmet, and my father looked chastened to her, as if rebuked by the elegance of the headpiece, the privileged angle of the head, as if my father suspected that my mother might have bought him this particular print for reasons not entirely testimonial. When my father talked about "making ends meet," was he talking less about money than his own cloven self?

She took down the Rembrandt from its place in the room that served as both parlor and bedroom. French doors camouflaged the bed that folded up into the wall, hidden away like dreams and sex. She took down the shirred organdy curtains she'd made from two yards she'd discovered in the remnant box at Woolworth's. In newspaper, she wrapped the photographs she'd kept on the bureau and placed them in a canvas satchel: her parents, two immigrants "keeping an eye" on their American daughter.

My grandfather was waiting for her at the station. It was snowing. The glittering flakes stuck to his thin white hair, to the shoulders and sleeves of his old tweed overcoat, even to the tops of his age-stained hands. As the train steamed into his view, my mother tells me, he lifted his arms in greeting, and the platform lights transformed them into shining wings. A crown seemed to shimmer on his head.

I called him "Pa" as my mother did, and he never objected. His was the thumb I grasped from my crib. His was the cheek against whose stubble my own softness was revealed to me. His arm was a raft I floated on inside the bathroom sink where he bathed me. "He was getting you ready for swimming," my mother says. "To be happy in the water." I took my first steps toward him, his voice speaking my name. He was the goal toward which I aspired, the reward of his hug sharpened in my instinctive ambition.

When he left the house for the store, I spent the hours of his absence mimicking him. I reinvented his presence by wearing his shoes, my tiny feet lost in the leather boats in which I sailed back and forth across the floor. I stood at the parlor window as he did, watching the street, observing the birds that nested in the maple, my hands clasped behind my back, my forehead pressed to the glass so that my breath clouded the pane. I chanted some loose imitation of the prayers he intoned when he woke and before he went to sleep, my body swaying like his, my eyes closed to this world. In the kitchen, I pulled newspapers from his stack beside the icebox, spread them open on the linoleum, pretended to lose myself as he did in the words I could not yet read; still, the print felt alive to me, the letters moved like tiny animals beneath my finger. Later I would come to understand that he was the man from whom I learned transcendence; but in those early years, before I needed words to justify devotion, I simply did what Pa did. I loved him. When he came home at the end of the day, I sat on the seat he made of his ankles, I grasped his hands, I rode the ship his body became, and we shouted together like sea gulls swooping down from the sky to the beach, up again, up, into the unpeopled heights.

By the time my father came home from the service, I was already my grandfather's child. My mother seemed to will the taxi into view—that was how deeply she concentrated on the corner around which it turned. It cruised down the block of one-time Victorian mansions converted now into rental units with dumbwaiters boarded up, closets for fancy wardrobes made over into bathrooms, and clotheslines strung across the yards in which wealthy families lolled once, or played croquet, or convalesced. My mother had bought me my first pair of Mary Janes and anklets edged with lace. She had dressed me in starched organdy and secured a pink bow in my wispy curls. My mother and grandparents were dressed up in their best clothes as well, their faces serious, anxious, as if they doubted that my father was truly returning or feared what his return implied. We waited in the front yard on that cool October afternoon, the sun's light thinned out, bleached, falling almost like a crust of ice on the leafless branches of the sycamores and elms. On that kind of day—as much the end of something as the beginning—we could have been a rich family of another time, awaiting a hearse or wedding coach, grieving or celebrating, it would have been hard to decipher which.

The stranger, my father, climbed out of the cab. He wore his Navy whites, and looked like the uniformed man in the photograph on my mother's dresser. She had taken me to the picture every evening before bed, as other children are led through prayers, or read to, or taught little rhymes with which they can console themselves in the dark. "This is your daddy," she would say, taking my hand and laying it against the glass. Was I supposed to feel my father's face coming to life against my palm? I did not understand her ritual and had not known what was expected of me. Nor did I now.

"That's your daddy," my mother said. Her voice broke. She ran down the front walk and embraced the stranger. He kissed her on her mouth. Daddy? I held onto Pa's leg, my face pressed against the familiar gabardine; his hand cupped my head, a proprietary gesture.

My father kissed my grandmother, shook Pa's hand, then hugged him with one arm. The other arm cradled a box bound by a thick red ribbon and an oversized bow; he'd left his duffle bag at the curb. Even as he greeted my grandfather, my father's eyes fixed on me. Tears clustered in his lashes and his gaze seemed to require of me a reciprocal intensity. Now he knelt down to my level. He held out the present to me. He said my name. He knew me. Later I would learn that he had kept my picture taped to the bottom of the bunk above his, so that when he went to sleep at night and when he woke in the morning, the first thing he saw was not a Betty Grable pinup, or even a photograph of his wife, but me—an infant on a blanket spread out on the grass in Franklin Park.

I said nothing. He was a stranger. I turned my face back into the fabric of my grandfather's trouser leg, and he allowed me the refuge. "Give your daddy a kiss," my mother instructed, but Pa kept his hand on my head, his claim to me clear.

Against such odds my father rose and took my mother's hand. They mounted the porch steps, his gift for me still unaccepted, the transaction unaccomplished.

Pa and I followed.

My grandmother trailed us all, sighing. Perhaps one of her many ailments—she would be dead by winter—had flared up, or this homecoming had disappointed her, or she was sad because in a few hours it would be time to take off her good dress and who could say when another occasion for wearing it might arise.

Nana died in January, three months after my father's return. My mother tells me her parents' marriage "wasn't good." She tells me anecdotes that support that interpretation. By the time I was born, Nana was a woman who stayed in bed, rising only to complain about something for which no remedy existed: the war, the weather, the

passing of time. She was too absorbed with her ailments, her depriva-
tions, her husband's lack of drive to offer her daughter or her
grandchild much notice. "Did I come to America to lose everything I
had?" Nor did our presence bring her solace. She was inconsolable,
which I have come to learn is a clinical term, a disease. Perhaps it was
chronic unhappiness that killed her, that rendered her less than alive to
me even before she died. My sense of her remains abstract and vague,
as much as my memories of Pa are concrete, sensuous, embodied. But
did they have feelings for each other that my mother failed to recognize? In spite of the bickering, the criticism, the silences, the averted
eyes, did they love each other?

For weeks after her death in the hospital, where she'd faded away
like a dimming lightbulb or a radio signal growing weaker until at last
it leaves the range of human reach, Pa walked the rooms of our flat not
so much searching for his wife as assuring himself of her disappearance.
A dozen times a day he spoke her name, silence answered, he nodded.
He held her shawl in his arms, the one she'd wrapped around her bulk
regardless of the seasons or the temperature in the house, and the near
weightlessness of the garment testified: *she is gone*. He sat on her side
of their bed and studied the emptiness, the sheer negation suggested
by the space where she had lain. One day I found him there, the fingers of one hand tracing the opened palm of the other. "This is
Lithuania," he said, stroking the map of his own flesh. "Your nana
came from . . . right here." He stared at the spot until it transformed
itself into a peopled town, a world I could not see. Even after he went
back to the store, resumed his life, took up again his newspapers, his
gardening, his grandchild—still some crucial part of him remained
where I found him that day, with the young girl he had married in a
town that no longer existed on any map—the Nazis had leveled the
place, obliterated it—save the one in his mind.

My mother's grieving took a different form: a series of illnesses that
seemed like a speeded-up version of Nana's life. In a single month, my
mother contracted bronchitis, middle ear infection, "stomach trouble," water on the knee. It was left to my father, at the time without a
job, to care for me. He took me to the park and I would not play: I
froze at the top of the slide until he let me climb backwards down the
ladder; I dug my toes into the ground to stop the swing he pushed; I

let the ball he threw me sail beyond me into the prickly bushes. He cooked meals I left on my plate. He filled the tub for my bath and I drained it. Finally, he withdrew from the effort, and I blamed him for this, too, though I knew I would resist all his appeals, all his suggestions. I knew what he refused to admit: Nana had died to make room for him.

In one way or another I was losing everyone. Pa was divided now between past and present, my mother always ill, Nana dead. I had even been evicted from the room I had shared with my mother. When my father had returned, I was moved to a corner of the parlor. A junior bed, a maple chest, a floor lamp, a small trunk that held my toys: these were the furnishings in the area that came to be considered my "room" as surely as if walls had risen around it, a door hinged to the invisible frame. I was learning the ways in which adults could impose on children realities for which no evidence existed: "This is your father, this is your room, there is no reason in the world for you to be so unhappy." In the room my parents occupied, the door closed "for privacy," I listened easily to every word of their arguments.

"It's time to make plans to go home," he said.

"He won't come," she said, referring to Pa, meaning herself.

"Then he'll live with your sister." Aunt Joan and her family had a bungalow in Revere, four blocks from the ocean.

"He can't get to his store from Revere," she said. "He'll be lost."

"I'm lost here."

He drove a milk truck for a few months; he worked as a letter-sorter for the post office; he sold Uncle Herb's Vitamin Tonic door-to-door. "In the yards," he said, "I'm established. I know my way around. I know the people."

After Nana died, she said, "Pa needs you, he needs an assistant. He wants you to have the position."

"He needs me like a hole in the head. There aren't enough customers for him to wait on himself."

"He means for you to have it after him."

"I don't want it. When will you hear what I'm telling you?"

I heard.

My mother told me, "We have to break up the house." I was five years old. When she had used those words weeks before to describe this day that had now arrived with no greater signal than the low whine of the moving van which had taken its place outside—when my mother had first said, "We are going to have to break up the house"— I had imagined terrible destruction. Windows would shatter, floors would buckle and splinter, ceilings and walls would cave in on themselves. At night, forcing myself to prepare for the day of terror, I could nearly smell the crumbling plaster, almost feel the night air whip through the shell of the dying house.

My mother had worked out all the details of the plan. The furniture would be sold to our landlord, Mr. Pinksy, who would disperse the pieces to furnished flats he rented out all over the city. My grandfather's store would be liquidated, and he would go to live with Aunt Joan (*I know that,* I thought; *I heard you plotting*). My mother and I would leave Boston on the night train to join my father in Pittsburgh where he had been waiting for months for us to "make the move already." As she made these decisions, finally, after months of tortured refusals and procrastinations, I imagine my mother was stunned by how simply, how logically, how inevitably the plan took form: as if each decision were a spoke on a wheel to which she had been bound without knowing it, on whose momentum she would travel the rest of her life, as surely as the night train would bear her and her child into the darkness.

I had gone with Pa to the store on his last day. I loved to visit there, dressing up in shabby costumes, listening to my grandfather converse in Yiddish with neighbors who came looking for a good winter jacket, a serviceable pair of woolen trousers. Now the old coats and suits and battered hats were gone from the racks and shelves. I helped him soap the windows. He swept the floor, pushing the broom heavily across the worn oak planks. Our voices sounded hollow, lost in the emptiness. In a cardboard carton, we collected the last pieces of litter and together we dragged the box to the curb. He padlocked the front door, and on the tarnished doorknob he hung the FOR RENT sign with which the landlord had entrusted him. He took my hand. Without looking back a single time, we walked home.

"You're seventy years old," my mother had told him that evening. "You deserve a retirement."

"Like Jonah deserved a whale."

"You won't make this a little bit easy for me?"

"You want I should show you how I really feel? You want I should jump off the roof right now?"

While the movers worked, I sat on a crate and watched them carry out piece after piece of the household I loved. They worked slowly, grunting under their burdens. It was July, hot, the air dead with heat, and the movers' faces gleamed with sweat. When they took off their shirts, their brown-skinned bodies looked like a piano's polished wood, each man a carved African idol, an ebony warrior. I had seen pictures of them in National Geographic, tribal icons discovered in the tombs of long-buried chieftains. Perhaps my grandparents' lamps and chairs and dressers and beds were offerings of some sort. Perhaps the huge van that rested out front like a giant coffin on wheels was a repository for treasures promised a thousand years ago to an undying spirit. That was no more strange than my mother's explanation: "Just because people love each other doesn't mean they stay together." Why not, I asked. "The world has its reasons," my mother said, as if the planet itself had a brain, and a heart. She shook her head mournfully. Her chin shuddered. "Don't think I understand it better than you do. I don't."

Pa did not jump off a roof. His suicide was more subtle, carried out in stages over the course of a year, kindly in that it allowed for other interpretations: hardening of the arteries, senility, geriatric diseases for which no names had yet been invented, but that surely could account for his decline. "He was old," my mother tells me. "You wouldn't realize. For you, he always had energy. But he was an old man."

First he stopped talking. Aunt Joan called from Revere: "I can't get him to say a word," she told my mother. "You try."

My mother coaxed and demanded. She pleaded. In the apartment we lived in now, the flowers and yards of my life in Boston abandoned for brick and alleys and hallways thick with strangers, I was emptying the dollhouse my father had bought me of all its fragile furniture. I stashed the pieces under my bed. I undressed the family of tiny dolls who were meant to live in the once-intact household and assigned each member, alone and naked, to a different barren room. My mother called me from the kitchen. I came to the doorway. "It's Pa," she said, as if I hadn't listened to her entire half of the conversation. She thrust the receiver at me. "He wants to talk to you."

But I knew that could not be true. I had heard her say, "This is a crazy thing you're doing, Pa, refusing to speak."

Well, crazy or not, he had chosen it, as he had not chosen anything else that had happened to him in the last year. I would not take the phone. I would not violate his freedom. I would not tempt him out of his dignity. Behind my burning eyes, my locked lips, my breath stilled like an ocean in which the tide suddenly ceases to operate, I joined him in his silence. "Talk to him," she said. I went to my room and got into bed. I was six years old, and I would never see my grandfather again. For five days, I kept mute, like Pa—we protested together—and no entreaty on my parents' part was strong enough to sunder that connection, no wooing or threat capable of interrupting that long, long conversation.

PALAIS
DE JUSTICE

Mark Helprin

In a lesser chamber of Suffolk County Courthouse on a day in early August, 1965—the hottest day of the year—a Boston judge slammed down his heavy gavel, and its pistol-like report threw the room into disarray. Within a few minutes, everyone had gone—judge, court reporters, blue-shirted police, and a Portuguese family dressed as if for a wedding to witness the trial of their son. The door was shut. Wood and marble remained at attention in dead silence. For quite a while the room must have been doing whatever rooms do when they are completely empty. Perhaps air currents were stabilizing, coming to a halt, or spiders were beginning to crawl about, up high in the woodwork. The silence was beginning to set when the door opened and the defense attorney re-entered to retrieve some papers. He went to his seat, sat down, and ran his hands over the smooth tabletop—no papers. He glanced at the chairs, and then bent to see under the table—no papers. He touched his nose and looked perplexed. "I know I left them here," he said to the empty courtroom. "I thought I left them here. Memory must be going, oh well."

But his memory was excellent, as it had always been. He enjoyed pretending that in his early sixties he was losing his faculties, and he delighted in the puzzlement of where the papers had gone. The first was an opportunity for graceful abstention and serene neutrality, the second a problem designed to fill a former prosecutor's mind as he made his way out of the courthouse, passing through a great hall arched like a cathedral and mitered by hot white shafts of grainy light.

Years before, when he had had his first trial, one could not see the vault of the roof. It was too high and dark. But then they had put up a string of opaque lighting globes, which clung to the paneled arches like risen balloons and lit the curving ceiling.

One day a clerk had been playing a radio so loudly that it echoed through the building. The Mayor of Boston appeared unexpectedly and stood in the middle of the marble floor, emptiness and air rising hundreds of feet above him. "Turn that radio off!" he screamed, but the clerk could not hear him. Alone on the floor with a silent crowd staring from the perimeter, the Mayor turned angrily and scanned halls and galleries trying to find direction for his rage, but could not tell from where the sound came and so pivoted on the smooth stone and filled the chamber with his voice. "I am your mayor. Turn it off, do you hear me, damn you to hell. I am your mayor!" The radio was silenced and all that could be heard was the echo of the Mayor's voice. The defense attorney had looked up as if to see its last remnants rising through rafters of daylight, and had seen several birds, flushed from hidden nesting places, coursing to and fro near the ceiling, threading through the light rays. No one but the defense attorney saw them or the clerk, a homely, frightened woman who, when the Mayor had long gone, came out and carefully peered over a balcony to see where he had stood. It was then that the defense attorney saw the intricate motif of the roof—past the homely woman, the birds, and the light.

Now he went from chamber to chamber, and hall to hall, progressing through layers of rising temperature until he stood on the street in a daze. It was so hot that people moved as if in a baking desert, their expressions as blank and beaten as a Tuareg's mask and impassive eyes. The stonework radiated heat. A view of Charlestown—mountains and forests of red brick, and gray shark-colored warships drawn up row upon row at the Navy Yard—danced in bright waves of air like a mirage. Across the harbor, planes made languid approaches to whitened runways. They glided so slowly it looked as if they were hesitant to come down. Despite the heat there was little haze, even near the sea. A Plains August had grasped New England, and Boston was quiet.

"Good," thought the defense attorney, "there won't be a single soul on the river. I'll have it all to myself, and it'll be smooth as glass." He had been a great oarsman. Soon it would be half a century of near-silent speed up and down the Charles in thin light racing shells, always alone. The fewer people on the river, the better. He often saw wonderful sights along the banks, even after the new roads and bridges had been built. Somehow, pieces of the countryside held out and the idea of the place stayed much the same, though in form it was a far cry from the hot meadows, dirt roads, and wooden fences he had gazed upon in his best and fastest years. But just days before, he had seen a mother and her infant son sitting on the weir, looking out at the water and at him as he passed. The child was so beautiful as the woman held up his head and pointed his puzzled stare out over river and fields, that the defense attorney had shaken in his boat—having been filled with love for them. Then there were the ducks, who slept standing with heads tucked under their wings. Over fifty years he had learned to imitate them precisely, and often woke them as he passed, oars dipping quietly and powerfully to speed him by. Invariably, they looked up to search for another duck.

"You shouldn't be going out today, Professor," said Pete, who was in charge of the boathouse. "No one's out. It's too hot."

He was a stocky Dubliner with a dialect strong enough to make plants green. When he carried one end of the narrow craft down the sloping dock to the river he seemed to the defense attorney to resemble the compact engines which push and pull ships in the Panama Canal. Usually the oarsman holding the stern was hardly as graceful or deliberative as Pete, but struggled to avoid getting splinters in his bare feet.

"I haven't seen one boat all of today." Pete looked at him, waiting for him to give up and go home. The defense attorney knew that Pete wanted to call the Department of Athletics and have the boathouse closed at two so he could go to tend his garden. "Really, not one boat. You could get heat stroke you know. I saw it in North Africa during the War—terrible thing, terrible thing. Like putting salt on a leech."

The defense attorney was about to give in, when someone else walked up to the log book and signed so purposefully that Pete changed his strategy, saying to both of them, "If I were you now, I wouldn't stay out too long, not in this weather."

They went as they did each day to get S-40, the best of the old boats. It was the last boat Pat Shea had built for Harvard before he was killed overseas. Though already a full professor in the Law School and over draft age, the defense attorney had volunteered, and did not see his wife or his children for three solid years. When he returned— and those were glorious days when his children were young and suddenly talking, and his wife more beautiful than she had ever been— he went down to the boathouse and there was S-40, gleaming from disuse. Pat Shea was dead in the Pacific, but his boat was as ready as a Thoroughbred in the paddock. For twenty years the defense attorney had rowed loyally in S-40, preferring it to the new boats of unpronounceably named resins—computer designed, from wind tunnels, with riggers lighter than air and self-lubricating ball bearings on the sliding seat, where S-40 had seasoned into a dark blood color, and the defense attorney knew its every whim.

As they carried it from the shadows into blinding light, the defense attorney noticed the other sculler. He could not have been much over twenty, but was so large that he made the two older men feel diminutive. He was lean, muscled, and thick at the neck and shoulders. His face was pitted beneath a dark tan, and his hair long and tied up on his head in an Iroquois topknot. He looked like a Spartan with hair coiled before battle, and was ugly and savage in his stance. Nevertheless, the defense attorney, fond of his students and of his son who had just passed that age, smiled as he passed. He received as recompense a sneer of contempt, and he heard the words "old man" spoken with astonishing hatred.

"Who the hell is that?" asked the defense attorney of Pete as they set S-40 down on the lakelike water.

"I don't know. I never seen him before, and I don't like the looks of him. He brought his own boat, too, one of those new ones. He wants me to help him bring it down. Of course I'll have to. I'll take my time, and you can get a good head start so's you'll be alone up river," said Pete, knowing that informal races were common, and that if two boats pulled up even it nearly always became a contest. He wanted to spare the defense attorney the humiliation of being beaten by the unpleasant young man who had meanwhile disappeared into the darkness of the boathouse.

As S-40 pulled out and made slowly for the Anderson Bridge, the young man, whom the defense attorney had already christened "the barbarian," walked down the ramp, with his boat across his shoulders. Even from 100 feet out the defense attorney heard Pete say, "You didn't have to do that. I would have helped you." No matter, thought the defense attorney, by the time he gets it in the water, places his oars, and fine tunes all his alloy locks and stretchers, I'll be at the Eliot Bridge and in open water with a nice distance between us. He had no desire to race, because he knew that although he could not beat a young athlete in a boat half as light as S-40, he would try his best to do so. On such a hot day, racing was out of the question. In fact, he resolved to let the young man pass should he be good enough to catch up. For it was better to be humiliated and alive than dead at the finish line. He cannot possibly humiliate me anyway, he thought. A young man in a new-style boat will obviously do better than a man three times his age in a wood shell. But, he thought, this boat and I know the river. I have a good lead. I can pace myself as I watch him, and what I do not have in strength I may very well possess in concentration and skill.

And so he started at a good pace, sweeping across glass-faced waters in the large swelling of the stream just north of the Anderson Bridge, gauging his speed expertly from the passage of round turbulent spots where the oars had been, and sensing on the periphery of vision the metered transit of tall ranks of sycamores on the Cambridge side. He was the only man on the river, which was glossy and green with a thick tide of beadlike algae. Always driven to the river by great heat, dogs loped along with the gait of trained horses, splashing up a wave as they ran free in the shallows. S-40 had taut blue canvas decking, and oars of lacquered yellow wood with black and white blades. The riggers were silver-colored, an alloy modification, and the only thing modern about the boat. The defense attorney was lean and tanned, with short white hair. His face was kind and quiet, and though small in stature, he was very strong, and looked impressive in his starched white rowing shorts. The blue decking shone against the green water as in a filtered photograph of a sailing regatta.

It seemed to him that the lonely condition upon the river was a true condition. Though he had had a lot of love in his life, he knew from innumerable losses and separations that one stands alone or not at all. And yet, he had sought the love of women and the friendship of men as if he were a dog rasping through the bushes in search of birds or game. Women were for him so lovely and central to all he found important that their absence, as in the war, was the stiffest sentence he could imagine, and he pictured hell as being completely without them—although from experience he knew that they must have filled a wing or two there to the brim. Often, as he rowed, he slackened to think of the grace and beauty of girls and women he had known or loved. He remembered how sometime in the middle Twenties, when he was courting his wife, he had passed a great bed of water lilies in the wide bay before Watertown. He grasped one for her as he glided by, and put it in the front of the boat. But when he reached the dock the flower had wilted and died. The next day he stopped his light craft and pulled deep down on a long supple stem. Then he tied it to the riggers and rowed back with the lily dangling in the water so that he was able to preserve it, a justly appreciated rare flower. But people did not "court" anymore.

He resumed his pace, even though, without straining, he was as dripping wet as if he had been in a sauna for five minutes. Rounding the bend before the Eliot Bridge, he saw the young man in his new-style boat, making excellent speed toward him. He had intended to go beyond the Eliot, Arsenal Street, and North Beacon bridges to the bay where the lilies still grew, where it was easy to turn (although he could turn in place) and then to come back. All told, it was a course of six miles. It would not pay to go fast over that distance in such killing heat. If they were to race, the finish would have to be the last bridge out. By the time he passed under the Eliot Bridge, with two more bridges to go, the young man had closed to within a few hundred yards.

His resolutions fell away as if they were light November ice easy to break with oars and prow. Almost automatically, he quickened his pace to that of the young man, who, after a furious initial sprint, had been forced to slow somewhat and retrieve his breath. The defense attorney knew that once he had it he would again pour on speed in the excessive way youth allowed, and so the defense attorney husbanded his strength, going as fast as his opponent but with the greatest possible economy. This he achieved by relaxing, saying to himself, "Easy. Easy. The fight is yet to come. Easy now, easy."

Though the young athlete was a hundred yards downriver the

defense attorney could see dark lines of sweat in his knotted hair, and could hear heavy breathing. "I'm a fool," he said, "for racing in this heat. It's over 100 degrees. I have nothing to prove. I'll let him pass, and I'll let him sneer. I don't care. My wisdom is far more powerful than his muscular energy." And yet, his limbs automatically kept up the pace, draining him of water, causing salt to burn his eyes. He simply could not stop.

He remembered Cavafy's *Waiting for the Barbarians,* which he—in a clearly Western way—had originally assumed to be a lament. Upon reading it he discovered that the poet shared in the confusion, for it was indeed a lament, that the barbarians were not still on their way. But for the defense attorney this was unthinkable, for he dearly loved the West and had never thought that to constitute itself it required the expectation of a golden horde. And he believed that if one man were to remain strong and upholding, if just one man were not to wilt, then the light he saw and loved could never be destroyed, despite the barbarism of the war, of soulless materialism, of the self-righteous students who thought to remake this intricate and marvelously fashioned world with one blink of an untutored eye. If a man can be said to grit his teeth over a span of years, then the defense attorney had done just this, knowing that it would both pass and come again, as had the First War, and the Second, in which he had been broken and battered repeatedly—only to rise up again.

He did not want to concede the minor victory of a river race on a hot day in August, not even that, not even such a small thing as that to yet another wave of ignorance and violence. He started with rage in remembering the sneer. Contempt meant an attack against perceived weakness, and did not weakness merit compassion? If this barbarian had thought him weak, he was up against the gates of a city he did not know, a stone-built city of towers and citadels. The defense attorney increased the rapidity of his stroke to meet his opponent's ominously growing speed.

The young man was gaining, but by very small increments. Were the defense attorney to have kept up his pace he would have reached the North Beacon Street Bridge first, even if only by a few feet. But two things were wrong. First, such a close margin afforded no recourse in a final sprint. Because of the unpredictability of the young man's capacities, the defense attorney was forced to build an early lead, which would as well demoralize his rival. Second, not even halfway to the finish, he was beginning to go under. Already breathing extremely hard, he could feel his heart in his chest as if it were a fist pounding on a door.

He was lucky, because he knew the river so well that he had no need of turning to see where he was headed. So precise had the fifty years rendered his navigational sense that he did not even look when he approached bridges, and shot through the arches at full speed always right in the center. However, the young man had to turn for guidance every minute or so to make sure he was not straying from a straight course—which would have meant defeat. That he had to turn was another advantage for the defense attorney, for the young man not only broke his rhythm and sometimes lost his stroke or made a weak stroke when doing so, but he was also forced to observe his adversary still in the lead. If the defense attorney saw the leather thong in the young man's haircomb begin to dip, and saw the muscles in his back uplift a bit, making a slightly different shadow, he knew he was about to turn. This caused the defense attorney to assume an expression of ease and relaxation, as if he were not even racing, and to make sure that his strokes were deep, perfect, and classically executed. He had been in many contests, both ahead and behind.

Though it was a full-blooded race, he realized that he was going no more than half the sustained speed of which he normally was capable. Like a cargo of stone, the heat dragged all movement into viscous slow motion. Time was caught in its own runners, and its elements repeated. Two dogs at the riverside were fighting over a dead carp lapping in the green water. He saw them clash at the neck. Later, when he looked back, he saw the same scene again. Perhaps because of the blood and the heat and the mist in front of his eyes, the salt-stung world seemed to unpiece in complex dissolution. There was a pattern which the darkness and the immediacy of the race made him unable to decipher. Intensified summer colors drifted one into the other without regard to form, and the laziness was shattered only when a bright white gull, sliding down the air, passed before his sight in a heartening straight line.

Though he felt almost ready to die and thought that he might, the defense attorney decided to implement his final strategy. About a mile was left. They were nearing the Arsenal Street Bridge. Here the river's high walls and banks stopped the wind, and the waters were always smooth. With no breeze whatsoever, it was all the hotter. In this quiet stretch races were won or lost. A completely tranquil surface allowed a burst of energy after the slight rest it provided. Usually a racer determined to begin his build-up just at the bridge. Two boats could not clear the northern arch simultaneously. Thus the rear boat had no hope of passing and usually resolved upon commencement of its grand effort after the natural delineation of the bridge. Knowing it could not be passed, the lead boat rested to get strength before the final stretch. But the defense attorney knew that his position was in great danger. A few hundred yards from the bridge, he was only two or three boatlengths ahead. He could see the young man, glistening and red, breathing as if struggling for life. But his deep breathing had not the patina of weakness the defense attorney sensed in his own. He was certain to maintain his lead to the bridge, though, and beyond it for perhaps a quarter of a mile. But he knew that then the superior strength of the younger man would finally put the lighter boat ahead. If it were to be a contest of endurance, steady and torturesome as it had been, he knew he would not win.

But he had an idea. He would try to demoralize the young man. He would begin his sprint even before the Arsenal Street Bridge, with the benefit of the smooth water and the lead-in of the arch. What he did was to mark out in his mind a closer finish which he made his goal—knowing that there he would have to stop, a good half mile before the last bridge. But with luck the shocking lead so far in advance of all expectations would convince the struggling young man to surrender to his own exhaustion. An experienced man would guess the stratagem. A younger man might, and might not. If he did, he would maintain an even pace and eventually pass the defense attorney dead in the water a good distance before the finish.

A hundred yards before the Arsenal Street Bridge, the defense attorney began his massive strokes. One after another, they were in clear defiance of the heat and his age. He began to increase his lead. When he passed through the dark shadow of the bridge, he was already five boatlengths ahead. He heard the echo of his heart from the cool concrete, for it was a hollow chamber. Back in bright light, clubbed by the sun, he went even faster. The young man had to turn every few seconds to guide himself through the arch. When he did so

he lost much time in weak strokes, adjustments to course, and breaking rhythm. But far more important was what he saw ahead. The old
man had begun a powerful sprint, as if up to that point he had only
been warming up.

Three quarters of a mile before the finish the defense attorney was
going full blast. From a distance he looked composed and unruffled,
because all his strength was perfectly channeled. Because of this the
young man's stroke shattered in panic. The defense attorney beat
toward his secret finish, breathing as though he were a woman lost
deep in love. The breaths were loud and desperate, abandoned and
raw, as if of birth or a struggle not to die. He was ten boatlengths
ahead, and nearing his finish.

He had no time to think of what he had endured in his life, of the
loss which had battered him, and beaten him, and reduced him at
times to nothing but a shadow of a man. He did not think of the men
he had seen killed in war, whose screams were loud enough to echo in
his dreams decades after. He did not think of the strength it had taken
to love when not loved, to raise faltering children in the world, to see
his parents and his friends die and fall away. He did not think of things
he had seen as the century moved on, nor of how he had risen each
time to survive in the palace of the world by a good and just fight, by
luck, by means he sometimes did not understand. He simply beat the
water with his long oars, and propelled himself ahead. One more
stroke, he said, and another, and another. He was almost at his end.

He looked back, and a beautiful sight came to his eyes. The
young man was bent over and gliding. His oars no longer moved but
only brushed the top of the water. Then he began to work his port oar
and turn around, for he had given up. He vanished through the
bridge.

The defense attorney was alone on the river, in a thickly wooded
green stretch full of bent willows. It was so hot that for a moment he
forgot exactly who he was or where he was. He rowed slowly to the
last bridge. There he rested in the cool shadow of a great and peaceful
arch.

COMPANY

Roberta Silman

When all the cousins in my family got together, it was me they locked in the closet. Or used as the patient when they played doctor. Or ran away and left me counting alone in the yard, hiding my eyes, eagerly anticipating where I would look for them until, finally, I realized that they had once again abandoned me. Lips quivering, I would find my Aunt Beadie. "Don't cry, Mona," she'd say softly as she stroked my hair. And then she'd lift single strands toward the light, trying to discover why my hair didn't shine like the other cousins' hair.

"Children can be very cruel," she always said. "It will be better when you're grown."

When I went to college—a good eastern girls' college, on scholarship, of course—there was one blissful night that first fall. About twenty girls in the scholarship dorm (they had us all in one house just in case we tried to forget we were poorer than the others) sat on the floor in my room and listened to my records of Dvořák's chamber music after the house meeting.

A few weeks later they elected me house president. Was I proud! Even after I discovered that I was the janitor. "She's president of her house at that fancy college they sent her to," Aunt Beadie bragged.

But even smart plain people need company. So if it isn't real company, if you're smart like I am, you make up company. There's no need to die for lack of someone to talk to.

You wouldn't believe what interesting friends I have. Once Virginia Woolf stepped into the car. It was a little awkward; she's very tall and I have a Datsun. But she managed, cape and all, and she hugged that beautiful mauve cape to herself and she stared at me with her marvelous sunken eyes and as we drove we talked. The usual, at first—the road, the fall colors (it was October), a bunch of geese flying south, the bearded philosophers in the sky (they looked like sheep to me, but why argue?). And then I said, "Virginia, with all your troubles, why didn't you ever visit Freud? Surely one of your friends could have gotten you an appointment." After all, sometimes the famous don't like to use their names—they prefer their friends. She sighed. I looked at her out of the corner of my eye, a little afraid I might have offended her. But she is, basically, despite the cape, very down-to-earth. "I was sure if I went to Freud I would never write again. The writing and the insanity were interlocked." She made it sound so simple that I didn't pursue it, though I'm sure she would have liked to be a better wife to Leonard.

Virginia comes back, though after that first time, never alone. Either with her sister Vanessa, or Leonard, or Bunny Garrett, once with Eliot. That was almost disastrous. He's so shy, and I was working so hard to get something, anything, out of his thin lips that I almost wrapped the car around a telephone pole.

At one time or another half of the people who are buried in Westminster Abbey have been in my car. And many who aren't buried there. I took a lot of English Lit at college, though I was a history major. My mother thought I would be another Mommsen. But who wants historians these days—not with the history we're making. So I took my master's in social work, finally succumbed to an afro (Aunt Beadie still says, feebly now—her shiny-haired kids put her in a home—"If only you had brushed it more as a child, Mona"), and I'm head of the social workers in one of those big New York hospitals. All day long I try to help people who have babies with birth defects, sisters with muscular dystrophy, brothers with heart trouble, parents with cancer. Not exactly the life I dreamed for myself. But at least there's money for the Datsun and weekends out of town. Every other weekend, there I am, on some parkway out of New York—to Vermont in the fall, to the Jersey shore in summer, or to Martha's Vineyard, Newport, Nantucket. In the winter it's the cities: Washington, Philadelphia, Boston—there are so many interesting places.

Kafka likes Philadelphia. He likes the quiet old Federal houses, and we have spent days in the Franklin Institute. Once I took him to Washington; he was fascinated by that wonderful pendulum they have in the Smithsonian. "I have finally seen time," he said when he saw it, but he won't go back. It was too noisy for him, the traffic frightened him, the crowds and lines depressed him. Even in Rock Creek Park, which is one of the most beautiful spots in the East, he seemed uncomfortable. "Look at her eyes!" I pointed to those incredible blue eyes of Mohini, the white tigress, stalking her cage. Kafka looked to please me, but he was miserable. "I could have written that lonely tigress," he murmured as we drove home. To divert him I started to talk about my job, but he said quickly, "Tell me something pleasant, Mona, please, just *happy* things."

When *Herzog* was published I had a definite sense of déjà vu. The people were different, but I had been doing it for years, and not just letters. Why write to someone if you can talk to him? Isn't that what the telephone ad says?

Today I am alone. Chekhov had to mulch his roses for winter, Henry James gets carsick on long trips, Napoleon had a stomachache, Bill Shakespeare had another date. Donne was free, but he's such dour company lately, I decided to pass. Occasionally I need to collect my thoughts a little. And it's pouring and there's a rainbow of leaves falling from the trees which, when they land, make the road slick. I need all my wits about me driving today. The slight element of danger in a slick road is exciting, though. Danger, no matter how slight, does make people feel adventurous, and with my hands on the wheel, I feel like those little boys who *vroom vroom* near the hospital all day long, imitating the ambulance call and the police whistle.

Vroom! Vroom! Now I'm in Vermont. I like crossing borders. New possibilities. So far I've been in thirty-six of the fifty states. I have a big wall map at home and I color in the states after I've been there. Sometimes I plan my vacations to see how many more states I can knock off. Once I drove my parents back to Florida just to color in more states. They didn't know that, of course. "You're such a good daughter, Mona," my mother crooned when we said good-bye. I am the only child, and they had high hopes for me, but this time I didn't get the usual lecture about finding a man and settling down and getting married like all your cousins are. Omission is sometimes bliss.

Jeesus Christ! I slam on the brake. I almost killed him! What an idiot to stand practically in the middle of the road wearing an orange jacket when everything else around is orange. He's young, probably in his early twenties, and wearing a pack. He throws it onto the back seat and then sits down beside me. He smells of wet wool and not too many baths recently.

"You're lucky you have all your toes," I say. Did I mention that he has a lovely dark beard? Fine and black and silky, and yes, almost shiny.

I almost never pick up hitchhikers because the car is usually occupied by my friends. But it is pouring and I practically killed him and, as I said before, I am alone. So why not? He doesn't look like the mugging type.

"I'm Louis," he says, "and you are very sweet to pick me up. It is raining very hard." He smiles a toothy smile, almost a caricature of a smile because he has such large, even teeth. He's glad to be in a dry place, that's clear.

"Are you from Paree?" He nods.

"Where are you going?"

"To Canada. I have a cousin north of Montreal. I'm going to stay there till Christmas and then I'll go home."

"Do you go to the university?"

"No, I am graduated, have graduated," he corrected himself. He speaks English slowly, but you can tell that he is getting the feel of the language.

"Where are you going?" He starts unfolding his map.

"Oh, I'm just out for a ride. No place in particular. Just out to see the leaves. But it rained instead."

"Yes." He smiles and gestures at the falling leaves with his skinny palms upward. "What is your name?"

"Mona."

"What do you do?" I can see he is making a guess in his head, and I wonder what I look like to him, but I can't exactly ask.

"Social work—in a big New York hospital. Help people face their lives." He nods.

"My cousin is an anesthetist in l'Hôpital de la Gare in Paris."

"Your cousin is a lot luckier than I," I say, but he doesn't get it.

Still, he's nice. And observant. And it's so good to smell an actual man in the car.

Maybe it was the smell that did it. Who knows? Who knows what makes people act the way I did? Because suddenly, after we had been riding for about half an hour, I wanted desperately to go to bed with him.

"Could you do me a favor?" I asked. His hand sought the window handle and he started opening it a little to get the fog off the windshield.

"Well, yes, that, too. But something else."

He raised his eyebrows.

"Could you go with me to a motel? Could you"—my palms were so sweaty they almost slipped off the wheel—"Could you sleep with me? It won't take long." I needn't have added that, because I could see, thank God, that he wasn't repelled. Just a little surprised. Well, maybe a lot surprised. So was I. But my surprise didn't make me take it back or try to make a joke of it or pretend I had had a moment of madness. The offer was still good, and as he paused before he answered, I could see that he was sizing me up.

Now although I'm not as good-looking as my cousin, who was freshman queen at Penn State, I'm not all that bad either. Plain, not really homely. I have sallow, slightly yellow skin that no amount of makeup can help, and going-gray dirty blond hair, but my figure is tidy and I do have a bust. A married doctor once lived with me off and on for about two years. I finally had to end that because the landlord was getting angry. He never wiped his feet when he came into the hall. It began to get under my skin, too. After he left the apartment I always had to vacuum. Where he found so much mud in New York I'll never know! The landlord was right; he had gotten to be boring anyhow.

Louis took his time. I didn't mind. There is something nice about having a real, actually substantial man looking at you. Kind of like Bishop Berkeley's question: Are you a woman if there is no one to see you as one? Well, Louis made me feel very womanly, and the more he looked the more I felt.

Finally he said, "Sure." That Americanese was perfect. I pulled into the nearest motel.

"My son would like to dry off and take a bath," I said to the clerk and pointed to Louis, who was still sitting in the car.

"You mean you're not staying for the night?"

"No, I'm sorry. We have to be on our way. My mother's dying in

Montreal. But my son had to change a flat tire and got soaked to the skin. With one member of the family dying I don't want to take any chances."

She gave me the room for half price.

Actually, I didn't feel like so much of a liar. As soon as the door closed, Louis asked if I wouldn't mind if he took a bath first. I said, "Of course not, take your time."

While Louis was in the bath I undressed slowly and got into bed naked and had an argument with Bill Shakespeare, who had gotten stood up and wanted to join me now.

"I already have a date," I told him in as harsh a whisper as I could muster, because Shakespeare is probably my favorite person in all of history.

Bill stroked his beard and looked at me kindly. "Enjoy it. You don't get a chance like this often," he said, and left quietly.

I lay there and looked around. It was the usual depressing motel room—avocado rug, green-flowered chair, and light green walls that reminded me of the hospital. Near the door was a large stain on the ceiling. I got out of bed and walked closer to it. The ceiling had been patched but it was just a matter of time before the leak would start again. When Louis came out of the bathroom with a towel wrapped around his waist I showed it to him. He smiled and went back into the bathroom and came out with a bucket that had obviously seen some use.

Louis's beard was not unlike Shakespeare's, and as we made love he whispered in French. Though I couldn't understand him, his tone was right. Everything would have been lovely if the leak hadn't begun about halfway through. *Plink, plonk. Plink, plonk.* The steady sound made me want to cry, but I tried not to show it. I guess I succeeded, because Louis looked very pleased with himself and promptly fell asleep in my arms. When he woke up we made love again, and although the water was still dripping I had gotten used to it. That time everything was better.

When I began to get dressed I noticed that a spider had begun to make a web in my underpants. My stomach was in a rage of hunger. I looked at my watch. We had been there four hours. But what better way to spend a rainy autumn afternoon in New England? We ate a little bread and jam from Louis's pack and then left.

"That must have been some bath," the clerk said when I returned the key. I could see in the mirror behind her that I no longer looked as if I had a dying mother. My sallow face was flushed.

"There's a leak in the ceiling of that room," I said brusquely, and ran to the car.

We had coffee and cereal and pancakes in a place up the road that served breakfast food all day. Louis didn't talk much; he kept looking at me with a puzzled expression.

"What's the matter?"

His voice was tinged with regret. "No one will believe me that this happened."

"Why do you have to tell anyone?" I said quietly. I hated to be laughed at over coffee cups.

"Because I'm not sure it will be real unless I tell anyone." He smiled his gorgeous smile. I nodded. That, at least, I understood.

"It's real if it's in your mind." I put my hand on his as he paused between pancakes. "Believe me. I know."

Back in the Datsun we rode peacefully. The weather was beginning to clear; there was going to be a sunset that would make everyone who saw it forget how much it had rained. From the vent on my side of the car I could feel the air getting crisper.

"Could you do me a favor?" I asked.

He spoke quickly: "I have to tell you, Mona, that my cousin in Montreal is a girl." I slowed down. All I had wanted was for him to open the window.

But he was uncomfortable. In Paris older women do live with younger men; maybe he thought I wanted to take him home. In a few minutes there was a picnic area on our side of the road, and I dropped him off.

Soon Shakespeare slid onto the seat next to me and we watched the sunset together in front of one of my favorite inns in all of New England. Then I had a long, leisurely dinner, and George Eliot and Henry Lewes stopped by for a nightcap, and I slept like a baby that night.

The first fifteen minutes at work Monday morning were filled with the usual resistance to the smell of the hospital. In short, I pressed my lips together while taking deep breaths through my nose to fight off nausea. By nine-twenty I felt as if I had been living there forever.

The waiting room to my office was filled. Criss-cross lines of suffering on the people's faces made me feel as if I were surrounded by a dozen pieces of human graph paper. And no matter what I did, arranged, or said, I couldn't help them. I was nothing more than Sisyphus in a white coat, a name tag, and a run beginning in my left stocking. Quickly I passed my puzzled secretary and all those resigned yet still hopeful pairs of eyes. I had to take a walk. If I didn't move my legs a little, I thought I would suffocate.

Emily Brontë joined me in the hall, and we closed our eyes and walked rapidly down the newly tiled corridors. We pretended we were striding along the moors. "Remember, Mona, how many died of tuberculosis then," she said. "And what good work they're doing here now."

"But it smells of death and dying. Why should good work smell of death?" I replied.

"The smell does defeat one," she admitted, and disappeared.

As I was going back to my office, my doctor friend stopped me. "Hi, Mona, how are you?" We're still friends. I don't believe in grudges. "Don't whine, Mona, and hold no grudges. They're dead ends," Aunt Beadie always said. She was right. Even history teaches you that.

"I'm fine," I said. "The foliage in Vermont was beautiful on Sunday after the rain. And I met a nice young man from Paris." Of course he didn't believe me. "And you?"

"The same." His mouth turned down a little at the corners; he expected some comfort, but I wasn't in the mood. I simply waited.

When he saw no sympathy forthcoming, he straightened his mouth briskly.

"Listen, Mona, you saved me a call. There are complicated problems in Room 201. The patient's wife had a heart attack over the weekend and is in Intensive Care. And in 117 there's a boy who was in a motorcycle accident. He'll be a vegetable. His parents are devastated. He was a Merit Scholar at Harvard," he added in a low, confidential voice. Obviously it was Harvard that impressed him. Whenever we talked, he never failed to remind me why I was relieved to see him leave my apartment for the last time.

"I know you'll see someone from both of those families today. Try to get back to me after four." He squeezed my elbow, either for Harvard or for old times, I suppose, and I headed back to the office.

It was a ghastly morning. One of the worst I've ever had. The stone gets heavier as we get older. By noon I was dripping wet—I perspire when I have to watch people cry. Before I went to lunch I changed my bra and blouse and then picked up a sandwich and coffee and headed toward Central Park. It was a school holiday and they had closed the park to traffic, so as I ate I watched the bicyclers. They looked happy; I began to feel a little better.

Then Rilke came along and sat beside me. Now there's a man. I wished I had combed my hair. We chatted quietly and then, because the sun seemed to be having one last burst of energy before the fall really closed in, we moved to another bench and arranged ourselves so the sun could warm our faces. Saturday's storm had knocked so many of the leaves off the trees. I started to mourn the lost leaves, but then Rilke said, "They'll come back, Mona." He covered my hand with his. "It is so good not to be alone in autumn," he murmured.

After a bit a breeze came up, and although I protested Rilke insisted on taking off his cape. Tenderly he spread it over my shoulders, and we sat there contentedly until it was time for me to get back to work.

ABOUT THE AUTHORS

BLANCHE McCRARY BOYD went to Duke University and graduated from Pomona College. She was a Wallace Stegner Fellow at Stanford University, where she earned her masters degree in 1970 and has been a recipient of a National Endowment for the Arts Fellowship. She is the author of *The Redneck Way of Knowledge* (1981), a collection of essays and reportage, and a novel, *The Revolution of Little Girls* (1991), which won the Ferro-Grumley Award for lesbian fiction in 1991. A different version of her story in this collection forms chapter three of that novel. Boyd is presently a professor of English and writer-in-residence at Connecticut College.

ETHAN CANIN is the author of *Emperor of the Air* (1988), a collection of stories, and *Blue River* (1991), a novel. Although born in Ann Arbor, Michigan, Canin was raised in Ohio, Pennsylvania, and California. He graduated from Stanford University in 1982, received an M.F.A. from the University of Iowa in 1984, and will complete an M.D. at Harvard Medical School in 1992. Canin is also the winner of a Houghton Mifflin Literary Fellowship (1988), and the recipient of a National Endowment for the Arts grant, the James Michener Award, an Ingram Merrill Fellowship, an Iowa Teaching/Writing Fellowship, and the Henfield/Transatlantic Review Award.

JOHN CHEEVER authored seven collections of stories (including *The Way Some People Live*, *The Enormous Radio*, *The Housebreaker of Shady Hill*, and *The World of Apples*) and five novels (including *The Wapshot Scandal* (1964), *Bullet Park* (1969), *Falconer* (1977), and *Oh What Paradise It Seems* (1982)). *The Wapshot Chronicle*, his first novel, won the 1958 National Book Award, and *The Stories of John Cheever* (1978) won the National Book Critics Circle Award and Pulitzer

Prize. Born in 1912, in Quincy, Massachusetts, Cheever died in 1982, shortly after being awarded the National Medal for Literature from the American Academy and Institute of Arts and Letters.

SUSAN DODD has written three novels, *No Earthly Notion, Mamaw,* and *The Return of Light,* as well as two collections of stories, *Old Wives' Tales* and *Hell-Bent Men and Their Cities.* She has taught creative writing at Vermont College and the Iowa Writers' Workshop. She currently lives in Cambridge, Massachusetts, and is a Briggs-Copeland Professor of Fiction at Harvard University.

ANDRE DUBUS was born in Louisiana in 1936 and currently lives in Haverhill, Massachusetts. After serving in the Marine Corps, he attended the University of Iowa Writers' Workshop, then taught at Bradford College until retirement in 1984. He is the author of eight books (including a novel, two novellas, five collections of stories, and a collection of essays). Dubus is also the father of six children, and has received two Guggenheims and a MacArthur Fellowship.

E.S. GOLDMAN, a Pittsburgh native, was born in 1913. After graduating from the Experimental College of the University of Wisconsin and the University of Pittsburgh, he skippered a U.S. Navy mine sweeper in World War II. "Way to the Dump," his first published story, appeared in *The Atlantic* in 1987, and was later anthologized in his award-winning story collection, *Earthly Justice.* Goldman, who now lives on Cape Cod and is married to the artist Virginia Goldman, is also the author of *Big Chocolate Cookies,* a novel, and *Going Back to the Sea,* a collection of poetry.

MARK HELPRIN, who was born in 1947, holds degrees from Harvard and Harvard's Center for Middle Eastern Studies. He is the author of several collections of stories, including *Ellis Island and Other Stories, A Dove of the East and Other Stories, Refiner's Fire,* and *Winter's Tale.*

DAVID HUDDLE was born in Ivanhoe, Virginia, in 1942 and holds degrees from the University of Virginia, Hollins College, and Columbia University. He currently teaches English and creative writing at the University of Vermont in Burlington. His poetry and story collections include *Stopping by Home*, *The High Spirits*, *Only the Little Bone*, *Paper Boy*, and *A Dream With No Stump Root in It*. He is married and has two daughters.

DAVID MICHAEL KAPLAN went to prep school and college in New England and still considers it to be his spiritual home, although he currently lives in Chicago. The author of *Skating in the Dark* and *Comfort*, both collections of short stories, Kaplan teaches at Loyola University. His stories have been anthologized in *Best American Short Stories* and *O. Henry Prize Stories* as well as in the PEN Syndicated Fiction Project Series.

JOYCE KORNBLATT was born in Boston in 1944. She has published two novels, *White Water* (1985) and *Breaking Bread* (1987) as well as a collection of stories, *Nothing to Do With Love* (1980). She is a professor of literature and creative writing at the University of Maryland, College Park. Her story in this collection won an O. Henry Award in 1986. She has a grown daughter and lives in Washington, D.C.

JOHN L'HEUREUX, a Massachusetts native, is the author of fifteen books of fiction and poetry. His novels include *A Woman Run Mad*, *An Honorable Profession*, and *The Shrine at Altamira*, and his stories have been collected in *Family Affairs*, *Desires*, and *Comedians*. Many of his stories first appeared in *The Atlantic*, where he worked briefly as an editor. He is a professor of English at Stanford University.

RALPH LOMBREGLIA lives in the Boston area although he was born in New Jersey and educated in Maryland and New York. A former Wallace Stegner Fellow at Stanford University, he has won many awards, including a grant from the National Endowment for the Arts. He is the author of *Men Under Water* (1989), a collection of stories.

SUE MILLER, a native of Chicago, attended Radcliffe College when she was 16. After graduation, marriage, and a series of various jobs, she won the Boston University Creative Writing fellowship, and later, a Bunting Fellowship. She is the author of *The Good Mother*, a novel, and *Inventing the Abbots*, a collection of stories.

SUSAN MINOT was raised in Manchester, Massachusetts, and now lives in New York City. After graduating from Brown University in 1978, she completed an M.F.A. at Columbia University, in 1983. She is the author of *Monkeys* and *Folly*, both novels, and of *Lust and Other Stories*, a collection of stories. In 1987 Minot won the Prix Femina Etranger for the French translation of *Monkeys*, and her work has been anthologized in such collections as *Best American Short Stories*, *The O. Henry Awards*, and the *Norton Anthology of Modern Literature*.

ROXANA ROBINSON was born in Kentucky and attended the University of Michigan. She is the author of *Summer Light*, a novel, *Georgia O'Keeffe: A Life*, and *A Glimpse of Scarlet*, a collection of stories. She is a recipient of a creative writing fellowship from the National Endowment for the Arts, and lives in upstate New York with her husband and daughter.

ROBERTA SILMAN is the author of *Blood Relations* (a collection of stories) and *Beginning the World Again*, *The Dream Dredger*, and *Boundaries* (all novels). Her stories have appeared in *The New Yorker*, *The Atlantic*, and *Redbook*, among other publications, and she is the recipient of both a National Endowment for the Arts Fellowship and a Guggenheim. A graduate of Cornell University, Silman is also the mother of three children.

ROBERT STONE is a novelist, screenwriter, and essayist. His first novel, *Hall of Mirrors* (1967) won the Faulkner Award and was made into the movie *WUSA*. Stone's second novel, *Dog Soldiers* (1974) recieved the National Book Award and was the basis for the movie *Who'll Stop the Rain*. Stone is also the author of *A Flag for Sunrise*, *Children of Light*, and *Outerbridge Reach*, all novels. He lives in Connecticut with his family.

CHRISTOPHER TILGHMAN lives outside Boston—where he was born in 1946—with his wife and two sons. After graduating from Yale in 1968, he spent three years as a gunnery and deck officer in the Navy. He is the author of *In a Father's Place*, a collection of stories.

JOHN UPDIKE is the author of numerous books, including *Rabbit*

Run, Rabbit Redux, Rabbit is Rich, Rabbit at Rest, Couples, Witches of Eastwick, and *Pigeon Feathers.* A graduate of Harvard University and Harvard's Ruskin School of Drawing and Fine Art, Updike has also recieved many awards, including the Pulitzer Prize. He lives north of Boston.

JOY WILLIAMS was educated at Marietta College and the University of Iowa, and currently lives in Florida with her husband and daughter. She is the author of three novels, *State of Grace, The Changeling,* and *Breaking and Entering.* She has also published two collections of stories, *Taking Care* and *Escapes.*